Used Aliens

A Novel
M. Sid Kelly

Interior Artwork and Back Cover by
G. Lasine Doumbia

Front Cover and Photos by
M. Sid Kelly
(The color is magnified abalone shell.)

DEDICATION

To
Julie and her sea slug
&
Jen and her spray paint

CONTENTS

ACKNOWLEDGMENTS

Thanks to my volunteer proofers/editors:
Greg, Julie, Dan, Rick, Michael, Paul, Larry, and Dad

A MISSION BEGINS

"Hey Skip, now can I wake up the bug?" asked Dee. "The poor thing's been in that box for an awfully long time."

"Sure. Just break the seal and let him come out here when he's ready," said Trukk-9, the owner and skipper of the ship.

"Sweet," said Dee. "I'll bet you guys five bucks it's a Flea. Those suckers are awesome. They are so bouncy! Plus, I hear they love to snuggle. And you can't hardly DENT those guys. Cuddly and tough... Yeah. I love Fleas."

"Okay then, I'm going to be optimistic too. I bet it's a Click Beetle," said Trukk-9.

"Oh, yeah... Those guys are tough too, and they're fun to wrestle with. You just have to watch out for that spike on their chest when you grapple 'em. I like your chances, Skip!" said Dee.

The ship's engineer drifted back from his station and said, "I'm in for five bucks too, Dee. I'll bet it's a Praying Mantis."

"A Praying Mantis, Stick? Are you sure about that, buddy?"

1

"Yes, the Mantis is my totem insectoid. Here, I'll imitate one for you."

"Totem insectoid? You have a totem insectoid? Stick, that is weird," said Dee.

"All of my people have them," said Stick as he took the approximate form of a six-foot-tall Praying Mantis. "There is a certain collective intelligence that we plasmanoids recognize and appreciate in insectoids. Blue-5 and ZZZZZZ-3 are sister planets from way back."

"That's a really great story, Stick. But don't you think they would have shipped a Praying Mantis in a tube? Sisters you may be, buddy, but insectoids are not plasmanoids. They have a rigid exoskeleton, Stick. You can't just moosh them into a little box. But, hey, good guess. I'll take your five bucks any day."

"Oh yeah... Okay, I'm going to say he's a Moth Technician then."

"Oh god, I hope not. They shed way too much and it gums up everything. And you can't rough 'em up AT ALL. A Moth would suck, Stick. The last time I was with a Moth Technician, that sucker got all riled up flying around in circles shedding all over and I sneezed and sneezed until I had a big ol' glob of sn-"

Trukk-9 interrupted. "Dee! Go unpack it. I'm sure whatever we got is fine."

"Sure thing, Skipper!"

Dee charged into the cargo hold, cracked the container seal, and then ran for the exit. He peeked back in through the small window and waited.

"Here it comes! I see a black leg with a pair of claws... I think it's a Flea guys. FLEA, FLEA, FLEA... WHOA! There he goes! AAAH HA HA HA HA. Oh man, look you guys! He did a flip and bounced off the ceiling! Now he's spinning around and around on his back. He's super shiny and has pretty red markings. He's nicely stout, and not too spiny. Flea, baby!"

Dee jumped up and down as he watched O'Buzznid-3 grasping about for something to hold on to.

"Oh! There he goes again! Off the wall and… Oh wow, he just knocked over my weight bench. I think he's okay though. Now he's staggering around. Should I dose him with some calming agent, Skip?" asked Dee as he hit the cargo hold calming agent button twice.

"No, not yet, Dee," replied Trukk-9.

"Oh… Should I let him come in here now, Skip?" asked Dee as he opened the cargo hold door.

"No – like I said, he will come out when he's good and…"

O'Buzznid-3 wobbled out onto the bridge. All of a sudden his wings unfurled and he flew headlong into the ship's viewing dome. He hit so hard that he left a spot of grease on the glass.

"Oops. You alright, little buddy?" asked Dee.

"I am fine. You placed my container upside-down so I could not wake up properly. Did you not see the big red arrows all pointing directly at the autotranslator-enabled voice instructions?"

"Maybe not," replied Dee.

O'Buzznid-3 removed the invoice that was taped to his thorax and handed it to Trukk-9.

Trukk-9 looked at the papers and said, "Welcome aboard Mister O'Buzznid-3. I'm Trukk-9 – he is Stick.E-5 – and the big furry loudmouth is Dee-15."

Dee grinned and waved.

"Yes, I know who you are. We insectoids enjoy the underground cinema too."

O'Buzznid-3 nodded in respect toward Stick.E, who still held his Mantis shape.

"I apologize for Dee waking you like that. I trust that you are in good health?" asked Trukk-9.

"I said I am fine. Can you please explain why I am on your ship instead of on a PLUMBOB mission?"

"Well, Mister O'Buznid-3, this IS a PLUMBOB mission. Haven't you been briefed?"

"No. I was simply packed away after my last mission. Also, you can call me Buzzy if you have trouble with insectoid names."

"Well, Buzzy, they asked me to participate in this mission because they want a high quality product this time. Anyway, there's our planet." Trukk-9 pointed at the blue and white planet outside.

"Yep, little buddy, we have arrived!" said Dee. "Um, you are a Flea, right? It's very important."

"No, I am not a Flea."

"Oh… Well you aren't a Click Beetle or a Moth either, right?"

"No. What I AM is ready to work. Where is my station, please?"

"Right there in the front. I believe all of the controls are insectoid compatible, and your software should already be loaded," said Trukk-9.

Dee said, "I'll be back here if you need me, buddy!"

"We have just arrived at the planet, correct?" asked Buzzy.

"Yes, all we know about this place is that it has a lot of water and a lot of satellites," said Trukk-9. "But even though we just got here, I feel good about this planet's chances. Gentlemen, I think you are looking at the next member of the Galactic Pool! What's our first task then, Buzzy?"

"Well, my first task might take a little while. What I must do is tap into the planet's computer information system and select representative captioned photographs. Our computer will analyze about a thousand pictures before it determines the meaning of the first written word. But the rate picks up quite dramatically as it gets the alphabets and languages worked out. It combines a photo interpretation subroutine into the same algorithm used by the galactic autotranslator."

"So, in other words, the thing sucks," said Dee.

"No, it is highly effective."

"So what can we do in the mean time?" asked Trukk-9.

"You do what is called simply 'the area study' – basically you get your bearings. Scan the geography, find the population centers, and look for some of the more obvious checklist items while you scan. You may notice landscape-level alterations like large water management projects and agriculture, for example. Then I will seek our initial objective," said Buzzy.

"Good, I'm looking forward to getting started," said Trukk-9. "Oh, and Welter-3 said I was to give you the official checklist."

"That will not be necessary. I have it memorized," replied Buzzy.

"He said you would say that. Here, I'm sending it to you."

"This checklist is very short, and most of the depressing stuff is missing. Some other crew must have all the bad stuff. It will suit me if we can wrap this up quickly. I cannot delay my breeding phase very much longer. I am already starting to feel the itch."

"Buzzy, old pal, that is too much information..." said Dee.

"Where is our PLUMBOB monitoring ship?" asked Buzzy.

"It's on its way. We are supposed to scout for checklist items so we'll be all ready to manipulate this planet's inhabitants when it arrives," said Trukk-9.

***

They flew around and scanned the surface while Buzzy ran the translation analysis.

"This planet's computer network is quite extraordinary. The technology is primitive, but the content is vast. They must use a tremendous amount of energy to store and process all this information. I found all the pictures we needed — seven-hundred million of them in just 0.19 seconds," said Buzzy. "And the very first picture up looks like a Bearman with a baby Bearman."

"Oh! Oh! Send it to me, send it to me, send it to me!" said Dee.

Buzzy forwarded the picture.

"Oh baby! Look at that! She is totally fuzzy and white as snow, and that cub is SOOO cute! I love this planet! Are there more?"

"The word for that animal appears to be spelled B-E-A-R, so do a search on that. You are connected to their network," said Buzzy.

Dee did the search. "Oh... my... god... This planet is a Bearman's paradise! Look at them all. So many different kinds, and all so beautiful..."

"The computer is still working on translation, but I already have enough to seek out our first checklist objective, which is 'greetings' of course. It says here that Dirtlings will expect alien visitors to greet them with 'Take me to your leader'."

"Oh, now that is totally lame! They should know that we want to give them hugs first!" said Dee.

"The dominant race is humanoid and it does not look as huggable as the bears in the picture, I am afraid," said

Buzzy.

"What!? How can the bears not be dominant? It's not like Dnooblians live here. It's outrageous. Are you sure about that, little buddy?"

"Yes."

"Well, I want to meet the Bear People myself. I will help them rise!" said Dee.

"I do not believe that they are sapient," said Buzzy.

"Fine, but I'm not leaving this planet until I get a chance to mix it up with them."

MONTHS LATER, JIMMY GOES FISHING

Jimmy Fresneaux got home from work and saw the long-anticipated package on his front porch.

He took the box inside and set it on the kitchen counter. He gazed at it and smiled. He allowed his excitement to build as he enjoyed an energy drink. He waited as long as he could – about thirty seconds – before tearing open the lid and dumping the contents onto his dining room table.

He unzipped each bag in turn, wafting his hand over the opening like a chemist as he sniffed from a safe distance. When he detected a savory smell, such as garlic or crayfish, he made a mental note of it and moved to the next bag. And each time he detected a sweet aroma, he put the bag over his face.

The translucent brown plastic grubs had a root beer scent, which indicated good quality control at the plastic worm factory, he thought. But the fat blue paddle-tail worms were mango-scented for some reason. And after a few huffs he decided that the gray sparkle leeches were bergamot.

He transferred handfuls of the worms into his own

custom-designed zipper bags. Each bag featured JIMMY JAMS! printed above a top-hat-wearing cartoon worm sporting a monocle and handlebar mustache. The worm was saying, "Old-fashioned Olfaction Bassin' Action!!!"

Jimmy was feeling pretty good. He loved these private moments with his plastic worms. But he would have felt violated if he'd known that a space alien just won five bucks for correctly guessing the contents of the box.

***

The afternoon had turned breezy, so Jimmy changed into his vented self-embroidered bass fishing sponsorship jersey. And he put on a new ball cap with the "CC" logo of Chompy Chunkbaits printed in crimson on the front.

Because it was the Friday of the first warm week of spring, the gas stations would be busy with happy people preparing for weekend outings. So once he had all of his gear together he towed his bass boat to the closest gas station.

On arrival, he jumped out of his truck like an actor taking the stage and announced, "Boy howdy!" to no one and everyone.

He removed his homemade Fresneauxlaroid Basses Glasses as two young women pulled up in a convertible sports car.

They were a blonde and a brunette, and each wore a floral sundress that seemed too short for this wind. The scenario was shaping up like a TV commercial, which is exactly what Jimmy was looking for.

"Hiya," said the blonde.

"That sure is a nice looking boat," said the brunette. "How about a ride sometime?"

Jimmy said, "Sure! I can pick you up at five o'clock

tomorrow morning."

The brunette giggled and said, "I don't know – that's about my bed time."

The two women glanced at each other, and then the blonde said, "Um, we are both hair stylists and we were just talking and… We think your hair is too nice to cover up with a hat."

"Yep, that's what we were saying," added the brunette.

Jimmy just smiled.

"Um… So… Can we maybe see your hair without your hat on?" asked the blonde.

Jimmy removed his hat.

The brunette said, "There you go – I wish my hair was that full. And you definitely shouldn't cover those eyes with those… those sunglasses."

"But I have to wear sunglasses and a hat in this profession. I like having my hair long like this, but it's starting to push my hats off. Do you happen to know of a way to keep hats on my head in the wind?"

"Well, you might go with a visor instead, and let your hair spill over the top – don't you think?" suggested the brunette.

"Yeah, a visor would work better," said the blonde. "We could see your hair then, and the band will grip your scalp. If you give me your hat, I have my scissors…"

Jimmy didn't recognize the teasing tone, and he said, "Sure, if you don't mind." He opened the hatch of his camper shell to get his box of Chompy Chunkbait hats.

The blonde cut the top from a hat and did a good job of trimming evenly around the logo. "There, that should work. But you really ought to switch to blue hats to bring out your eyes."

Jimmy tried the visor on.

"There, now use your fingers, like this, to pull your hair

up through the top," the brunette said as she helped fluff up Jimmy's hair. "What brand of conditioner do you use — something in mango?"

"Oh, no, my conditioner is fragrance-free, ma'am. The mango scent is probably Jimmy Jams Mango Manglers. Tell you what — you can really stick some hawgs on those fat babies. Here, I'll show you." Jimmy tried to give a fist-full of Mango Manglers to the women.

"Oh, that's okay... But can we have a couple of your hats instead, maybe?" asked the blonde.

Jimmy watched the two Chompy Chunkbait-logoed women drive off wearing their trophies.

***

At gas station number two, Jimmy noticed another fisherman filling the tank of a small aluminum boat.

Jimmy checked the sun position and wind direction so he could position himself and his rig for maximum product branding effect. The man glanced over at the brilliant stormy sunset colors and rainbow of sponsor decals topped off with "J. Fresneaux" on the outboard motor in tasteful lightning bolts. Jimmy reeled the man in with an inviting smile.

A breeze blew between the two gas pumps where Jimmy was waiting. His vented shirt billowed to twice its normal girth and rippled with logos. The low angle of the sun made his sponsorship colors glow as if lit from within. His visor held tight.

"Howdy," said the man. "I was noticing some of your sponsors. So how do you like those Chompy Chunkbaits?"

"I'm glad you ask. I've stroked some toads on those bad boys — won my last tournament on 'em, in fact. It was out-of-state, so you might not have seen it on the news. But the

Chompy Chunkbait will cast real nice – even into the wind – and they have a very natural presentation in both clear and turbid waters. The bass just love 'em! Tell you what – I'm out of samples right now, but I have a logo hat for you here."

"Oh, thanks," said the man as he accepted the hat. "Okay, um, how about those Persimmon Grips? They work pretty good, huh?"

"I tell you what – you know how sometimes when you're fishing and your hands get so cold that you can't even unzip your pants to take a leak?"

The man nodded and said, "My problem is that I can unzip, but then I can't zip back up again."

"Exactly! But with Persimmon Grips, even under those tough conditions, you'll have the grip you need to reel in a big ol' bass. And they come in sizes to fit every model of reel."

Jimmy knew that the man just wanted some free samples, and he wished the man would ask about Jimmy Jams instead.

"How good do the Slidewinder Reels cast?"

"Amazing distance, almost impossible to backlash, and they have the lightest titanium body in their class. They have fish pumping torque – especially when equipped with the matching Persimmon Grip. There's even a USB port so you can track your cast data on your home computer."

"Wow! Mind if I check one out?" asked the man, believing that there really was such a thing as a Slidewinder Reel.

Jimmy explained. "Well it's an up-and-coming brand trying to get some name recognition before starting to manufacture. I'm doing them a favor by sporting their decals and answering enquiries. I should be getting some of their hats soon too – blue ones. I'll look for you on the lake and I'll see if I can't get you a Slidewinder to test drive when they come out."

***

Jimmy attracted the attention of another customer as he re-vacuumed at gas station number eight.

"How's it going?" said Jimmy, when he saw the man looking at his boat.

"I'm well. How are you?"

"I'm fantastic! My name is Jimmy. What's your name, friend?"

"Gregory."

"Are you a bass fisherman, Greg?"

"It's Gregory, actually."

"Oh. So do you fish Gregory?"

"No."

"Oh. Well, I tell you what – I'm up at the lake most weekends. That is unless I'm fishing out-of-state in a big tournament like the last one I won. But look for me if you ever want to check out the latest gear and git to fishin'!" said Jimmy.

"That's unlikely to happen. But, actually, I'm on my way to meet up with an associate who lives near the lake. We search some bluffs on a creek up there for fossils. The exposure is on a tributary to one of the creeks way up the river. Normally it's flowing water up that far, but with the reservoir high like this, I bet you could get there in this boat."

"Sure enough, I know the bluffs you mean. I ripped a bucket-mouth and some bank-runners back there on a Jimmy Jams green and red watermelon worm one time. Here, let me show you."

"Oh, that's okay. I was just daydreaming about how

much easier it would be to get to that spot with a boat like this. A boat with this paintjob must be pretty fast huh?" Gregory cleaned his glasses with the tail of his shirt, wiped his nose on his sleeve, and then leaned in to examine the details in the boat's paint.

"Son, she could get me a ticket if I drove her on the freeway!"

"What are these sparkles made of?" asked Gregory.

"Huh? Oh, in the paint? It's the same glitter that's in plastic worms, I think."

"Does it have the same purpose?"

"You mean like attracting fish? Well, let me show you something about these Jimmy Jam's Watermelons. See? Black glitter. That's like a watermelon's seeds, and is an indication of the quality control that big bass notice."

"Sure. Well, good luck," said Gregory as he accepted a Chompy Chunkbaits hat.

Jimmy sniffed the worms to see if they were actually watermelon. They were American cheese.

***

The next morning on his way to the lake, Jimmy stopped at his favorite mini-market. He noticed a commotion in the parking lot as he was paying for drinks and a bag of donuts.

"Hey, it looks like you got a problem out there. A serious problem… Oh boy… There's blood and everything. Ohhh… yikes! You better call 911!"

Jimmy stuck around with the cashier until things were under control. They couldn't be sure what had happened, but they gave statements to the police anyway. And the cashier showed his appreciation to Jimmy by giving him the bag of donuts for free.

By the time he made it to the boat ramp, there was

already a long line. And every boat ahead of Jimmy seemed to encounter one problem or another as they launched.

Once he was finally on the water, he ran his boat far into the upper reaches of the foothill reservoir as if he were trying to leave the morning's madness behind. And sure enough, there were some bluffs near the end of a long flooded creek channel. Jimmy smiled with the satisfaction of having found a place that another guy had directed him to.

"Well, howdy folks! Welcome to my bassin' hole for the day!"

Jimmy's imaginary fishing show was called Jimmy's Bassin' Hole.

"This spot looks very similar to the spot where I won my last tournament. I think we're going to get 'em today!"

He didn't choose his fishing spots based on the behavior of bass or habitat conditions. He chose the locations for scenery and seclusion. And by that standard, the curious scruffy fellow's gas station tip had served him well.

"I'm at a great little spot up-river on my local lake today, y'all. The recent weather conditions lead me to believe that a lot of nice bass could be back here in this warmer water seeking prey. The wind has dropped, and the big bass are in pre-spawn mode. That means they'll be feeding heavily to store away energy for nesting time."

But the water in the narrow canyons where Jimmy floated was several degrees cooler than the water in the shallow coves on the main reservoir – where the fish were biting.

"Friends, it's time for Tip of The Week! – brought to you by Stanky Shad. Stanky Shad makes life-like lures with a whole threadfin shad emulsified into each soft plastic body. They're available at a fine retailer near you."

Jimmy made a long cast.

"Okay friends, let's say that you've made a long cast way back into a little creek mouth. And then you notice a big ol' mossback sow-belly bass boil on a luckless minnow down the bank at a ninety-degree angle to your original cast. What you have to do is retrieve your lure, get it back into the air, and drop it right on that boiling bass water ASAP. Now watch and I'll show you how."

Jimmy demonstrates by pretending that he sees a big bass jump in his peripheral vision. "Look! It's a big one over there!" he says as he jerks his head to the side and points.

"Okay friends, now your hand must become a machine. You need to produce quick, smooth, even cranks using your wrist – not your elbow. See how my Persimmon Grips facilitate the speed I need. Hold your rod low, and just before your Stanky Shad gets to the tip, quickly turn your rod like this and give a backhand flick directly at the action. The key is to keep the lure low to the water as it travels toward the target at maximum speed."

Jimmy executed this cast and said his lines without a flaw over and over again for a couple of hours using every one of his 'sponsors' products without a single bite.

He sat down for a snack.

He felt better after some donuts and another energy drink. Then he drove his boat out to the main body of the reservoir and pushed the throttle all the way down. He zigzagged over his own wake a few times. Then he went back to the bluffs.

Jimmy held a large lure up to the camera and said, "Friends, I'm going to start the day with this Mega-Mouth Poppin' Minnow! The fish are probably going to be aggressive, and this bad boy, which is the newest pattern in my line of all-natural hand-carved top-water lures, will surely attract their attention!"

Jimmy cast his homemade Mega-Mouth Poppin' Minnow into what seemed like as good a spot as any. And mustering all of his enthusiasm, he explained, "A hungry bass will just explode on a lure like this! The Mega-Mouth Poppin' Minnow is equipped with three laser-sharpened AccuPoke treble hooks, which are sure to solidly hook a big bass in the chaos of the strike!"

Jimmy liked the way that sounded, so he repeated it – adding "frenzied" in front of "chaos" on the second take.

"Now, y'all, I like to let my lure sit on the water until all the ripples have died down. As I like to say – if you ain't got patience, you ain't got fish… Because friends, through years of experience I've learned that a bass will strike more often on a top-water bait that seems to suddenly come to life. Okay, now I'll just give it a little twitch…"

And KABOOM! A huge largemouth bass exploded on the lure. This startled Jimmy into forgetting that he was supposed to be in character.

"OUAAAAAH! Oh, uh… Boy howdy! There she is! WOOOOOOOOOOO! This is a bigun folks! Tell you what!"

The huge bass jumped with its head thrashing and threw the lure.

"GHAAAAAAHHHHHH!" Jimmy's line went limp and he came close to crying. But the giant fish came back and re-exploded on the lure.

Jimmy snapped to attention and regained some composure. "Folks, they do love that Mega-Mouth Poppin' Minnow! I do believe that this is the same fish I just lost. Leapin' armadillos!"

Most of his previous netting experience came from practicing on his neighbor's chickens when they strayed into his yard. But he got this big bass into the net like a real pro.

He felt weak in the knees.

"Folks, I feel weak in the knees. Oh man... This wall-hanger must weigh eleven or twelve pounds," said a breathless Jimmy. In reality, the giant bass weighed over sixteen pounds.

"As you know, my fishin' friends, Jimmy Fresneaux always lets the big ones go. These are the fish that make the next generation of biguns," said Jimmy as he snuck his trophy bass into the back livewell.

"Now y'all, it's a good idea to tie a new knot on your lure after fighting a big fish like that one."

His hands shook, but he figured that it would add drama to the moment. He cast the lure to another spot, but nothing bit.

As he began to reel the lure in to cast again, a fish broke the surface at the exact edge of his peripheral vision. Jimmy executed his Tip-of-the-Week cast to perfection. The lure zipped inches above the water and dropped right into the center of the widening rings. The lake surface exploded under the Mega-Mouth Poppin' Minnow.

"WOOOOOOOOOOOO!" yelled Jimmy. "We got us another bigun! Big fish! BIIIIIIG FISH!"

Jimmy worked the fish to the side of the boat and saw that it was actually three fish – one on each treble hook.

"Oh my, y'all... Oh my... I've poked three pigs! Come on, come on…" Jimmy pleaded as he grabbed the net.

He netted them as easy as three chickens. "This is how it's supposed to happen," he thought out loud. "Friends, oh my friends, these fish'll go at least six pounds each. Oh wow…"

The fish weighed twelve, ten, and nine pounds each. Jimmy pretended to release the three bass.

"Okay, my fine angling friends, I'm sure pleased that you could join me today. Ain't we havin' fun, y'all?! You too can have the kind of success that Jimmy Fresneaux enjoys. The right cast with the right lure is the key. And it looks like we might be onto a pattern here."

Jimmy cast at another random spot. This time there was commotion under the lure as soon as it touched down. "There's a big fish right there, folks. I can see a shadow and movement…"

And the water erupted under the lure.

"Another good one, folks!"

As Jimmy fought another big bass, additional underwater shadows swam in from all around, and more watery explosions erupted from the lake's surface.

Jimmy found himself reeling in a whole school. The fishes struggled at the surface with all their faces stuck together around the Mega-Mouth Poppin' Minnow, making it look like a nightmarish pom-pom.

Jimmy got his net around a couple of the bigger fish and heaved the entire mess into the boat. He stood there with his mouth wide open looking down at the fish struggling on the deck of his boat.

Stuck to the nine points of the big lure's three treble hooks were: another big largemouth bass of about eight pounds, a four-foot long alligator gar, the biggest bowfin Jimmy had ever seen, a huge striper, a slab crappie, a monster bigmouth buffalo, a respectable channel catfish, an ancient yellow bullhead, and a carp. The tenth fish, a bluegill, seemed to jump into the net voluntarily as Jimmy landed the other fish.

"Ohhh, mon Dieu… Uh, Lordy… Oh Lordy, Lordy! That has to be the greatest fishing feat by anyone ever. Oh Lordy, and I got it on video. I'm so blessed. Folks, I'm so happy you could be here with me today. That Mega-Mouth Poppin' Minnow… Oh, uh…"

Jimmy's emotions got the best of him. He dropped to his knees, shivering like an abandoned puppy lost in a crowd of flopping fish.

Then he noticed the other improbable events unfolding around him, and his fishing feat no longer seemed quite so extraordinary.

FLEENCE-18 MEETS THE DNOOBLIANS

PLUMBOB stands for Planets Under Monitoring For Baseline Observations. The old agency acronym was CAPMA, which stood for Candidate Planet Monitoring Agency. But the new Galactic Pool administration wanted better 'corporate identity' so they manufactured a new agency name to form a nicer acronym.

Now everyone thinks there are either two different agencies, or that the administration is just dumb. But these people underestimate the power of confusion.

***

Fleence-18 simultaneously entered and exited the final wormhole of her month-long journey. Soon she would arrive at the Tertiary Tongue Terminal Outpost. This was the farthest she had ever been from home, and was much farther from the center of the galaxy than most people will ever travel. She was filled with excitement and anticipation for what she expected would be the first of many grand adventures.

She was on her way to meet a couple of Dnooblians who ran the PLUMBOB Field Office at this outpost.

Fleence was optimistic about working with Dnooblians, and she was intrigued by them in general. She knew about the restraining order that forbids a sub-adult Dnooblian to approach any species of humanoid. But she also knew that trained bull Dnooblians were perfect gentlemen as long as you didn't startle them. What Fleence did not know, however, was that the two Dnooblians were not expecting her.

Fleence stopped her ship when she got to within visual range of the outpost. It didn't look as nasty as she had expected.

The outpost was an enormous brown cone with a matte-finish, and an anti-reflective crisscross pattern embossed into its lower hull. It was ten miles long from top to tip. The tip was meant to point down when viewed from an approaching ship.

The superstructure was a white hemisphere that covered the full circumference of the cone's top. Dark brown tubular hangars, there for the use of visiting ships, were sprinkled about its top. And a red-tinted radar and communications dome crowned the outpost.

The only objects hovering outside the outpost were maintenance craft that had put a fresh coat of paint on the superstructure. They were now cleaning paint dribbles from the side of the substructure.

There were no hulking freighters bearing mysterious insignia, no souped-up smuggling cruisers doing fly-bys, and no charred bodies of exotic aliens hurtling out into space. There were no big burn scars on the outer surface, no plasma jets shooting out of random pipes, and no neon signs advertising the vices within.

This place was nothing like outposts in the underground

cinema. Maybe it was a cesspool inside, she thought. Still, she waited until afternoon before approaching in case she'd awaken someone hungry or dangerous.

"Hello Tertiary Tongue Terminal Outpost," Fleence announced as she flew in closer.

"Identify your port of registry, space vagrant," replied an alert-sounding bureaucratic voice, which Fleence wasn't expecting.

The owner of the voice was seated in the red control dome atop the superstructure, but she was too small for Fleence to see.

"I've come directly from Chuffed-18, my home planet. I'm an egocite handler. I'm supposed to meet Maghosh-10 of PLUMBOB."

Announcing oneself as being from Chuffed-18 always elicited a certain type of reaction from other humanoids. But the radio voice's reaction belied that it belonged to a non-humanoid.

Insectoid, thought Fleence. Probably Cricket...

"Really?" replied the radio voice. "Is Maghosh-10 expecting you? He did not notify us of your pending arrival." The radio voice put this juicy bit of gossip aside for the moment. "Are you currently in possession of egocite?"

"Yes, I have a fresh ingot. It's for the mission that PLUMBOB is planning to a planet called Dirt. I have all the paperwork in order."

"Good. Fly to the hangar closest to the red dome – the one with the big C-O on it – and I will have a customs officer meet you there. I will try to reach Maghosh while you are checking in."

***

The customs officer was a plasmanoid, so he didn't

notice anything stunning or radiant about Fleence. He did, however, study her as a template for the next time he needed to take on humanoid form. Her perfect bilateral symmetry would be much easier to imitate than the complicated humanoid species he usually encountered.

But if a humanoid male from this part of the galaxy tried to describe Fleence to you, the exact tone of the translation would vary depending on who YOU are.

Depending on how you were raised, what culture you belong to, and how educated you are, you might hear the galactic autotranslator offer, "Fleence is very pretty. I like her hair and the way she dresses."

Or you might hear, "Fleence is a most lovely and fetching woman. She has a palette of flowing locks and a fabulous wardrobe."

Or you might hear, "Fleence is a smokin' hot BABE. Blonde, red-head, whatever! And you can change her clothes with your eyes! WOOOOOOOOOOOOO!"

To a listener who has 'WOOOOOOOOOOOOO' in his vocabulary, 'lovely and fetching' may not convey the speaker's true feeling about the matter.

***

The two Dnooblians had been reunited the day before when Dluhosh-10 returned from a year-long mission to PLUMBOB's present candidate planet. He and his supervisor, Maghosh-10, felt justified in leaving Dluhosh's data and ship as-is, and taking the rest of the day off for some fish wine and hanging out.

That seemed like a good idea yesterday.

Maghosh's buzzer buzzed for a full minute before he realized what it was.

Dluhosh was curled up unconscious in the wastepaper

basket in the back meeting room. He was wise to have contained himself like this, but he hadn't quite got situated properly before passing out. Now most of his tentacles were asleep.

Maghosh found his radio handset stuck to the floor in a puddle of congealed wine, and answered the call.

"Yeah… Maghosh here."

"Hi, Maghosh! How are we feeling today?" asked the Cricket dispatcher.

Dluhosh awoke at the unpleasant noise and wiped the dried spit from around his beak with the only tentacle he could pull free. His siphon was congested. His normal brick-red and roughened skin had turned gray and dewy. As he listened in, he opened one of his eyes only enough to expose the narrowest slit of pupil above the rim of the basket.

"Is it not funny that one would forget to secure one's own memory wiper unit? You do realize the penalty for unofficial possession," teased the radio voice. "Good thing your transgression is going to save me two rounds of paperwork today, Maggie. Because…"

"Get on with it," said Maghosh.

"Be nice now… I just have one little itty bitty question. Are you boys expecting an egocite handler today for a new mission?"

"Uh…wha…?" The galactic autotranslator turned his grunts into something that the radio voice thought was very funny.

"She is here. Her name is Fleence-18 and she will be at your office in approximately two minutes. She seems very fit and enthusiastic, just like Dnooblians like them. Am I right?"

Dluhosh opened his eyes all the way and said to Maghosh, "Um, Eighteens are humanoid. I don't think I can handle seeing a humanoid in person right now. And there aren't any Dnooblian children on the outpost, are there?"

"No. Look, you stay back there and I'll take care of it. It must be a mistake," said Maghosh.

Dluhosh managed to wobble the wastebasket over and spill himself onto the floor - where he waited for his tentacles to regain feeling.

***

Fleence was dressed in her standard baggy blue canvas fatigues. She paused for a moment to consider the unfamiliar insignia posted on the office door. It was an arrangement of folded and refolded lines. She counted the ends and determined that there were three of these lines — black on a white background.

She entered the office right on time and said, "Hello."

Maghosh maintained his bodily constitution at the first sight of Fleence. But then Dluhosh, still in the back room, vomited at the thought of a humanoid's lips saying 'hello' in Dnooblian. And then Maghosh vomited at the sound of Dluhosh vomiting. It was horrible.

Fleence took a look around thinking that this was more like how an outpost was supposed to be. She didn't know that the odds of encountering and surviving two hung-over Dnooblians were almost zero.

Maghosh apologized, but was hopeful of getting this over with soon. "So there's been some mistake about a mission?" he asked.

"I hope there's no mistake. I've been traveling for a month. I have these orders to be your egocite handler for a PLUMBOB mission leaving for the planet Dirt tomorrow."

"Dirt? Uh, can you be more specific? There are several

planets that could be called something that would translate into Dirt. We recently had a mission to a planet called Ground, for example…"

"No, they were very specific that it is called Dirt," said Fleence.

"Are you sure you're at the right outpost?" asked Maghosh. He sounded less hopeful this time.

"Well, I think so. A 'Maghosh-10' is carbon-copied on all the paperwork I have. And there's supposed to be a Dluhosh-10 as well…" Fleence's words trailed off as she glanced toward the meeting room where the initial sounds of puking had come from. "Really, you don't know about this? Trukk-9 is already there scouting locations."

A voice from deep within the meeting room croaked, "Trukk-9?"

Fleence handed the papers to Maghosh, who gagged when he saw her fingers.

Fleence noticed him struggling, and said, "I know that Dnooblians find humanoids to be sickeningly hideous, so you should know that you can mentally dress me in anything you want. Imagining me covered up by something might help."

Maghosh managed to cover her hands just in time with imaginary Dnooblian catcher's mitts. And then he covered the rest of her in a humanoid-sized beekeeper suit. He shuffled through Fleence's orders, which he had not previously seen.

Dluhosh crawled in. The rules allow either a crawl or a hike over this distance while indoors, as long as laziness isn't the deciding factor. Dnooblians generally accept fish wine poisoning as an adequate mitigating factor in the decision to crawl.

"Trukk-9?" Dluhosh asked. Then he decided he should stick to business before getting so excited about Trukk-9.

"But even if we have a mission, my ship isn't scheduled for a new fuel supply for months."

Maghosh pulled a stamped document with his 'cc' on it from Fleence's stack of papers. It appeared to be a legitimate fuel order. "Well, if this is actually a fuel order and we can actually get the fuel, then I'll suspect that this isn't a hoax."

He called the radio voice back. "Hey, do we have a fuel order available?"

"Yes," replied the radio voice with a hint of a giggle.

"Seriously, you have a fuel order on file – for us – right now?"

"Yes. I am looking at it right here – just came in – with your 'cc' on it. When would you like the fuel delivered, ccHosh?" The radio voice sounded like it was enjoying itself.

"I'll get back to you on that," replied Maghosh. "Do we have an order for fresh self-destruction tablets?"

"No – looks like somebody got lucky on something at least!"

"You'll hear from us again shortly," said an exasperated Maghosh.

"Byyyyeeee," sang the radio voice, accompanied by the sound of her legs rubbing together.

"Uh, I don't suppose they sent fresh self-destruction tablets along with you, did they Fleence?"

"No, they said you'd have mine for me here."

"Alright, well, I'd better call Welter-3."

Welter-3 was a humorless Blister Beetle and top bureaucrat at the PLUMBOB headquarters. He had an oblong red head with a long fluted black proboscis with fleshy lips at the end. His six thighs bore rows of long spines, each with a dew-like drop, scented like marzipan, at its tip. And he had his species' habit of swaying, butt-up, as a warning display whenever it was official business.

Most species preferred to speak with Welter-3 electronically whenever they had to talk to him. He had become very proficient at making the video conference equipment work properly.

Welter-3 said, "Hi guys, we need to make this quick."

Maghosh wasted no time. "Uh, hi, Welter-3. Say, what do you know about a mission to a planet called Dirt? We have an egocite handler here who seems to know a lot more about it than we do. I never received the orders that she has with her."

"Yes. We have orders directly from the administration on Planet One. You were carbon-copied on them. I am not sure why you did not get them."

"When did this Dirt become a candidate planet anyway? Did we completely skip the petitioning process? How is it that the egocite handler got orders a month ago, with my name on them, but I didn't get them until just this minute? And why no self-destruction tablets?"

"I wonder all that myself, but that is not really for us to worry about, is it?" replied Welter. "I assume that you and Dluhosh are able to prepare this mission. Because, that is your job after all – to prepare and execute missions. You will need to be members of the team on this."

Dluhosh chimed in. "Why is Trukk-9 involved? And why is he already at the planet? He must have left months ago."

"I find that interesting myself. What a great opportunity it is for you to work with Trukk-9, Dluhosh. I will try to get back to you with some answers. Good luck gentlemen, I have to call into another meeting." Welter-3 clicked out.

Maghosh turned to Fleence. He took a deep breath and said, "Sorry Fleence, uh, Dluhosh and I need to sleep on this. You might as well get set up in Dluhosh's ship. It's right through that bay door across the hall. His previous egocite handler was an avianoid guy, so your cabin might be awkward. Please check to see that the duplicator has appropriate food for you. I don't know why they haven't given us time for a regulation humanoid conversion."

"Well, it will probably be better than living in a mine shaft. I'll check it out," said Fleence.

"I'm going to make copies of these orders, and then we should take them to the hot springs this evening," said Maghosh to Dluhosh.

"Uh, Fleence, you can come with us if you like. Dluhosh and I will need to soak, but that will be a good place to talk about this development. Hopefully you can meet up with us. There's a map of the outpost on the wall there."

Maghosh reached across the room with a tentacle and touched the spot that indicated the entrance to the EnviroPods.

"Our pod is called Dnooblian Hot Springs. It's about two miles from here. We have to go at full speed. But if you like to sprint, it's a nice trail. We'll see you there at nineteen-hundred hours, okay?"

***

Fleence went to Dluhosh's ship to get settled into her temporary home.

Dluhosh's ship was about the size of Fleence's ship, but was partitioned for two live-aboard passengers. Unlike her ship, there were no decorations on the bridge. The bridge's bulkheads were flat gray. The bridge control stations had no cup holders or foot rests. The floor was bare unheated metal. Fleence could see that the administration took no chances of spending unnecessary budget on this operation.

Fleence's quarters featured a horizontal wooden bar

hanging from ropes over a paper-covered floor. A sculpture made of braided rope and perforated plastic balls with bells inside hung from the ceiling in front of the wooden bar. And a long glass tube with an empty water reservoir at the bottom was attached to the wall. The only other furnishing in the room was a scuffed-up mirror. There was no bed, so she'd have to go get the mattress from her own ship.

The toilet looked like it hadn't been used in a long time, but seemed to be functional. She found a three-foot-long thin blue feather in the shower. She poked the beautiful feather into the hanging sculpture. She needed very little space for clothes since most of her wardrobe was imaginary. The avianoid computer interfaces looked humanoid-compatible.

Once she was familiar with all of the basic ship operations, she relaxed with some acceptable humanoid duplicator food. She entered the details of these experiences into her sketchbook. She drew a picture of the outpost from space, and did a portrait of the plasmanoid customs officer. She wrote about her first impressions of the Dnooblians – leaving out certain details of the hangover parts because she couldn't think of the right words. She parted for the BioPods early to find a good vantage point from which to sketch the Dnooblians sprinting.

***

Maghosh's original set of orders happened to arrive while he and Dluhosh were sleeping.

The two recovering Dnooblians crawled into the hall outside of their shared living quarters and prepared to sprint to the hot springs. The trail wasn't very challenging, so the Dnooblians were required under the rules of terrestrial ambulation to sprint there in two-wheel drive.

Each Dnooblian extended the third tentacle on his right side, and the eighth tentacle on the left, and then whipped them into spinning hoops like fat lassos. The base of each tentacle, where it attached to the body, wound up like a rubber band in a toy airplane.

Then Dluhosh and Maghosh rocked back and forth, alternating traction between the two spinning tentacle wheels. One wheel dropped and propelled while the other lifted to rewind. They continued to rock back and forth like this as they zipped down the hall and onto the forested trail at the entrance to the BioPods.

Fleence had stationed herself on a rise that presented the longest unbroken view of the trail to Dnooblian Hot Springs. She sat with her sketch book, and was ready when she saw the two Dnooblians shooting toward her right on time.

They used their non-wheel tentacles as stabilizers, shock absorbers, and steering levers. Tentacles flailed in seeming chaos. But each tentacle pushed off of a boulder, or looped around a tree trunk to swing the Dnooblians around tight turns. And they swatted leaves and low branches away from their eyes as they streaked by. She sketched what she thought was a reasonable representation of Dluhosh's sprint and labeled the drawing with the date and the place.

Fleence was an excellent runner, but she felt like she ran in deep dry sand as she tried to catch up. When she arrived, Maghosh and Dluhosh were in the hot spring soaking in silence. But they began speaking as soon as they saw her.

Maghosh said, "You might not realize how unusual this is for us."

Fleence was beginning to realize.

"Dluhosh has completed three missions. You may remember the voting processes for the last two rejected planets – Hardpan and Territory?" asked Maghosh.

Fleence nodded.

"Dluhosh did those. And I've been Project Leader on those missions and dozens of others, and I did the monitoring on ten planets myself, including Free-15 and Sphere-16," said Maghosh. "And we've never had a surprise mission like this."

"Wow, you've been doing this for a long time. And Free-15 must have been very interesting. Wasn't it dangerous?" asked Fleence.

"It certainly was interesting, but not that dangerous. Those Bearmen are pretty tame, even sweet, once you know how to handle them. There should be an ursoid Bearman with Trukk-9 if he has his regular crew – so I'll give you some advice. If he tries to get smart with you, just fire right back. The biggest bear will turn into a cub if you shoot him down the first time."

"Sounds like most men…" said Fleence.

"Perhaps. Anyway," said Maghosh, "we always have several months of lead time for a new mission – for preparations and briefings, for recruiting personnel and modifying their quarters, and to update the ship's computers. And there's also time built in for seeing family members, and having a fish wine or two with an old friend."

Fleence stuck her finger into the spring water. It wasn't scalding – only tepid. The spring had a strong mix of organic and mineral smells – nothing like the sterile tubs on Chuffed-18.

Maghosh continued. "Our missions always begin with our monitoring ship leaving in tandem with the video production ship. The video director and his team are always career bureaucrats. We've never had this work handled by private consultants before. Dluhosh just returned from a year on an alien world, and now he has to turn right around and head to another one. We know nothing about the mission. This is unprecedented, and I feel like something isn't right."

"And why Trukk-9? Why would the king of underground cinema want to do a routine government job?" asked Dluhosh.

"Welter stressed that Dirtlings had landed people on their moon less than seventy years after inventing combustion-powered aircraft – he said that Trukk-9 was interested in making a film about that," said Fleence.

"Wow that IS impressive. They went from combustion-powered flight to antimatter technology in only seventy years?" assumed Dluhosh.

"Anyway," said Fleence, "he thinks Dirtlings will be highly intelligent and accomplished, but perhaps also excessively prideful. So he said it was critical that we get egocite data from many Dirtlings."

"How long ago was their first moon landing? Did he say?" asked Maghosh.

"He said it was about forty or fifty years ago now," said Fleence.

"Well, it sounds like it might be a good idea to contact the Dirtlings before they find us first," said Maghosh.

The two Dnooblians extracted themselves from the hot spring. Their skin absorbed the remaining water, and they turned back into their normal rough and reddish selves. They put their thongs back on and tucked in their shells without needing to towel off.

Then Dluhosh asked a final question before they returned to the office. "I don't suppose they provided any information on Dirt's fossil record?"

"No, of course not," replied a pulsing purple Maghosh.

THE EGOCITE DOCUMENTARY

Dluhosh's vessel wasn't the newest or most sophisticated ship in the fleet, and it was too small to be given an official name. But Dluhosh had converted the sink in his quarters into a small hot tub, so it was as comfortable as it needed to be for him.

The ship was saucer shaped in top view, and cigar shaped in side view. The bridge was situated in a clear dome on top of the saucer. A small communications receiver and V-shaped antenna were mounted atop the dome. The living quarters and engine room were below.

A ring of alternating red and white lights flashed around the ship's edge, giving it the illusion of spinning. And the fuselage emitted a green glow and a whirring sound when the ship flew uncloaked in an atmosphere. It had twin antimatter propulsion systems, and was equipped with a cloaking device that was about to miss its regularly-scheduled phase recalibration.

Fleence wore her blue fatigues with the baggy pants tucked into heavy boots. She kept her long brown hair tucked up under a wide-brimmed cloth hat, so that she might as well have been bald. The hat also caused her brow to furrow, which, by design, made it look like she wore a permanent scowl. All of her skin, apart from hands and face, was covered, and the heavy canvas rendered her virtually shapeless. She wore make-up that made her lips appear thin and dry. And her shirt had a single shoulder pad to help offset her symmetry.

The outfit didn't disguise her enough for Dnooblians, however. But Dluhosh was ready for Fleence's appearance this time.

"Okay, I'm all set to go," said Fleence as she came up the ladder from her quarters onto the bridge.

Dluhosh turned to respond and broke out in a big beaky grin. He had put her in a wooden crate with air holes in it. Realizing that imaginary air holes probably aren't necessary in an imaginary crate, he closed them up. "You don't need air holes or peep holes, do you?"

At this, Fleence laughed until it sounded like she was gasping for air. So Dluhosh imagined some air holes again just in case.

Dluhosh realized that he shouldn't feel awkward about any of this. So he changed Fleence into a Dnooblian moose costume complete with giant head, plush antlers, and plastic fangs. Now they were both laughing.

Maghosh called in, "Hey Dluhosh, Welter wants to have a quick video conference – maybe he has some answers."

Welter began. "Hello people, here is what I have been able to find out for you. Apparently your orders went to the wrong outpost. And supposedly the administration is giving Dirt an expedited review because of the possibility that they will achieve intragalactic travel much more quickly than normal."

"Well, I guess that makes sense," said Maghosh. "These Dirtlings must be something really special."

"I suspect so," replied Welter. "And as for Trukk-9, I am told that he just wants to do a film about the process. He volunteered, and who says 'no' to Trukk-9?"

"Not me, that's for sure," said Dluhosh.

Welter continued. "And today – I am serious about this – I had a call from Wulu Griffer-1's Administrator for Internal Affairs. The Vice President himself wants briefings on your progress."

"Really?" said Maghosh. "What legitimate interest does he have with a PLUMBOB mission?"

"Maybe Griffer-1 is a big fan of Trukk-9, do you not think? Just let us know as soon as Dluhosh makes it back, and then we can begin regular briefings on your editing work. Anyway, gentlemen and lady, I have to click on another meeting. So good luck." Welter clicked out.

Dluhosh went back to what he was doing.

"Do you mind if I ask what the insignia on your office door means?" asked Fleence.

"Oh, it's the Dnooblian Golden Rule. The three lines represent truth, accuracy, and obedience. This is the rule that rules all Dnooblian rules. The particular bends in the lines indicate that rules should be taken seriously, made objectively, and implemented precisely – so that the rules are just. Then only fools break the rules. It's always printed in black-and-white like this to indicate that, as long as you know the rule, your decision is between black and white."

"That sounds wise. Does it work?"

"Well, let's just say that there are plenty of fools out there," replied Dluhosh. "But I try to live by it. This PLUMBOB work is rule-intensive, which is why Dnooblians are suited to it. Unfortunately, we always have to answer to insectoids, and their only rule seems to be to do whatever the Ones want."

Fleence changed the subject. "What are you

downloading?"

"Oh, a full collection of Trukk-9's films – plus some training materials for you," said Dluhosh.

"Yeah, sorry about you having to leave so suddenly and then having to train me too."

"Oh, no problem. I'd much rather be working in the field than be stuck in the office editing and writing. Besides, I've never had a rookie with me on a mission. It should be interesting to see your reactions to stuff."

"Well, that's a relief," said Fleence.

"I'll still have to work on the report for my last planet, so I'll have to review those abduction videos anyway. Watching those videos with me should cover most of your training needs. So it's really no extra work."

"That sounds great," she said. "But I want you to know that whatever strangeness you sense with this mission, it's a mystery to me too. It's all strange and mysterious to me, even without the intrigue. This is so far beyond my life experience that I feel like a beaver in a brick factory. But that's why I signed up."

***

The Trukk-9 films that Dluhosh had downloaded included his award-winning masterpiece called The Slaves of The Egocite Mines, which tells the story of Fleence's people, and served to expose the last known pocket of slavery in the Galactic Pool.

"You know Fleence – I don't really know anything about your people. Do you think it would be helpful if I watched his egocite mines film?"

"Yes, please. I'd like to watch it with you too, if that's okay. My mother is prominent in the film and supposedly I'm in one scene," explained Fleence.

"Really!? You're kidding!"

"Nope."

"Wow, does your mother know Trukk-9 personally?"

Fleence's giant moose head nodded.

"Have you met him?"

"Not since I was a little girl, and I don't remember anyway. But my mother wants me to say 'hi' to him from her. I can't wait."

"Yeah, I can't wait either. I also can't wait to see this film. It's the only Trukk-9 production I haven't seen. I guess I've always been squeamish about the idea of watching a film about sexy humanoids."

"I understand, but it's kind of ironic. That's the reason most men watch it, of course."

"Watching it would be a nice work-related item to ease into the mission with. And it would help take a little of the sting off the R&R I'm missing," said Dluhosh.

"Rationalizing like a lumberjack spreading jelly with his chainsaw!" said Fleence.

Dluhosh gave a courtesy laugh as he began the ship's departure sequence. He didn't really get that analogy. He figured it was too culturally specific for the galactic autotranslator. But the analogy seemed colorful and he was feeling better about things.

"Okay. Hang on Fleence! We've got about three months of scanning for wormholes and staring at video screens ahead of us."

Dluhosh announced their intended departure to the outpost control room. "This is Dluhosh-10 and Fleence-18. We are ready for departure."

"Affirmative, sweethearts, do not do anything that I would not do," replied that same annoying radio voice. "Hangar doors unlocked. Airlock breeched. You are hereby and henceforth under general flight rules. Hopefully we will still be here when you return."

"I hope you get a promotion by then," replied Fleence.

"Engine on. Course set. And here we go," said Dluhosh, already reaching for the video play button.

Fleence asked, "Do you mind if I keep the remote control so I can stop the film occasionally to point things out?"

"Not at all. It'll be like a guided tour," replied Dluhosh.

***

The film begins with a zoom down to the moon's surface from a high altitude. As the camera gets closer to the ground it appears to speed up, and then it turns to fly through the landscape of a rugged red rock canyon.

A minimalist string quartet piece builds tension. The sun is low and directly behind the shot, so the glow of late afternoon alternates sides of the canyon as we meander through it – on and on – occasionally bursting through patches of fog. The astute viewer might feel as if they were seeing someone's inner landscape.

At the canyon's terminus stands a dusty woman dressed in homespun rags. She does not speak as the camera hovers in front of her holding her gaze for an awkwardly long moment. She seems not to know what to do.

Fleence paused it. "That's my mother."

"You're kidding!" Dluhosh turned and mentally removed Fleence's moose head. "You do seem to look like her, but it's hard for a Dnooblian to tell."

"Yeah, no problem. I couldn't tell you and Maghosh apart. Like two nuts in a sack."

Dluhosh flinched.

"The only way I could tell it was Maghosh is that he kept getting those beautiful colors on his skin. Is that some kind of an emotional response?"

"Yeah, he was feeling the drama, that's for sure."

"Can you change colors voluntarily, or is it more like a humanoid blushing?"

"Eww… Uh, well, no… Uh, it's sort of like blushing, in that it can be triggered by emotion. But it isn't due to blood rising up under see-through skin like…" Dluhosh felt the dew rising on his own skin. "Anyway, yes, we have innumerable pigment cells that open and close to produce a wide spectrum of colors. Some emotional responses, like what Maghosh did, are very difficult to produce voluntarily. It would be like a humanoid blushing at will. If you can learn to produce those emotional color patterns voluntarily, you can win a fortune playing Dnooblian poker."

Dluhosh produced a deep-blue and white striped pattern that moved in wavelets across his skin like sunlight through rippled water.

"Wow! That is amazing! Does it have a meaning?"

"That is the color for swimming in shark infested waters. That pattern looks conspicuous in the air, but in water it breaks up my shape to confuse my prey and conceal me from my predators. This pattern occurs involuntarily when a Dnooblian goes swimming in the ocean. I learned how to produce this pattern voluntarily by visualizing the ocean very intently."

He morphed into a green and brown dappled pattern to look like a small shrub. Papillae of skin moved to look like leaves vibrating in the wind.

"This one is for hiding in the forest. It's more difficult because it has color, texture, and motion. But making patterns is like playing an instrument – just takes discipline and practice. You can learn almost any pattern."

"Do you do silly ones for fun then – or artistic ones?"

"Here's my impersonation of a volcano."

Dluhosh inverted the point of his head and produced a bright red color around the rim. Tongues of this red moved down his black body like lava flows. Then he said, "BOOM!"

Fleence jumped, and then laughed.

"Sorry, I knew that would get you. I learned that one for a project in school. Here's a thunder cloud."

Dluhosh flattened and spread the top of his head to look like a tiny cumulonimbus incus cloud. Then he flashed blue lightning bolts across his sides.

"That was great!"

"I can do a tropical reef too, with fish and everything, but I'll need to hone my chops before I show you that."

Fleence restarted the video.

The film now shows ancient footage of a sad looking man speaking a language that we cannot understand. He bleats and baws like an animal. The effect on viewers who have only lived under the galactic autotranslator is to give an impression of seeing into the distant past.

Trukk-9 narrates.

"This very pitiful man is from an extinct race of Goat People from Precipice-7. He is speaking an unknown and very very strange language. He was the last known member of his people. No one could understand his language, and he could not understand anyone else. He was a man alone. I like him very much."

Trukk-9 has implied here that since the egocite mines used slave labor, the use of egocite to enable the galactic autotranslator links everyone to this atrocity.

The scene changes to a view from space of a red moon eclipsing a green planet. Trukk-9 continues narrating.

"This is the moon of Cache-6. This is where all the egocite in the galaxy is mined. What you are about to see may be disturbing. However, you will witness the final liberation of a people and perhaps better understand the soul of displaced humanity. The very history of the Galactic Pool is the story of these enslaved people."

The scene cuts to another old grainy clip.

"And here we see some shocking footage uncovered by my team. It shows the invasion of Bounty-2 by soldiers from Planet One. These were the first sapient biological species that either people had encountered. The Bountyans possessed only primitive technology, so the invaders graciously used only primitive weapons against them. But these poor people probably had no way to understand the profound and very terrible horror that rained down upon them from the heavens."

The scene shows armored soldiers jumping to the ground from a low hovering ship. Dust and leaves blow toward the camera.

"As you see, each of these soldiers is armed with a pole bearing a double-edged bayonet at one end and a loop of rope at the other. These monsters used one end of the pole to stab and slice through Bountyans trying to protect their families, and then lassoed their female targets with the other end. No one should be permitted to see this very horrible film clip."

The video shows the clip a second time.

"This is the only known footage of the invasion of Bounty-2. Shortly after this invasion, the administration of Planet One abruptly declared Bounty-2 to be an off-limits wildlife refuge and erased all information about its location. Most scholars view this decision as a cynical move designed to maintain a strong market for the limited number of captured slaves and a tightly controllable limit on the production of slave clones."

The video now shows grainy footage of a meteor streaking through the Planet One sky.

"However, conspiracy philosophers cite administration insiders who reportedly hinted at an intervention and threat from some unknown entity. The philosophers see additional evidence of this intervention in the sudden decrease of their foot size, and a flurry of meteor near-misses at about the same time."

Dluhosh interrupted. "Fleence, can you pause it? I had no idea that humanoids could be so brutal toward other humanoids. I'm sickened."

"Well, no one had any idea how the invasion actually happened until Trukk-9 found this footage. I guess we always believed that they were captured by an old-time grabber beam. Of course, some deniers claim that this film is a fake and that the women voluntarily left Bounty-2. Or some even claim that we were rescued from Bounty-2 before the planet was destroyed somehow. Some say Bounty-2 never existed at all, and we were some kind of artificial chimera."

Out of respect, Dluhosh removed Fleence's moose costume to reveal her fatigues again.

Fleence pressed play.

The scene changes. Trukk-9 is standing in a vast chamber full of books and various other paper records. He gazes around the room with all eleven of the different colored eyeballs scattered about his head. He blinks them all simultaneously. His antler stubs are freshly ground down, so apart from the extra eyes, he looks like an ordinary humanoid.

"I'm standing in the Great Library of ZZZZZZ-3. These halls contain the entire recorded history of this planet, including detailed graphical interpretations of the first alien invasions here."

Trukk-9 opens an ancient volume and interprets its elaborate drawings.

"This beautifully drawn scene depicts an invading Planet One army encountering large insectoids of many different species. As you can see here, these very terrible humanoid soldiers are firing on these unarmed insectoids, but most of the bullets are passing through with no apparent damage. Individual insectoids of the different species are depicted here setting upon helpless soldiers – stinging, piercing, ripping, crushing, and literally sucking the life from the humanoids. Dozens of men never returned to Planet One."

Trukk-9 turns the large page of parchment, and the camera scans the images.

"And this image depicts the retreat of the humanoid raiders. These Planet One invaders were scouting for things to plunder, and had hoped to meet little resistance."

The next set of drawings depicts the Planet One invaders returning to spray insectoidicide.

"This spraying program continued for many years as Planet One tried to wipe the insectoids from ZZZZZZ-3. The effort was, of course, unsuccessful. As we know, the numbers of insectoids initially decreased, but they became more resistant to the poisons over successive generations. Eventually even the resistant insectoids grew weary of the assaults, so they negotiated a treaty with Planet One."

The camera pulls back to reveal Trukk-9's insectoid host.

"I'm sitting with Dr. T'kleezitch-3. Hello, Doctor."

"Hello, Trukk-9. It's a pleasure to welcome you to ZZZZZZ-3. And if you have trouble with insectoid names, you can call me Doctor Tickly."

"Thank you. Doctor Tickly, can you tell me what the terms of this peace treaty were? And also please help us understand how it continues to influence the relationship between ZZZZZZ-3 and Planet One."

"Yes. The terms of the treaty stated that Planet One would stop spraying us with insectoidicide if we did whatever they wanted."

"That leaves open a lot of possibilities, doesn't it Doctor? How did the treaty play out?"

"Well, they did not want us living on Planet One, so they set up factories here on ZZZZZZ-3 and made us work in them. Because we are so hard to kill, they moved all of their hazardous manufacturing processes and waste storage facilities here."

"And then a very strange thing happened. Can you explain the next phase in your relationship, Doctor Tickly?"

"Yes. They began dumping their convicts here."

The doctor turns to a page in the middle of a large book. The artwork depicts groups of desperate humanoids being rounded up by Ant Police.

"Of course, we did not want these dangerous criminals running around on ZZZZZZ-3 where ordinary citizens would be forced to chomp them in half or sting them to death. So we built prisons to house them in. Every time Planet One dumped off a load of convicts, we rounded them up and imprisoned them – for their own good, mostly."

"But you didn't know what these prisoners' crimes were or how long their sentences were supposed to be. Am I right, Doctor?"

"That is correct. We expected Planet One to come get them when their sentences were done. But this never happened. Then they came to collect a prisoner that was needed as a witness. The delegation from One was amazed at how well-run and efficient our prisons were compared to their prisons. That is when they realized that we could be valuable as organizers and administrators."

"Right – and that continues to be a major role of your people today."

"Yes, we still run most of their institutions."

"Doctor Tickly, allow me to ask you this. Have you ever fed upon a humanoid from Planet One?"

The Doctor seems stunned by the question. He appears not to be sure how to play along – which is what Trukk-9 wants.

"Well, Trukk-9, I am, uh… we, I mean my people… We are a species of Pleasing Fungus Beetle. I have cured the fungal infections of a few Planet One patients by licking off the infected layers of skin, yes. But I would never harm a One. They are lovely people, sir."

Trukk-9 says, "Lovely people…" And then he thanks Doctor Tickly for his time and good humor.

Trukk-9 continues his narration over footage of the tropical jungle of the planet Fermament-4.

"Fortunately for the Fermamentians of Fermament-4, the Ones discovered them only after the insectoids had gained considerable influence. The insectoids reminded the Ones how much the wasted insectoidicide had cost during the invasions of ZZZZZZ-3. The insectoids encouraged the Ones to discover value on this next world via a diplomatic approach. So the Ones compromised and sent a heavy ship to Fermament-4 to, as they claimed, 'accidentally' melt a mountain."

The camera lifts through jungle fog at the top of a waterfall to reveal The Great Melted Mountain of Fermament-4. Children recite a nursery rhyme.

"This is the mountain of Fermament-4
The melting of which opened our door
Planet One did it once, and they did it some more
The Galactic Pool added these planets four
Blue-5 and Cache-6 avoided war
Precipice-7 is what Goat People are for
Millet Fields-8 gave us birdies galore

And that is the Compromise of Fermament-4!"

"Every schoolchild recognizes this very special place as the first of the five melted mountains in the Great Melted Mountains Galactic Parks. The Ones' tactic was to go to a planet, melt a mountain, and open diplomacy with profuse apologies. This attention getting device is now referred to as the Fermament-4 Compromise, and was used to great effect on the next four Galactic Pool member planets."

The camera pans over each of the Melted Mountain Parks on each of the planets from equally dramatic vantage points.

"Now, at the time, the Fermamentians were a pre-industrial civilization with vast mineral resources that they had not developed any need for."

The film shows historic footage of a Fermamentian garden and market square. Smoke is heavy in the air as grotesquely asymmetrical Fermamentian humanoids go about their business tromping through mud and shit. All the extra noses poking out through random tufts of greasy hair make them especially sensitive to their own stench.

"I should say that the Fermamentians themselves regard Fermamentians to be an ugly species. To be kind, one says that each individual Fermamentian has a 'very complex symmetry'. But like other humanoids, they naturally consider more bi-laterally symmetrical individuals to be more beautiful."

The video now shows rare footage of a Fermamentian beauty contest that has been decided on penalties after an over-time draw. An accompanying dirge is sung by the Scablands-17 Industrial Accident Choir.

"Therefore, the Fermamentians eagerly accepted a deal for some of the most symmetrical, high-grade Bountyan clone slaves in exchange for mineral exploration rights and certain royalties. The resulting mining activities turned Fermament-4 into a very wealthy planet almost overnight. And the mineral wealth generated for Planet One financed a series of planetary conquests."

Dluhosh asked, "Can you pause it for a second?"

Fleence hit pause.

"Was your clone line involved in this trade deal?"

"Yes. I can trace my lineage back to a young woman who was taken from Bounty-2. She is my great-great-times-twenty-eight-grandmother. My twenty-third great grandmother and all of her sisters and daughters were traded to Fermament-4 in this deal."

"And so you are from one of the high graded clone lines then?" asked Dluhosh.

"Yes, well, I hope this doesn't sound vain, but the legends say that all of my grandmothers were marketed as the most beautiful women in the galaxy. Supposedly a war was fought between rival counties on Fermament-4 over a single genetic sample from one of my grandmothers. And a Fermamentian Viscount is said to have traded the most lucrative nickel mine in the galaxy for one of my grandmothers when she was eighty years old."

"So humanoid men must behave strangely in your presence?" asked Dluhosh as he twirled a tentacle tip around at the side of his head in the universal sign for nuttiness.

"Well, yes, I guess you could say that I never get to know how humanoid guys normally behave. And to make things worse, I have another awkward telepathy that you'll see described coming up in the film. Basically, I have to be very careful about saying anything nice to men. Plus this wardrobe function wasn't really necessary, but I was young and wanted to remain tied for the most desirable humanoid in the Galactic Pool. But now I'm stuck with it."

"It will be interesting to observe our male abductees on Dirt. I'll make sure they don't get too randy."

"Oh, you probably don't have to worry about me," said Fleence.

"Good. So then you were born into slavery, right?".

"Right. I think Trukk-9 is about to explain it."

Trukk-9's narration continues. "Over many generations, freed clones on Fermament-4 gained power and began to advocate for an end to slavery."

Now the scene is of early protest marches on Fermament-4. The marchers are both native Fermamentians and Bountyan clones. Ugly men with chains and shields hold back large dog-like animals all along the parade route.

"The protests succeeded, and for a long time we all believed that slavery was a thing of the past. But then I found something very inexplicable when I started research for a film about egocite."

The scene is now hidden-camera footage of a buzzing office full of various insectoids processing paperwork and slamming rubber stamps on documents six at a time.

"I couldn't get a visa to visit the egocite mines. Ostensibly this was because of the toxic nature of the high levels of egocite in the atmosphere. The consulate of Cache-6 said that only robots and insectoids could survive there."

The scene switches to a view of Trukk-9 sleeping under a clear dome.

"I had the feeling that this was not true. So I stole an extremely weathered ingot of egocite from a university laboratory. Here you see that I am in a sealed chamber breathing egocite-saturated air. I lived in that box for two weeks with no apparent harm. My doctors documented this, and we presented the results along with another visa application to the Cache-6 officials."

A large hairy hand slaps the clear dome above a sleeping Trukk-9's head and he startles awake. He hits his forehead on the dome and we hear roaring laughter.

"The insectoid administrators then made the excuse that the robot miners were not capable of distinguishing humanoids from other dangerous animals and they couldn't be trusted to not kill me. It should be noted that the good Squirrel People of Cache-6 played no part in these affairs. So I simply flew to the moon in my cloaked ship and the insectoids never suspected a thing. I was appalled at what I found."

The video returns to the image of the red-dust covered woman at the egocite mine. The camera pulls back to reveal that she is now standing with all of her identical sisters.

"The real secret hidden on the moon was the legendary Lost Lineage of Bountyan clone slaves! And, as you can see, their beauty is literally the stuff of legends."

The camera pulls back farther to reveal some hills beyond the desert that are covered by long swaths of green.

"But it turns out that the real profit from egocite mining came from something other than the egocite itself. My trusted crew and I remained aboard my cloaked ship as we studied the situation."

The video now shows a group of well-dressed multi-nosed fellows holding beverages and bragging about their exploits.

"As you see here, we observed the daily hikes that these Fermamentian men take through these immaculately groomed green hills. They are hiking in groups of thirty-two, and all appear to be engaged in some sort of sport that involves hitting small balls into slightly larger holes from a tremendous distance with a long stick."

The scene changes to a man taking practice swings and then placing a small dimpled ball on a hover tee.

"Each man has a bag of sticks and a ball, and they each hit their ball toward the hole in turn. There appears to be an energy field on either side of the grass lane acting as a bumper to keep their balls in the center. Each thirty-twosome is followed by a small six-wheeled basketbot. The bot is outfitted with a single-purpose grabber beam that collects the egocite ingots as they form behind the group of men."

The camera zooms in behind a group of hiking men.

"Now, you must watch this scene very closely. Watch the ground directly behind this group... There! An ingot seems to leap up from the ground as if it were a silver egg being laid by the fairway itself. A single ingot forms behind the hikers about once per hole. As you see here, the ingots are a metallic version of the little ball that the men are hitting."

The scene is shown a second time, but in slow motion and zoomed to the spot where the ingot forms.

"The ingot takes the form of the object that represents the thing that the men are most proud of. And it requires the combined egos of this many men, all excessively proud of the same thing, to pull the egocite together from its gaseous state. But once the crystal forms, the material is relatively stable. However, its crystalline configuration can be altered by a single sufficient ego."

Dluhosh interrupted. "Is that as ridiculous as I think it is, Fleence?"

"Yes it is. Everyone thinks that egocite mining is absurd. Well, maybe not those thirty-two guys... But they are so full of themselves that they're like sea slugs in slingshots."

Dluhosh had no idea what that analogy could possibly

mean, but it seemed funny, and they both enjoyed a good laugh.

"Anyway," said Fleence, "it is the only way they've been able to make egocite crystallize in an efficient manner with a convenient shape."

Fleence restarted the video.

The scene now cuts to a view through a bay door of the ingot packing warehouse where robots and their insectoid monitors are working. The soundtrack plays the actual ambient sound from the warehouse.

The audio captures the distinctive ringing sound of the egocite as it is handled and jostled by the robots. It sounds something like cicadas buzzing on a hot afternoon accompanied by a hundred tuning forks being swung around on steel strings. The robots themselves produce a low frequency hum under the ringing. The scene is hypnotic and lasts a very long time.

Trukk-9 narrates again as the warehouse audio fades.

"We've been observing this very strange warehouse for several days, and it appears to process about ninety ingots per day. This production rate would require eight or nine teams of thirty-two men playing this bizarre game for full ten-hour days. But these men are not slaves. In fact, as it turned out, these men are paying vast sums to belong to this country club."

The scene now shows an egocite vapor spraying operation preparing its equipment.

"As you can see here, the raw egocite ingots fit into these air-tight, ego-proof pods. Each pod then fits into one of the drones that are used to spray the vaporized egocite into the atmosphere of each planet in the Galactic Pool. This aerial spraying program creates the so-called egotrails that were originally described by conspiracy philosophers."

The video cuts to footage of a plump Planet One

humanoid wearing a white tank-top and track pants. His tabby hair is cut in a then-popular style. He stands outside of his desert hover-home and points at a vapor trail in the sky while his ears twitch. The man is saying something, but his voice is nothing but unintelligible grunts and squeaks.

Trukk-9 continues. "It only takes a very low concentration of vaporized egocite to activate the galactic autotranslator. Here you will witness how an observer uses a new egocite-enabled camera to capture the final moments of pan-galactic misunderstanding. Listen closely to the voice of the philosopher."

"Gluh frubub screeeee... tellin' ya, I don't believe in no goddamn coincidences!"

Trukk-9 continues, "Additionally, a few of the ingots are reserved for scientists who will use them for experiments and psychological testing."

The scene changes and Trukk-9 is speaking in a tense whisper in front of what look like cave entrances at the base of a hill a hundred meters distant.

"We want to document the daily lives of the slaves, but we need to infiltrate their community in order to film inside the old mine shafts where they live. What I am about to do not only puts me at great peril, but is certainly illegal. And I have no idea how these clones will react to a stranger. I am going to present myself as a doctor who is here to evaluate the stress of their work."

Trukk-9 strides toward the shafts. The music rises as he walks. It is an aria sung in the plaintive voice of a Dnooblian tenor. The video view changes to a hidden camera on Trukk-9's lapel, and he narrates off camera.

"They were surprised that I wasn't an insectoid doctor, but they seemed comforted to know that I wouldn't be licking them. I was relieved to find that they were warm and welcoming. I liked these people very much."

The scene is now of Trukk-9 being surrounded by the women.

"Here I am explaining to them that they are the only slaves known to still exist in the Galactic Pool. I'm telling them that I need to document their living conditions in order to take the evidence back to help them win their freedom."

The scene cuts to an interior of a luxurious bedroom.

"The women allow me to secretly film one of their so-called coaching sessions with the Fermamentian country club sportsmen. Because these women were born and raised in an egocite saturated atmosphere, they have certain... I'll call it 'abilities' that most people don't have. I advise strong guidance for your children and other sweet darlings if you choose to allow them to view this shocking footage."

The video now shows a pair of clone women, who look like Fleence, standing over a young man as he reclines on skins of unknown animals. The women kneel and start to coach.

"You have the most beautiful swing I've ever seen! Please, please let me sing its praises. Ah, there... What did you shoot today? Oh, that's my favorite number!" And they begin to sing.

"Oh, handsome man, you shot a 143
And you did it just for she and me
You hit the ball too far to see
And we worship thee

Oh, handsome man, your putts were true
And you drove the ball into the blue
The eagles and the birdies flew
And we worship you

Oh, handsome man, of low handicap
Your ball rarely, if ever, finds the trap
But when it does, your skills you tap
And we worship you, chap!"

This goes on for several minutes as both women take turns flattering this man and his 'exquisite technique' with skillfully improvised verse. The man writhes on the floor under the spell of their telepathic sexual powers.

Trukk-9 continues. "As you can see, each man has his ego built up to very specific dimensions."

The scene now shows the slaves' living area.

"And here you can see how the slaves live in these abandoned mine shafts that are left from previous, less profitable, egocite mining techniques. The slaves are allowed to clone themselves and have families, which, of course, provide the next generation of slaves."

The scene changes to something that appears to be unrelated to anything else in the film so far. A glistening yellow Swamp Master is skinning eels on the planet Swampy-12 in the radiant glow of the setting sun. In the director's commentary Trukk-9 explains that, despite the various hypotheses of many film scholars, the scene looked nice and he wanted to use it in something.

"I thoroughly documented the practices and conditions that these last of the slave clones had to endure. And I smuggled out this woman to present as evidence to the Galactic Assembly in order to plead for these people's freedom."

The scene changes to Trukk-9's famous speech to the full membership of the Galactic Assembly. His companion stands at his side as he prepares to speak.

The camera scans the interior of Assembly Hall, which is crowded with delegates. Giant Squirrels cling high up on the hall's pillars. Hulking Bearmen and Bearwomen form a scrum in the center, where they jostle each other with a rough, but playful, spirit. Plasmanoids adopt various imitative shapes as they weave their ways through the crowd. Humanoids, some with excessive eyes or extra noses, form tight nervous groups. Beautiful tall blue and green birds perch in the balconies. A few Dnooblians and Snake Apes appear to be self-sequestered against the back wall. Swamp Masters and Mudskippers slide and flip, respectively, into and out of a large shared tub in one corner. Goat People observe from narrow ledges along the hall's walls. Crab People peer out from under a large low table. And, of course, various insectoids are busy flitting from task to task in their role of organizing the event.

Trukk-9 begins his speech. "Ladies and Gentlemen of the Galactic Assembly, I present my new, very great friend. Her name is Kyleence."

Mentioning Kyleence's name without using a customary planetary numeric designation after her name would normally be a big *faux pas* in such a formal introduction. This small shock to the delegates' sensibilities served to underscore that she was a woman without a homeland.

"She is a slave from the egocite mine on the moon of Cache-6. I have smuggled her from the mine at great risk to us both, as well as to my loyal crew. Slavery still exists in the Galactic Pool! And it appears that it's being done with the knowledge of the Fermamentian Oligarchy!"

Trukk-9 is forced to yell above much loud chattering coming from the pillars, "I have to say, however, that the good Squirrel People of Cache-6 appear to have no knowledge of this activity!"

The chattering ceases and the hall falls silent.

Trukk-9 is one of the few civilians who could make accusations like this in front of the Galactic Assembly and be taken seriously.

The remainder of the film is a montage of images from television news reports that show the liberation of the slaves, the ensuing hearings and trials, and the abdication of the throne by the Fermamentian King.

The final scene is of the sights and sounds of red dust blowing in drifts against mine shaft entrances in the late afternoon sun. Small flocks of domesticated fowl with nothing left to eat but themselves traverse the barren landscape.

"Fleence, that was intense. That's your mother at the Galactic Assembly too, right? And you are one of the children we see playing outside the mine shafts?"

"Yes, that was her. As for me, I can't tell for sure, since we all look alike, and I don't remember Trukk-9 being there. But my mother says I'm running around with the other kids in that scene. She has told me so many stories so many times that I almost feel like I remember. I think she still has a thing for him. I suspect that they had primary contact during his visit. She's like a little churdle wishing for her tusks."

Dluhosh had no idea what a churdle is or why it wants tusks, but he laughed and said, "Fleence, I have to say, it's an honor to be working with someone who was born into slavery AND has been in a Trukk-9 film."

"Well, thanks, but I didn't have much say in it, of course."

"So anyway, Fleence, what happened when you all moved to Chuffed-18?"

"Right, so the rulers of Fermament-4 offered to provide a sterile planet for us. And for its part, Planet One provided the terra-forming work. I have to say, they did a very nice job. They brought in all sorts of plants and animals from all over the galaxy. We have beautiful oceans and forests, and the climate of Chuffed-18 is like perpetual spring."

"Well, I guess that's a good start," said Dluhosh.

"Yes, and many tens of thousands of Bountyan clone women left Fermament-4 and Planet One and settled there. My mother and her sisters of the Lost Lineage found themselves to be quite a sensation. Humanoids from all over the galaxy, especially wealthy Fermamentians, offered huge sums of money just to have us be nice to them while they reclined on skins or in hot tubs. My mother set up the first clone conversation club and constructed a course so men could pretend like they were egocite mining. The entire industry built up around her concept."

"Your mother must be a very successful woman."

"Yes, she is one of the ten richest women in the galaxy."

"No way," said Dluhosh. "That would make her richer than the Queen of Dnooblia... It's like you are a princess of some kind."

Fleence had to laugh at this. "It's definitely a slave-girl-to-princess kind of a story. But I did my time working for five years as a conversation hostess. It was very lucrative, however. For example, if you were a Fermamentian Viscount, and you wanted to spend a year like this with me alone on this ship, it would cost you a cool hundred million. And if you touched me even once, I'd kick your teeth out and bill you double."

"I'm glad I have a beak," said Dluhosh.

"Anyway, I retired and got bored, so I bought a ship and put myself through egocite handler training. And here I am."

"Well, I have to say that I'm very happy to have you along. And I'm happy to know that I'm making a Fermamentian Viscount very jealous right now." Then he asked how Fleence's wardrobe trick worked.

"Ah, well, that only works for those of us who were born in the mines where the atmosphere is saturated with egocite. So it only takes splicing some rather simple code into my cells to create the link between my natural telepathic field and a person's imagination."

"Huh… That would be like someone else having the ability to change my colors for me, come to think of it."

"Yeah, it was hard to get used to."

"So how do they mine egocite now?" asked Dluhosh.

"Oh, basically in the same way. The slaves were replaced by well-paid women from a variety of species, including somewhat symmetrical Fermamentians and very leggy Leaf Hoppers. It turns out that a woman doesn't have to be a telepathic high-grade clone to convince a man of his mastery of the little ball."

BACK TO TRUKK-9'S ARRIVAL

Trukk-9 and his crew arrived on Dirt at about the same time as Fleence and Dluhosh set out from the outpost.

Their journey had been uneventful. But Trukk-9 and his crew had never before encountered such a high density of wormholes leading from all directions to one place, despite their having travelled throughout the civilized galaxy. Trukk-9's ship exited through the end of the final wormhole uncomfortably close to Dirt.

Trukk-9's crew included his ursoid cinematographer, pilot, bodyguard, and best friend, Dee Ay En-15. Dee looked like an upright grizzly bear with humanoid hands. He was a Bearman's Bearman. Dee had saved Trukk-9's life on several occasions. And he had an uncanny ability to interpret Trukk-9's spherical vision. Trukk-9 was fond of saying that, "Without Dee as my cinematographer, I could never translate my vision for two-eyeds."

His engineer, gaffer, key grip, sound man, and another long-time collaborator and friend, was a plasmanoid named Stick.E-5. Being a plasmanoid with unlimited appendages, he could handle even more simultaneous tasks than a

Dnooblian. Stick.E was blue and translucent. He normally took the form of a bi-pedal humanoid to make everyone comfortable. But when being lazy about holding his humanoid shape, he tended to become very long and thin with a bulbous head and large, black, almond-shaped eyes.

Stick.E's specialty was using his custom-built array of grabber beams that he could operate en masse with high speed and precision. He used these beams to great effect by manipulating objects, including people and animals, for some of Trukk-9's most successful films.

And his fourth crew member was a veteran PLUMBOB Research Assistant and computer text translation specialist – an insectoid named O'Buzznid-3. He was personally selected for the mission by Welter-3 who mailed him to Trukk-9's home packed in a refrigerated case with instructions not to revive him until they got to Dirt.

Trukk-9's ship was his own personal craft. The Cruiser Duke Sukk-9 was recognizable by most people in the Galactic Pool because it had been a feature of so many of Trukk-9's films. The Duke, as the ship was known, was several times larger than Dluhosh's ship, but was the same general flying saucer shape. The similarities ended there, however.

The Duke's observation dome had variable tint control, and the antenna on top was a modern hoop design. The outer hull was gold plated, and multi-colored lasers replaced the normal perimeter lights. The floors on all decks were electronically carpeted to suit the preference of any crew member at any time. Each crew member's cabin had a personal duplicator and en suite bathroom.

The inner walls of The Duke were decorated with exquisite works of art from all over the galaxy, and various awards, including Trukk-9's Galactic Loop Prize. The cargo hold doubled as a gym with all the latest equipment, and there were elevators as well as spiral staircases between decks. Had Trukk-9 been able to secure permission for a quantum radio, The Duke would have been the most modern and luxurious civilian flying saucer in the galaxy. Plus it was a workhorse.

Trukk-9's instructions were simple and the opportunity was exciting. He saw only benefits in his involvement. His cinematic stylization techniques were perfectly suited to PLUMBOB work. His artistry and spherical vision would present a truer image of the Dirtlings, and would, therefore, advance democracy throughout the Galactic Pool. Plus he would make a pile of money and win some more awards.

***

Buzzy said, "Okay, I have a list of potential greeting examples. Do you want to start with complex greetings, or would you prefer to start in a place where they barely acknowledge each other? There appear to be plenty of the latter, but I think you might be interested in the greetings of a country called Hippopotamus."

"Really? You mean it's named after an animal like a Swampy-12 flippopotamus?" asked Trukk-9.

"Yes, that is what I had in mind. But these Dirt ones are much bigger and they do not appear to flip."

"Are they huggers?" asked Dee.

"I do not believe they are built for hugging. They are very large quadrupeds with stubby limbs."

"Not the flippos, Buzzy! I mean the humanoids! HAAHAA!" said Dee.

"I am not sure if these particular humanoids hug. But it says they have many clever benedictions and they use ritualized insults in greetings."

"Well if I can't get hugs, I'll settle for insults! Let's go!

Oh, sorry Skip, I mean I would vote that we go there."

"Yes, Dee. Let's go there Buzzy."

Buzzy said, "On other planets I have found that following public transportation is an effective way to observe greetings. We need to document transportation too, so we might get a couple of checklist items out of it."

"Good," said Trukk-9. "I'm excited to get started."

They flew to the biggest city in 'Hippopotamus' and checked the main roads leading out of town. Stick.E saw something with potential.

"Hey, check this out guys. This van looks like it's leaving from a transport depot. I see a number of well-dressed, highly symmetrical humanoid passengers with baggage. My guess is that they would be travelling home from here."

Stick put the scene up on the shared video monitor.

A beat-up green van with about twenty-five people in it kicked up a red dust cloud in the middle of a green savannah next to a large river. Several of the passengers wore flowing robes in shining blues and purples with elaborate golden embroidery. The light was good.

As they tracked the van, Buzzy shared a few of the example greetings he had read about.

"From what I am able to translate, I think these people use elaborate ritualized greetings, and some of the special types include the use of insults. For example, when they meet another individual with a particular family name, they will launch into a string of insults, such as 'You eat beans', 'Your kids are ugly', 'Your wife dresses in rags', and things like that. They will engage in these ritualized insults even if the other person is a stranger, but they often pile it on heavy if they are the best of friends."

"Okay, Dee, get us up right next to the van," ordered Trukk-9. Their cloaked vessel tracked alongside as the crew listened in. Stick.E created an egocite delivery tube with a grabber beam, and pumped the vapor into the van.

One well-dressed man spoke. "I'll be getting off at Balontan in a few minutes," he said to the eldest man. "Old Pilgrim, I have enjoyed your company and I wish you peace and prosperity. Please greet your family and your many children and grandchildren for me. I wish you and them the best of health."

The old man said, "Right on! They will hear it. You Numun. Iron hammering man, you and your work! May you find your house in perfect order. Greet all the people of Balontan, and enjoy good health."

The well-dressed man, who was named Numun, replied, "Right on! Right on! Right on! Amen!" And as the van pulled into Balontan, Numun gave the other passengers similar farewells and benedictions.

Dee asked, "Are you guys getting a translation on all those 'freaking awesomes' the men keep saying? It's what they are saying repeatedly between greetings. That can't be what they're really saying, is it? I think that damn autotranslator is stinking it up again."

Trukk-9 said, "I think you mean what I'm hearing as 'right on' – sort of like an 'all's well' perhaps?"

Buzzy confirmed this and added, "I am hearing 'Splendid! Splendid! Splendid!' right there."

***

Numun's eventual arrival at the village was expected, but the exact arrival date was unknown. A small boy saw him disembark and ran to tell Numun's family. A crowd of dozens of family members and friends of all ages gathered around. This festive scene was noisy and colorful.

Numun began his greetings and benedictions with the

eldest men and women and worked his way down the age groups.

The youngest men seemed to be in awe, as did a few of the young women. Numun ignored the children until he had greeted and asked after all the adults. Then he opened a sack and gave candy and small gifts to the children, who had a great time beating the crap out of each other until all the gifts were fairly distributed.

Trukk-9 was impressed. "Wow, listen to him go. He must have said 'right on' a thousand times. How can he possibly keep track of all those people and names? That was impressive. How do the shots look, Dee?"

"Sweet."

"Sound?"

"Nice and clean," replied Stick.E. "I haven't heard any insults yet though."

Trukk-9 said, "I think we should stick with this scene for a while. It looks like there might be a party. That would give us another checklist item, right?"

As things settled down in Numun's family concession, a couple of teen boys brought in a small charcoal stove and a silver tea set with four demitasse glasses. They had enough tea and sugar to fuel this party all night long.

Numun retired to a small walled-off space with a bucket of hot water and a plastic kettle. The boys made tea while Numun bathed.

As the party built up steam, many people came and went, greeted and chatted, slurped tea, played cards, and danced to very loud and distorted pop music. Still, no one exchanged insults.

Finally, a man of Numun's age, and similarly dressed in a bright blue flowing gown, arrived.

The younger men playing the music and cards stopped chattering and turned down the volume. The new visitor strode in through the concession door like a big shot. The man said, not yet looking at Numun, "I hear that my beast of burden is back. Yes, I can hear the shrieks of ugly children. You should know that your wife has taken up with a donkey while you were away – maybe your next child will be better looking!"

"I smell cow shit! Someone let a cow in here. A cow that's obviously been eating beans…" said Numun.

"We have insults! And good ones too!" said Dee.

These two men were bound from birth into a custom handed down from time immemorial. Djiana was a herder and Numun was a blacksmith. They were born in the same month of the same year. They grew up sniping at each other like this. They had been at it for over thirty years. But Numun had been away since the end of the last dry season, so they had some catching up to do.

They finally looked at each other and then went through another fifteen minutes of 'right on!' and 'amen!' and about ten different kinds of handshakes. They stopped to gossip for a minute and then went right back to greeting like they had just met. They asked after everyone who they mutually knew.

They sprinkled in the occasional 'bean eater' and 'my slave' insults, and got down to catching up over some serious tea, cigarettes, and cards. Numun had brought kola nuts from the city too. Boys dragged in a handmade foosball table, and the party raged through the night.

***

"So, Buzzy, what's the purpose of all these wonderful insults?" asked Trukk-9.

"According to what I have read, these two men are allowed to say anything they want to each other. In fact, they have to be able to say anything, and their counterpart has to accept anything that is said without being insulted or disagreeing. The men are called 'joking cousins', or something like that, and they work together to help settle disputes. For example, if two Djianas have a dispute, they find a Numun. They know that a Numun will not lie to them. And because he is a joking cousin of theirs, they have to accept the ruling as final – no disagreement, no resentment."

Trukk-9 was very pleased. He liked the term 'joking cousin' very much. The other crew members also liked the term, though each heard a slightly different translation with more-or-less equivalent meaning. Trukk-9's translation was 'jocular playmate'. Dee heard 'grapple cubby'. Buzzy heard 'leg-rubbing co-pupa'. And Stick.E heard 'easy melders'.

"You know, I think that this would play really well on your planet, Dee," said Trukk-9.

"Yep, this could be huge on Free-15, Skip. We love this sort of jocular backslapping."

"Brilliant work guys," added Trukk-9.

The crew continued to film the party until it ended well into the dawn. When the last card was slammed onto the table, Numun said, "Those insects I hear must be your children calling for their father."

Djiana responded, "Well, then I better get home before your children swoop down and eat them."

Buzzy moaned. "Well, for this planet to have a chance, I think you will need to edit out that last insult for the voters on ZZZZZ-3."

THE DNOOBLIA DOCUMENTARY

During a long stretch of empty space, Dluhosh suggested they watch the Trukk-9 film about Dnooblia.

"Sure, I was hoping you would suggest it. Is it a good portrayal?" asked Fleence.

"Yes, in fact, The Dnooblian Academy of Accuracy awarded Trukk-9 its highest honor for the film. He's the only non-Dnooblian to ever win it. The Academy wanted to recognize Trukk-9's stylization technique for its unconventional way of getting at the accurate truth."

"So it's the accuracy you enjoy?" asked Fleence.

"Yes – therein we find the ecstasy. I'm not at all interested in cinema with little or no truth in it. To me, nothing is worse than some outer-space science-fiction farce with special effects and crazy space aliens and impossibly heroic deeds. My friend Mudhosh enjoys all of that, but for me this film is the acme of truth through art."

Dluhosh punched it up on the computer.

The film begins with an aerial sequence that flies the viewer through a misty gray and dark green forested landscape. The camera then breaks out of the fog to reveal miles and miles of Dnooblians sitting in cages. The cages sit at the top of a long cliff where they overlook ocean vistas. The Dnooblians sit as if frozen – many with mouse nests in their mouths, spider webs in their ears, and ravens or robins perched on their heads.

The camera zooms in to Trukk-9 where he stands at the edge of a forest above a sea cliff in an area free of Dnooblians. He shouts over the sound of wind and surf.

"This is what they do – every one of them – for a year – before becoming adults! This, I believe, is what gives Dnooblians their amazing observational skills and highly disciplined and truthful nature! I like them very much!"

The camera zooms in for a close-up of Trukk-9's face.

"I can see easily into the soul of a humanoid, and I use this vision to capture the soul on film. But I cannot yet see the soul of a Dnooblian. The soul of a Dnooblian is too deep. So I, myself, will sample the Dnooblian Drying Out Time rite. For one month I will sit in a cage at the top of a cliff. And then, and only then, will I make my film about the Dnooblians."

The view changes to focus on the empty cage that Trukk-9 is standing next to.

"We have duplicated my cage in the style of a traditional Dnooblian cage, except that it is much larger, of course, and what appears to be wood is reinforced concrete. And I have a sheet-metal floor. We are in the deep wilderness in an area that closely resembles a traditional Drying Out Time area. I have secured permission from the Dnooblian High Council to set myself up here. They will not guarantee my safety, but this area is not frequented by Dnooblians, so I should be able to hide for a month."

Fleence paused the video. "So you've undergone this Drying Out Time too?"

"Yes," replied Dluhosh. "The Drying Out Time must be completed before we are taught how to tolerate humanoids."

"I'm trying to picture you in one of those cages with a nest in your mouth."

"Picture me with weasels in my siphon instead – me and a pack of vicious Dnooblian greater flying weasels and small animal carcasses stripped to the bone scattered all around. The weasels kept all the other living animals away from my cage."

"That's too bad," said Fleence.

"Not really – spiders didn't built webs in my ears, and mice didn't nibble my beak. And because the tops of our heads sometimes collapse into a bowl shape, birds will build nests in there and shit all over my eyes. So I was able to see more detail and to concentrate enough to make out slowly shifting patterns in moving features – the fluctuations in river flow, the tides of the sea, the slowly migrating waves of sand dunes, and the movement of stars across the sky. I learned to see in time lapse, essentially. And the weasels were interesting companions until my parents showed up. The weasels almost killed them."

"Oh no – what happened?"

"Well, I was protected from any bites due to my dried skin, of course. But my parents were freshly soaked in preparation for the big day. They arrived in the traditional way – in a sprint with their tentacles linked together to form the wagon bed they'd carry me out on. And the pack of weasels attacked them."

"Oops."

"My parents had difficulty untangling their wagon as they screamed and flashed colors of panic. Their instincts directed them to the closest water, which was the estuary at the bottom of the cliff. And while obeying the rules of terrestrial ambulation, they sucker-crawled their way down to the river and rode the current out to sea."

"Wow."

"They hadn't had their flesh ripped enough to kill them immediately, and they had just enough strength to swim ashore and crawl to help. They were hospitalized in an induced coma for two weeks. I sat there wondering whether they were dead and who was going to let me out of the cage. Then three weeks later a team of wildlife biologists showed up and trapped the weasels."

"And your parents recovered okay?"

"They made full recoveries. And actually, we got lucky with the weasels. The Dnooblian greater flying weasel was critically endangered. The wildlife biologists used my pack of weasels in a captive breeding program. We became known as the family that saved the weasels – it was even on the Galactic News Channel."

"And the weasel population made a full recovery?" asked Fleence.

"Uh, well, no. Their problem is habitat loss, so they still only exist in zoos."

"Okay, well, on that note let's continue," said Fleence.

She hit play and a frantic Trukk-9 came on the screen.

"I am on my first night in my cage! I've been here for two hours, but I've only this moment been able to set up my camera. I've been fighting off these gigantic wasps the whole time. I think I've won, at least for now. Here, look at this!"

Trukk-9 holds a dead wasp up close to the camera so we can see its long stinger and robust mandibles.

"From the looks of it, I've been stung three times on one arm, two times on the other arm, and once each on three eyelids! But, honestly, it feels like I might have been stung a hundred times! Okay – I need to catch my breath…

I think I'm fine. I hope I don't have to fight wasps every day."

Now it is morning and Trukk-9 is speaking to the camera in the cage.

"My first night wasn't too bad. No more wasps came back after the third wave. My arms still sting, but they are itching now as well, and some of my eyes are swollen shut. In fact, my whole head feels swollen."

Trukk-9 repositions his in-cage camera toward the floor.

"As you can see, I have a sleeping pad and a wooden chair. I cannot dry out like a Dnooblian, so I will need a supply of food and water. Like a Dnooblian, I hiked to this spot over many miles across the wild land. But unlike a Dnooblian, I brought as much water as I could carry. Stick.E will re-provision me once a week using a grabber beam blindly from The Duke hovering miles above. No matter what happens, I must remain truly alone."

The scene fades and dissolves back to time-lapse footage of a rolling marine-layer fog bank and scattered beams of sunlight sweeping by. Vines twist around the cage. Shrubs encroach. A flower with a humanoid-looking face seems to stare at Trukk-9.

The top of Trukk-9's head is out of focus in the lower foreground. All of his eyes are open. His green, yellow, orange, and purple eyes are visible in the shot.

Another Dnooblian tenor sings another aria of great foreboding. The music continues as the scene rapidly changes over the first week's time. Then it cuts to normal time and Trukk-9's antlers have grown into small, velvet-covered forks.

"Today's the day I get my ration supply from my crew aboard the Cruiser Duke Sukk-9. There's been a Dnooblian algae bear sniffing around the past couple of days. I saw it this morning."

Stick's grabber beam sets the ice chest against the side of the cage.

"Ah! Stick is a genius with a grabber beam. Okay, let me get this…" He starts to pull the individual items out of the chest and through the bars. He pauses, and then yells, "Hey! Go away bear! GO!! Damn it, GO!!"

The bear runs up and grabs the ice chest. Trukk-9 tries to pull it away, but he can't. The bear gets all of the food and most of the water bottles. It destroys the chest and all the contents as it lazes in a comfortable patch of moss.

"The bear has eaten all of my survival bars and punctured all of the water bottles. I know that I can survive for a month with no food. I am no stranger to starvation conditions. But I'll need to carefully ration my remaining water until next week."

He turns the camera to show the bear chomping the plastic water bottles.

"He is a beautiful beast, but to me he may as well be the bile of Death himself. The beauty of his sharky blue-gray coat and the glistening emerald algae growth on his back simply mock me."

The scene changes to quick cuts of views from the cage. Trukk-9 uses the camera in attempts to capture the beauty of the forest's flora and fauna. He wants us to recognize the misery of existence by showing us the uncaring beauty of nature.

"I draw your attention to a large flower that appears to be looking at the bear as it naps under that tree. This is the Dnooblian face plant. I think it is safe to say that no Dnooblians have been here recently."

The video zooms to the face plant, which looks remarkably humanoid with its nose-like pistil, anthers that resemble eyes, and sepals that curl into smiling lips.

"The face plant photosynthesizes in the infrared spectrum, and in low light conditions they will turn to follow animals as they walk by. The face plant is essentially feeding itself from the bear that is feeding from me."

The bear wakes up, stretches, and walks away to defecate in the woods. The face plant turns to follow the bear until it becomes obscured by vegetation. The plant then turns as if to regard Trukk-9, who is the next most radiant infrared emitter.

Trukk-9 narrates over the scene. "Scientists agree that the face plant is probably connected to the Dnooblians' humanoid revulsion. The plant is toxic, but poses little danger to an adult Dnooblian. However, this may not have always been the case. Earlier in the evolution of terrestrial Dnooblians, this plant, if abundant, would likely have been a dire hazard."

The video now shows a scene from the Dnooblian humanoid tolerance camp. A humanoid is being flung around by an irate trainee as two Magnificent Bull Dnooblian guards attempt to intervene.

Trukk-9 continues to narrate. "Scientists believe that humanoids are simply the unfortunate victims of a cruel coincidence. Dnooblians may retain an ancient instinctual fear of the face plant as a result of their evolutionary history – similar to how humanoids find snakes and spiders repulsive and want to kill them on sight. One thing is certain however – if a Dnooblian hiked through here, that face plant would be a goner – as might I be too."

The bear returns and regains the flower's attention. Trukk-9 now narrates in live action.

"I have survived on half rations of water and have been saving my meager urine in empty bottles. I get my rations again today, and you-know-who is still over there."

The ration chest appears and bangs against the cage. The bear wakes and pounces. Trukk-9 manages to grab a water bottle and then tries to thrust at the bear with his three-point antlers. But the antlers are still in velvet and bump uselessly against the bars of the cage. The bear takes the cooler back to the spot where the crushed water bottles are. The face plant follows the action.

"I'd yell for help. But my friends are miles above. I have maybe two days' worth of water, and then it's no food or water for five days."

The music is Swamp Master tantric chanting, accompanied by acoustic plasmanoid guitar and a Click Beetle on percussion.

"I'm down to urine," Trukk-9 says as he starts the fourth day without water. "It is not delicious, but it is precious. I caught and ate a Dnooblian scorpion last night. I need moisture in any form I can get it."

Trukk-9 opens his mouth in front of the camera to show how dry he is. An unknown amount of time passes, and Trukk-9 begins speaking.

"The weather seems to be changing. The wind is from the north now and I think I can see a distant cloud bank. If this is rain, it might save my life. I've been able to dent the floor of my cage slightly by jumping up and down on it. I think it could catch and hold a day's worth of water."

And it rains. Trukk-9 is drinking from the shallow pool in the middle of his cage floor as fast as the rain fills it.

"I have to get the next supply of rations. If I don't, and it doesn't rain, Dee and Stick will find a dead man next week."

The third cooler lands and the bear gets it after a mighty tug-of-war with the poor caged filmmaker. Trukk-9 breaks a tine from his fully-formed four-by-four antler spread during the struggle.

The next scene shows Trukk-9 a week later laying in the fetal position on the floor of his dry cage. There is no more urine.

He gags on his swollen tongue and utters what he thinks will be his final words. "Existence is a kind of hell, and the entirety of nature watches with the indifference of a face plant. I feel no more misery than the pain of life itself. A man's curse is his knowledge that death can come with such agony, so this is only the fulfillment of a terrible prophesy. As I go silent, let nature screech in my stead."

And then another wave of wasps arrives. The first stings don't register, and Trukk-9 doesn't react until one wasp stings him through the eyelid and penetrates his orange eyeball. He will be forever blind in one eye as a result, but the wasp also gives him the gift of life. He eats it – and then another and another. He regains strength until he is able to detect the wasps before they sting. He gorges.

Dee appears next to the cage. He unlocks it and swats away all of the uneaten wasps.

"Time's up, Skip!"

"Water," croaks Trukk-9.

"No water, Skip. We'll get some on the ship – unless you still want to travel on foot back to where we dropped you."

"No water?" gasps Trukk-9.

"Buddy, a Bearman doesn't need to carry a damn plastic water bottle every time he leaves the ship," says Dee as he lifts Trukk-9 over his shoulder.

"Well, friend, you've saved my life in the nick of time once again."

"Sure, but you almost croaked before the clock ran out, Skip. You sure know how to make my job difficult. But that was a hell of a performance you put on."

"Huh?"

"Yeah, that was perfect timing on that death poem you came up with. 'Fulfillment of a terrible prophesy' – was that it? I'm sure that stupid autotranslator didn't do it justice though. Anyway, I won five bucks from Stick on you drinking your urine. So that was good."

"I told you not to monitor me," says Trukk-9.

"I know, Skip, and we find it insulting. Stick and I are absolutely loyal – you know that. Seriously, Skip, your fans are gonna love it. It was awesome, and I'm glad you lived."

"Watch out for the bear," says Trukk-9.

"Yeah, I know about that greedy little bastard. He's not a problem. We just need to get you back on The Duke to give you a good probaluation."

"Yes, but do not repair my eye. Death is my constant companion and my future friend. And I must be reminded of these things."

"Uh, sure Skip."

They turn toward a clearing for pick up.

"Don't forget the camera in the cage, and leave it running," directs Trukk-9.

As Dee goes back for the camera, the algae bear appears. Dee tries to spook it away by roaring and twirling Trukk-9 around over his head in an effort to appear even bigger. Trukk-9's voice returns as narrator.

"The Dnooblian bear has never seen a Free-15 ursoid before, so the poor animal doesn't feel threatened. Dee tried his best to scare it away. But he failed."

The bear walks right up as Dee says, "You poor fella – you're no Bearman. Sorry I have to do this, buddy."

Dee drops Trukk-9 and assumes the universal ursoid wrestling position. The bear accepts the challenge. They grapple, and with one fluid move Dee puts the Dnooblian bear flat on his algae-covered back.

Then Trukk-9 comes back to narrate in voice-over. "I now know something of the Dnooblian soul."

Fleence paused it. "Does he really?"

"Well, inasmuch as we have what he calls a 'soul', I don't see why not. What he had to endure was more physically challenging than what we Dnooblians do. There's also a rumor that during the making of this film Trukk-9 volunteered to be the subject of a humanoid tolerance test, but the footage was too gruesome to include. Supposedly he was quartered before the guards could intervene. They say that after they rebuilt him he refused to have his memory wiped."

"Well, maybe you'll get a chance to ask him if it's true."

"Oooh, I don't know about that…"

Fleence hit play again.

Trukk-9 continues narrating, "Like no other race in the Galactic Pool, the Dnooblians are obsessed with their origins. Yes, like the rest of us, they believe that they evolved from life that was formed during chemical reactions on a young planet. BUT, they don't know what planet! Dnooblian mystics practice a lifestyle similar to the monks of old. But their paraphernalia is the tools of science – telescopes, microscopes, nano-hammers and plasma-brushes – all used in the quest to find out where they came from!"

The scene shows Dnooblian paleontologists at work on a dig.

"You see, Dnooblia's fossil record goes back to the origin of life on Dnooblia. However – and this is very startling – the Dnooblians' ancestors appear out of nowhere about sixty-six million years ago. Seemingly all at once, the progenitor of the Dnooblians appeared along with many similar-type animals. Each of these animals had in common a chambered shell, but the shells are of many shapes and sizes."

The video shows a Dnooblian fossil shrine with many beautiful specimens. The camera zooms in on an iridescent corkscrew-shaped shell.

"THIS is the Dnooblians' earliest known ancestor!" says Trukk-9 as he lays his hand on the fossil shell.

The video then shows an artist's depiction of the live animal in its original habitat. There is a head with many small tentacles sticking out of the aperture of radiant nacreous mother-of-pearl shell, and the animated animal swims over a reef using jet propulsion.

Dluhosh interrupted. "Dnooblian children always laugh when they first see a recreation of our ancestor. In perspective, he looks like a normal guy but with a giant shell. And since we normally now keep our shells sheathed, it looks kind of funny."

Trukk-9's narration continues. "Dnooblians have retained many features of their earliest known ancestors. In addition to tentacles and large eyes, huge neurons and a sharp beak, they have a shell. But Dnooblians no longer live within their shells as did their ancestors. The shell is now primarily a secondary sex characteristic that – much like a beancock's tail – plays an important role in evolution by sexual selection. The more ribbed and iridescent his shell, the more attractive the male Dnooblian is to the female."

The video shows several Magnificent Bull Dnooblians showing off their shells.

"A Dnooblian male's corkscrew-shaped shell hangs down on his lower back and is tucked into a traditional thong pouch. The shells of female Dnooblians are much reduced – like a pearl – and covered within a small fold in their mantles. Still, Dnooblian males enjoy catching a glimpse of one from time to time!"

"Ooh, they're handsome," said Fleence.

"Yes, I suppose they are," said Dluhosh.

Trukk-9 continues narrating. "I spoke with Chief Curator of the Dnooblian Fossil Museum, Doctor Tclarkhosh-10."

Doctor Tclarkhosh-10 is standing there as if waiting for a question and not knowing what to do with his tentacles. He waits and waits…

"Doctor Tclarkhosh-10, do you think that out in the galaxy somewhere perhaps somebody is wondering where all the ancient Dnooblians disappeared to?" Trukk-9 asks from behind the camera after a full minute of Doctor Tclarkhosh sitting there awkwardly with orange blotches flickering across his skin.

Doctor Tclarkhosh seems to relax as he pondered the question. "Well, yes, why not? Presumably, there could be a planet out there with a fossil record that stops where ours begins. And maybe an intelligent race there would wonder why the Dnooblians went extinct. I think it's unlikely, but it's fun to think about."

Trukk-9 continues with this suppositional line of questioning. "I suppose it's possible that only a portion of the original Dnooblian ancestors were taken from the original planet. In that case, those that remained might have continued to evolve. Do you think they'd be anything like you?"

"Well, if the genetic mutations, selective pressures, and stochastic events were the same for both of us over sixty-six million years, then maybe they would evolve into something just like us. That would be exceedingly unlikely though. I mean, we Dnooblians do have a very effective body plan, but evolution works in mysterious ways," replies Doctor Tclarkhosh, looking pleased with his response.

"Well, what do you expect to find, Doctor, if the Dnooblians are lucky enough to learn the answer?"

"I, personally, imagine that we will find our ancestors on a planet without a dominant species like a Dnooblian. Some think that our ancestors were sucked up by a random wormhole and deposited on Dnooblia. I think that's unlikely. Perhaps we were intentionally transplanted by advanced beings. But it was so long ago that I don't expect to ever meet them."

A Dnooblian cellist plays in a minor key and the scene is a series of dramatic landscapes and violent natural phenomena – volcanoes spewing lava, giant waves crashing, swollen rivers full of uprooted trees. And the film ends with a 360-degree pan from within a twisted mass of rusted-out wreckage that isn't even on Dnooblia.

"Wow," said Fleence. "That was intense! You Dnooblians are amazing! Will you tell me more about your childhood, Dluhosh?"

"Um, we aren't normally very comfortable talking about ourselves too much. It always sounds like we are bragging. But ever since Dnooblia became a Memory Wiper Power, we have put the technology to peaceful use by requiring ourselves to produce what we call a 'memory biograph'. After we pass all of the rites, we must formulate an accurate mental biography of our childhood, from birth, as a way for others to verify that we aren't too full of ourselves."

"That sounds like a great idea. I know some Fermamentian Viscounts who should do it," said Fleence.

"It requires weeks of meditation. When you are done, you make an appointment at the memory wiper facility and copy the file onto a hard drive. The events have to be verified and approved by parents, siblings, teachers, etcetera – and grandparents just love them. Then they can be useful for college applications and stuff. We tell the story in third person tense and the spoken dialog and visuals are recreated from our minds as accurately as possible. The narration is, of course, in my voice, so it's difficult for me to listen to."

"Do you have a copy that I could, um, experience?"

"I have the resume version in my PLUMBOB file. It just hits the required highlights, which is probably good since the full version is pretty long and boring. I should warn you though that some of it would be quite gruesome to a humanoid's aesthetic sense. You know about that… business, right?"

"I'm aware."

"Okay, are you ready then?"

Dluhosh pulled up the file, unlocked the memory wiper unit, and made the transfer to Fleence's mind. Fleence closed her eyes and let the story unfold.

***

In a warm tidepool at the edge of the Southern Continent, a babe was born.

"Look at this one!" said the father. "He's the biggest one. I bet he's going to be a great fisherman! We should name him Dlu after your brother, Mama."

The two adult Dnooblians named hundreds of larvae that afternoon, and they bid each one farewell with the traditional benediction for this occasion.

"Don't get eaten!"

Little Dlu took a look around. He saw the forest at the top of the beach cliffs. He noticed a few of his siblings in the pool. Everyone seemed to be trying to figure out what to do. Dlu knew what to do. He swam toward the sea beyond the tidepool. He went over a ledge, into the depths, and hid under a rock.

There were other animals living under the rock. Dlu did not know what the animals were, but he did not fear any of them. Certain ones made him feel hungry. And he ate them.

Dlu grew. On foraging trips he occasionally glimpsed siblings and other larval Dnooblians. He encountered fewer and fewer of them as each day passed. And Dlu grew faster than those who remained.

One day, as he investigated a deluxe-looking flat rock, another male larval Dnooblian appeared from an entranceway.

Dlu did not think about what he did next. He puffed up to his full size, which was about as big as a grape, and flashed electric green ocellated spots across his brick red body. His skin sprouted thorn-like papillae. His many baby tentacles snapped at the ends like miniature whips, producing tiny cavitation bubbles and pinpoints of intense heat.

The rival larva turned gray, inked himself, and disappeared into the abyss.

Dlu felt sad to have frightened away such a friendly-looking fellow. But he did upgrade his living quarters.

He saw many dangerous-looking creatures swim past as he lurked in the doorway. But he either avoided detection, or enjoyed a large meal after vanquishing an attacker.

One night, when Dlu was about the size and shape of an avocado, he dreamt of the dry shoreline. The dream images were more like feelings than visions in little Dlu's mind. The forgotten high cliffs and forest came back to him. He experienced the bewildering sense of a face looming over him, and he awoke with a start. None of the feelings made sense. But the pull of the shore was now an irresistible force.

Dlu sucker-crawled into shallower water. He followed a somehow-familiar scent into a tidepool. Two massive versions of himself sat waiting.

"There's one!" shouted his mother.

"It's little Dlu!" said his father.

Dlu was not afraid as the two relatively large adult Dnooblians picked him up and cradled him in their tentacles.

"Look how big he is! I just knew he'd survive!" said his mother. "Oh, he's beautiful Papa... Just look at his little tentacles! And oh! He's turned blue! We are wondrous to him, darling."

"Yes, he has my father's quality of blue. And I think he has your mother's beak. He's a handsome lad," said his father.

It was like sweet music to Dlu's ears.

His father held him up to his eyes and said, "Little larva, you have passed the first rite. Now the real trials of life begin. You start kindergarten next week. And we shall now call you Dluhosh. Welcome into the House of Hosh, Son."

"Oh, I love you little Dluhosh. Come home with us. I have your pool all ready. And there's plenty of space in case you are lucky enough to have a surviving sibling," said his mother.

Dluhosh's parents wiped tears of joy from their eyes as they hiked home with the only baby that survived from their first brood.

***

Now Dluhosh stood at attention. He held himself rigid and upright with his tentacles curled beneath him. Though he was still a teen, he was fully grown. In erect posture he was almost a meter tall.

"I'd rather be fishing," he said to no one in particular.

The drill instructor looked with disapproval at the group of trainees.

"Do any of you larvae know what we are looking at here?!"

Dluhosh raised his tentacle. "Um, I don't know about the red matter in the glass carboy, but the thing on the left looks like a medical probaluator, and the other thing is a hospital-grade duplicator."

"That's right, larva. And do you know why we need these very sophisticated and expensive devices today?"

Nervous laughter and a flush of orange spread through the group of trainees. Dluhosh replied. "With that technology, you should be able to rebuild a dismembered humanoid rather easily, I would suspect."

"Well, larva, you think you know what a humanoid rebuild is like? You don't! Your practice mannequins don't even have bones or intestines. And you probably never considered humanoid blood. We have to pre-duplicate gallons of it!"

Many of the young Dnooblians turned gray and dewy-skinned. A few went white upon realizing what was in the carboy.

"Many of you will fail – a higher number than usual from the looks of it. And humanoids are often rendered unrecoverable by failures like you. So please remember not to fling him or any of his constituent subdivisions against hard surfaces. Come with me, now!"

Dluhosh and his fellow trainees crawled together until they faced the iron bars and force fields that protected the humanoid inside the bunker. The force fields were there to keep Dnooblians out. The iron bars kept the humanoid from fleeing in panic when the force fields dropped.

"Dluhosh! You're first! Now remember – if you can – that when you go through the gate, the humanoid will be directly to your left. Go!"

The drill instructor deactivated the outer force field, and Dluhosh slipped between the bars.

Dluhosh's skin shimmered in its full spectrum of colors, which made him appear iridescent and almost metallic. He turned to face the humanoid. This was the first one he'd ever seen in real life. The videos and mannequins had not desensitized him. He vomited.

Two bull Dnooblians stood guard to protect the humanoid in case any of the bulls- and ewes-in-training failed the test. The guards focused on Dluhosh's tentacles.

Dluhosh ground his radula against the roof of his beak. The tips of his tentacles snapped like whips. He tried to suppress the mental images of the various ways in which he could kill this humanoid. But he couldn't block the seductive image of disembowelment with a tentacle flicked like a rolled up wet towel. He pumped air through his siphon in blasts of rage, which soiled the naked humanoid.

Three minutes felt like three hours. But Dluhosh passed and the humanoid was uninjured. The guards hosed them both down with tepid salt water.

Many more young Dnooblians faced the humanoid that day, and only a couple of them failed the test. The humanoid's potentially fatal injuries were repaired and his memories of the events were erased. He was paid very well, and he did not mind that his ears were reattached upside-down.

***

Dluhosh was honorably discharged, and he returned home much earlier than he or his parents had expected.

And he was eager to get on with his remaining rites of passage.

Dluhosh had chosen for his sculpture rite to carve a series of ceramic tiles. He then used these to construct a fountain for the family hot tub. The tiles depicted various stylized, but proportionally accurate, Dnooblian shelled sea creatures.

For his essay rite he produced a piece called "Art as Discipline – The Dnooblian Way". In it he made the case in support of the traditional Dnooblian philosophy that the arts are disciplines meant to serve as examples of mathematics and accuracy, which were the true pleasures of life. The essay was said to be convincing.

"Mother, Father, I have almost two months before I begin sprint training, and my essay and sculptures are complete. So I would like to attempt the family reliance rite in the meantime."

"But Dluhosh," said his worried mother, "you don't have your sprinting license yet. How can you hike that distance and then swim to the concession and back? You realize that's at least twelve miles round trip, not including chasing the fish…"

"Yes, Son," said his father, "that would be quite a task for ONE day, but thirty consecutive days? That's a lot of fish. You'd have to rise early."

"Please don't encourage the boy!" said Dluhosh's mother.

His father continued. "It might not be possible, but it's better than sitting around playing video games. And if you pulled it off, you might be able to get into university a semester early."

"I'm sure I could catch the fish, and I can hike at almost six miles per hour uphill while carrying a limit. If I get up at sunrise, I can get down the hill, swim to the concession, and then have three or four hours for the hunt. I can easily be back before dinner. I'll start tomorrow morning! Um, with your permission, of course."

"Oh, Dluhosh… Please reconsider."

Dluhosh interrupted. "But Mom, when was the last time you had fresh tuna? You both deserve tuna, and even a nice halibut, after all you've done for me during my rites."

***

So Dluhosh plunged into the ocean on the first morning and grabbed a limit faster than he had predicted. He focused his efforts on trout, but he had the opportunity to grab a halibut for dessert.

On the third day, a school of tuna swam through the concession and he grabbed five large ones in five consecutive thrusts with his two hunting tentacles. It took him about ten seconds to grab all five tuna and secure each one with a free tentacle. And he swam the mile back to shore in a single breath.

Sharks didn't attack him very often, so he enjoyed the hunt. And the daily hike gave him the opportunity to practice his singing. The vigorous exercise had added a deep luster to his colors.

Dluhosh was surprised at how easy the rites had been compared to the horror stories told by fresh under-bulls. Kindergarten calculus was supposed to be a nightmare too, for example. And he'd pulled off his own baby tentacles as soon as they became loose rather than whine as they fell off little by little like all the other crybabies in his class.

***

Dluhosh and his parents sat in the audience as all the successful bulls- and ewes-in-training were presented with their sprinting licenses. The large and proud community of Hosh held the ceremony at the town's track and field arena. The podium was in front of the high-jump pit, and the audience covered the entire field out into the grandstands beyond the javelin sector.

The master of ceremonies tried to say something unique about each recipient. Dluhosh expected that he might go last since he was the only one to have completed all the other rites as well. The time crept by until, by his calculation, only he and perpetual bull-in-training Mudhosh were left.

"Mudhosh, please advance toward the stage!"

Mudhosh had finally passed the sprint training rite. He had failed his sculpture and essay rites again though. His sculpture was a painting of an enraged Queen of Dnooblia, and his essay was called 'Painting as 2-D Sculpture'. His rendering of the Queen's colors had been an exquisite display of accuracy, but the judges burned the work 'for his protection'. On any other planet Mudhosh could have become rich drawing cartoons or writing silly science fiction stories. But on Dnooblia he was considered 'aesthetically inverted'.

Dnooblians who fail the rites sometimes end up going rogue. Rogue Dnooblians, though rare, often became a menace to society. But poor Mudhosh was still advancing, and Dluhosh admired his persistence.

The master of ceremonies continued. "And lastly, I'd like to introduce an exceptional recipient – Dluhosh-10!"

The crowd was caught by surprise when they heard Dluhosh's name combined with the number ten. And this was the first time Dluhosh had ever heard his name uttered in public by someone using the formal adult appellation. He advanced at hike speed, which was the legal speed for a Dnooblian in this formal situation.

"Dluhosh-10, you have passed your sprinting exams with a score of one-hundred percent on the first try!"

The audience applauded.

"Because you have already passed your essay and sculpture project, and you have learned to sing 'Dnooblia, My Dnooblia' in the original radula, AND because you have passed your humanoid tolerance test with only one minor slip..."

Everyone knew that 'one minor slip' meant that Dluhosh had vomited.

As the crowd giggled, Dluhosh gave a sheepish bow with the tip of his head. He peeked and saw a wave of aquamarine move across his body – a color that indicated self-deprecation. He was relieved that the color wasn't yellow. He felt no shame at being a puker, and he became more confident that he would never see his yellow again.

The distinguished master of ceremonies continued. "I have the honor of presenting you with something that I don't ordinarily get to present. Because – quite impressively I might add – you have already passed the family reliance rite! So you become the first Hosh this generation to pass it BEFORE earning your sprinting license!"

A murmur rose from the crowd, and it escalated into a cheer as one-by-one the gathered Dnooblians stood in ovation.

"Therefore, it is my pleasure to accurately address you as Dluhosh-10, of Dnooblia-10, House of Hosh!"

The crowd now stood as one.

"But wait, there's more! Under my authority, I hereby bypass you directly from under-bull to full Magnificent Bull Dnooblian! Here, Dluhosh-10, I present you with your sprinting license AND your shark-skin shell thong. May you wear your thong in accuracy. And as if this weren't enough, you have been selected to sing 'Dnooblia, My Dnooblia' to close tonight's ceremony!"

Dluhosh turned to face the crowd and changed into his black and white formal performance pattern. He slicked back the peak of his head, snapped a tentacle tip in 9/8 time, and gyrated his lower body in rhythm. He began the song with a flourish by humming a variation of the theme in a series of prime-numbered frequencies.

"Mmm, mmm, mmm…
Dnooblia, my Dnooblia
Shabooblia, shabooblia
Your oceans of blue-blia
Your halibut and salmooblia
Your tuna and wahooblia
Your ocean sustains me
Dnooblia – mmm, mmm, mmm – my Dnooblia"

Dluhosh hiked back to where his happy parents sat. The promotion to Magnificent, the presentation of the thong, and the invitation to sing had all come as surprises, so Dluhosh stole a glance down his body to make sure he wasn't bursting green stars.

As he hiked back down the aisle, the adult bull and ewe Dnooblians in the crowd offered congratulatory tentacle shakes, and his buddies gave him mantle slaps as he passed. He made brief eye contact with his bride-to-be. He managed to control his colors, but he felt a longing that would only be the beginning of his longing. He would miss her every day until they could afford to purchase a house and a family fishing concession together. Only then could they live together and start a family.

But for now he could at least start at university and dream of a career in galactic exploration. The end.

***

"That was amazing, Dluhosh! No wonder you are self-conscious about bragging. And that's so sweet about your bride-to-be. And I'm sure your friend Mudhosh is going to be fine."

"Thanks. I sure hope so."

"That was a strange experience though. It was almost like having a chapter from an interactive video-enabled audiobook inserted directly into my mind. Do I get to keep it?"

"If you like, but I'm not sure why you would want to," said Dluhosh, flashing a pulse of orange.

HOW TRUKK-9 DISCOVERED JIMMY

Dee thought it would be fun to have Buzzy as his joking cousin. Buzzy had no say in the matter.

Dee had the advantage of being an ursoid Bearman with a strong background in jocularity. And he was a contractor who worked within the lawless underground cinema. So he operated under a much looser set of behavioral norms than Buzzy the agency bureaucrat.

"Hey Buzzy, you're right, you don't look like a Flea. You look more like a giant Cockroach!" offered Dee.

"Fuck off you fucking gorilla," offered Buzzy back.

"Oh come on Buzzy, old Cousin. It's not me. You're just hearing that mean ol' galactic autotranslator playing tricks on you, buddy. I swear I hate that autotranslator. If I ever find out where that sucker is, I'm going to dump a big ol' nuts-and-berries cra-"

Trukk-9 interrupted. "Buzzy, see if you can come up with another hat-trick of checklist items."

Trukk-9 opened all of his eyes so he could see Dee behind him. "And let me offer some advice, Buzzy. I've known that Bearman for a long time. He's chosen you as his playmate. There's not much you can do but play. Don't take it personally."

Dee nodded and flashed his big toothy smile.

"Okay, I might have something for you here," said Buzzy. "I was looking for the 'water projects' item, and I have found that the Dirtlings store water in large reservoirs to be used for irrigation, industry, and recreational purposes. I think we can bag several checklist items. Here, have a look."

Buzzy punched up a live scene with pairs of people sitting in many boats. They floated on a calm pre-dawn cove next to a large marina. The boat motors idled and exhaust was heavy in the air.

"Is this some kind of boat race?" asked Trukk-9.

"Well, I think it starts out that way. But from what I can gather, this is going to be a fishing contest. These Dirtlings are about to drive their boats out into the lake to try and catch fish. They weigh the fish and hand out prizes to the winning fisherman," explained Buzzy.

"So, does the winning fisherman get to keep all the fish then?" asked Stick.E.

"No."

"They kill the fish and throw them away?" asked Trukk-9.

"No, they supposedly keep the fish alive and then let them go after they show them off to the crowd," said Buzzy. "They lose points if the fish die."

"Bizarre. They use grabber beams?" asked Trukk-9.

"They use a lure that resembles fish food. The lures have metal hooks that snag the fish in the mouth when it bites," said Buzzy.

"Oh man, that's brutal. This should be interesting," said Trukk-9.

"Plus, this covers at least three items from the checklist:

Dirtlings interacting with nature, competitive sports, and advertising culture," said Buzzy.

"Nice hat-trick Cousin! But if they want to win a fishing contest they should put hooks on little replicas of you!" said Dee.

"That is not clever," said Buzzy.

***

At safe light, a man standing in one of the boats started calling off numbers. The boats shot off one by one out to the main lake.

Dee pulled their ship up to the first boat that slowed. The fishermen jumped up and cast before the boat stopped. They caught nothing and said nothing, and they were unkempt and gross-looking around their mouths.

So Dee piloted the cloaked ship off to find the next boat – no fish, and boring. In the third boat a contestant was netting a fish for her partner. They measured the fish and threw it back into the lake. They caught two more fish each that they didn't bother to measure before tossing back. They were catching fish on almost every cast, but they seemed disappointed. So the ship sought another boat.

The ship went back out to scan the entire main lake. All but one of the boats had stopped to fish. One boat was still running up toward the end of the reservoir about twenty miles from the marina. Jimmy Fresneaux was driving to a spot suggested by his randomly assigned fishing partner.

The ship fell in behind and followed. The crew was impressed by the speed of this boat.

The fishermen pulled up to a small point on the last bend before the lake turned into river. As they slowed to a stop, Jimmy jumped to the front of the boat and lowered the foot-controlled electric trolling motor. His partner was already casting when Jimmy reached for a rod. Jimmy made a cast, and as he waited for the lure to sink he grabbed his lunch box.

As his lure sat on the bottom of the lake, Jimmy sat in the front swivel chair of his bass boat looking at a sandwich in a plastic bag. "Zipper bags sure are a great invention, huh? Look how many I have right here," he said to the other fisherman as he gestured toward an open tackle box.

The other fisherman didn't look.

"I probably have forty or fifty zipper bags with plastic worms in 'em. And I have a sandwich in one too. Two of my favorite things – plastic worms and sandwiches… How can the plastic zipper bag not also be a favorite thing?"

The other fisherman asked, "Hey, if you aren't going to fish, would you mind if I control the front of the boat here?"

"Oh, sure, go ahead," replied Jimmy, and the two men switched places.

"Would you like a tuna salad sandwich?" asked Jimmy, expecting that the other fisherman would politely refuse the offer.

The other fisherman said, "Sure."

Jimmy re-sealed the zipper bag and tossed his only sandwich to the other fisherman. The other fisherman set the sandwich down behind his swivel seat without looking at it and went right back to fishing. Jimmy went back into his lunch box and pulled out a foil pouch.

On the ship, Dee said, "Hey that shiny package looks futuristic."

Jimmy opened the package, and the guys on the ship saw two flat, rectangular pink pastries with colored sprinkles on the top.

Stick.E asked, "Do you think he'll offer one of those pastries to the other guy?"

"No way. That guy's not even eating the sandwich," replied Dee.

Jimmy shined the sun's reflection from the toaster pastry's foil pouch on the other fisherman's cheek. "Did you know that in an emergency you can signal for help with one of these foil wrappers?"

The other fisherman gave a deep "Rrrrrrrrr".

Stick.E said, "Huh, Dirtlings growl – how interesting."

The growling fisherman hooked a good-sized bass and yelled for the net. Jimmy dropped, and then stepped on, a pastry as he tried to grab the net. The other fisherman got the fish into the boat by himself without the net. He put the fish into his livewell, and took another cast.

Jimmy put the second pastry in his mouth to take a bite and heard "FISH ON!" from the front of the boat. Jimmy grabbed the net and managed to get the fish into it. But as he did, he bit through the pastry and it dropped into the net with the fish.

The other fisherman dropped the fish into his livewell, tossed the slimed pastry into the lake, and went right back to casting.

Jimmy went right back to his lunch box.

"Is the brightly colored guy in the contest? Or is he a mascot or a religious figure of some kind? Maybe his first cast was ceremonial…?" asked Trukk-9.

Nobody knew the answer, but they knew that Jimmy was the one to watch regardless.

Jimmy pulled out another zipper bag filled with little orange crackers. As Jimmy pulled the bag apart, the other fisherman yelled "FISH!"

This startled Jimmy and all of the crackers exploded into the lake.

"Hey, did one of you guys do that?" asked Buzzy. "You know you are not permitted to manipulate anything until the PLUMBOB monitor gets here."

"No." replied Stick.E. "My grabber beams are offline. It was pretty funny though. That poor guy has lost a lot of food. He's only had one bite of a pastry so far."

Jimmy opened a yogurt. He forgot to bring a spoon, so he tried to make one out of the foil top. "Foil also makes a good spoon. And they make those survival blankets out of foil too. I bet thousands of lives have been saved by foil."

Jimmy laughed. The guys on the ship laughed. The other fisherman did not laugh.

The other fisherman did, however, hook another big bass. As Jimmy went for the net, a glob of yogurt fell off the foil spoon and ended up all down Jimmy's sponsor jersey. Then he tried to wipe it off with his hand and got yogurt on the net handle. The other fisherman waved him off and boated the fish without the net.

"Aren't you going to fish?!" asked the other fisherman.

Jimmy put his yogurt container on the floor and picked up a rod.

The other fisherman hooked the biggest bass yet and got yogurt all over his hand as he netted it himself.

"Whoa, that's a money fish there for sure!" said Jimmy.

Jimmy managed a cast and the other fisherman took several casts with no more bites. So the other fisherman pulled up the trolling motor, and asked Jimmy to drive to a similar point on the opposite bank.

Jimmy grabbed his yogurt thinking that he could pour some into his mouth as he drove, but he found that a bee had landed in it. So he panicked and threw the container and bee into his lunch box and slammed the lid. The two men took their seats and Jimmy fired up the main engine.

"Ha! Trukk-9 would have eaten that wasp!" said Dee. "Oh, sorry Buzzy, no offense…"

"Oh, where do I start?" asked Buzzy. "Any resemblance

to me is superficial, and even so, only an idiot would call that a wasp. It is clearly a bee."

But Dee continued talking as if Buzzy were just a fly.

"No, I'm serious Cousin! Trukk-9 almost starved and dehydrated to death on Dnooblia once. He ate wasps to stay alive! And not just any old wasps – these were GWASPS! Those bastards even stung him in his test-"

Trukk-9 interrupted and said, "Yes, but that is a very unimportant fact – the kind of truth that only an accountant would need to know."

They chased Jimmy and the other fisherman to the other rocky point. Jimmy kept his eye on the sandwich as he drove. He zigzagged over the wake of a houseboat hoping that the bouncing would move the sandwich to a more favorable location for its reacquisition. His skillful manipulations caused the sandwich to drop from the front deck onto the floor.

The other fisherman shoved cookies into his mouth as fast as he could chew. He didn't offer any cookies to Jimmy though.

When they stopped, Jimmy wanted an energy drink. But he was afraid to open his lunch box.

"Did you like that sandwich?" Jimmy asked as part of his strategy to get the sandwich back for himself.

The other fisherman said, "Yeah, it was good."

Jimmy wasn't sure what that meant. But the other fisherman's back was turned, so Jimmy reached his rod tip and lure over the location of the hidden sandwich as if ready to make a long cast. Then he tried to snag the plastic bag.

The lure's hooks missed the sandwich and snagged the handle of a tackle box. The tackle box tipped over and the tackle spilled into the bottom of the boat.

The other fisherman paid no notice. He just kept

casting.

"Oh man, I'm sorry. I got it. Sorry," said Jimmy as he got down on his knees to clean up the mess.

"He has the sandwich!" yelled Dee, as Jimmy snuck the sandwich from under a pile of plastic worms.

The other fisherman caught another fish but he refused Jimmy's help with the net. He already had a limit of bass in the livewell, so he would need to throw back the smallest of his six fish.

"Hey, if you aren't using that back livewell, I'm gonna put this fish in it so I can cull after the bite dies down," said the other fisherman.

Jimmy put the sandwich down and opened the livewell cover.

The other fisherman dropped his bass in and said, "Hey, I should be glad that you aren't catching my fish, but you're driving me nuts with your fiddling around. I put us on some fish here, so fish dammit!"

Jimmy tried not to think about the sandwich as he cast. The morning was warming up and the sandwich was in the sun with condensation forming inside the sealed bag.

The other fisherman caught another keeper-sized fish, which he also put in the back livewell. The two men fished for another hour, but the other fisherman only caught fish too small to keep, and Jimmy caught nothing.

Jimmy took the sandwich out of the bag and looked at the translucent mayonnaise around the edges. He put the sandwich back into the bag and held it out toward the other fisherman. "Hey, you wanna trade another sandwich for some of those cookies?"

The other fisherman ignored him.

On the ship, Trukk-9 asked, "What's it going to be? Is he more afraid of the sandwich or the bee? Or can he tough it out for the rest of the day?"

Dee said, "I think the man is hungry. He's going to go back in for the yogurt. He's probably thinking that the wasp is all gummed up and harmless by now, so I'm betting five bucks on him going in…"

"Okay. I'm in for five on him toughing it out for the rest of the day," countered Trukk-9.

"I don't understand the problem with the sandwich, but I'm in for five bucks on him finally pestering the other fisherman into giving him some cookies," said Stick.E.

"What about you, Cousin? Is that wasp as edible as your mother?" asked Dee.

"You guys know that I cannot gamble on official business," said Buzzy.

Jimmy scratched himself in a couple of spots, and the guys in the ship scooted forward in their seats.

Jimmy opened the lunch box and the bee flew right out and stung the other fisherman on the lip. The other fisherman detected yogurt on his lip when he rubbed at the sting, and he yelled out a string of expletives before saying, "If you don't mind, I know a ledge in the main channel where bass sometimes congregate after the sun gets high. Will you kindly drive your boat there if I point the way? And will you kindly try to catch a damn fish when we get there?"

"Sure," replied Jimmy.

"Good. Drive that way, please."

So Jimmy pushed the throttle down and the boat leaped up onto plane, hitting sixty miles per hour within seconds. They had gone about a half mile when a very large carp jumped, as they are wont to do, in front of the speeding boat. The fish glanced off the trolling motor shaft and the other fisherman looked up just in time to see the carp before it hit him in the forehead.

Buzzy scanned the fisherman and the carp and

announced that they were both dead.

"Did you get that on tape, Dee?" asked Trukk-9.

"I sure did, Skip. Did that fish do that on purpose do you think?" asked Dee.

"You mean like a revenge attack?" asked Stick.E.

"I do not think that these fish are intelligent enough to plot suicide attacks. Recall how they are so easily fooled by the silly looking lures," said Buzzy.

"Good point," said Trukk-9. "Keep rolling."

Jimmy got on his radio and called the marina. "Marina, this is Jimmy Fresneaux, I have a medical emergency. My partner got hit in the head by a carp at high speed."

"Okay, what is your location?" replied the marina chief.

"I'm a few miles up the lake where the channel starts to narrow. I'm headed toward the marina now, but my partner needs help – if he isn't already dead."

"We have a first responder on staff and we'll meet you as you come in. We'll be in a ridged-bottom inflatable with flashing lights. Are you in the bass tournament – in a bass boat?"

"Yes, a wrapped bass boat – stormy sunset colors. And I'll be flashing a foil toaster pastry wrapper."

"Okay, good, what is the condition of the victim?"

"He's in the bottom of the boat with his head bent like he's probably dead. I can't tell if he's breathing. He has scale marks on his face."

"Sounds like a neck injury, so you probably shouldn't move him. What is his name?"

"Uh, I don't know. I forget. I only just met him at the draw this morning. He's not very talkative – kind of skinny and irritable," replied Jimmy.

"I'll contact the tournament director for his details. OK, the response boat is about ready. Stay close to the south bank, and keep your radio on. See you in a few minutes."

The guys on the ship were impressed. "Couple of checklist items there, I believe," said Trukk-9. "I must say, I didn't expect such a rapid and coordinated response. I guess when you play as hard as these Dirtlings you need to build in some safeguards. I like these people very much."

Jimmy ate the other fisherman's cookies as he drove.

"Stick wins!" said Trukk-9.

Dee protested to no avail. "That was not pestering, you guys."

***

The emergency boat arrived and the crew strapped the dead fisherman to a board to transport him over to their boat. The marina chief thanked Jimmy and introduced him to the tournament director. The director boarded Jimmy's boat and the emergency boat took off back to the marina.

"Howdy! I'm P.K. Dale, tournament director for Global Bass. I believe we've met. Jimmy, right?"

"Yes sir, P.K. It's Jimmy Fresneaux. Welcome aboard!"

"I think it's pretty clear what happened here, but there'll probably be police reports and stuff for us to deal with. So I hope you plan to stick around, even though you won't be able to continue fishing in the tournament without a partner. Do you have any fish yet?"

"Yes sir, two in the back and a limit in the front."

"Oh, good job! I can serve as a witness so you can weigh them in. I'll take a picture of your fish right now, and I'll sign your weigh slip later," explained Mr. Dale as he bent to open the front livewell. "It's your boat, so I can assume these fish up front are yours, right?"

"Yep."

"That's a nice limit there and that kicker is a hawg!" said P.K. "That's gotta be in the money, my friend. Nice job.

Does your partner have big fish too?"

"Naw, just a couple of solid keepers," replied Jimmy.

***

Jimmy got to spend the rest of the day hobnobbing with tackle sponsors and the Global Bass folks who were setting things up for the weigh-in and awards ceremony. A camera crew was there to do a live webcast, and Jimmy tried to stay close to them at all times. He handed out bags of Jimmy Jams to gawkers, and was quick with his business cards.

By the time the coroner removed the dead fisherman and the police completed their investigation, tournament time expired and the rest of the boats came in to the marina. Trukk-9 and his crew stuck around too.

The official weigh-in ceremony kicked off with bass boats zooming past the marina in the 'missing man' formation. And the master of ceremonies asked the gathering to observe a moment of silence. Then he asked Jimmy to weigh his partner's two fish first, and Jimmy solemnly complied. The crowd applauded when the other fisherman's name was posted at the top of the leader board.

Then the MC, determined to lighten the mood, said, "Well, folks, a man died doing what he loves. We should all be so lucky. And speaking of lucky, wait until you see the bag of fish that Jimmy Fresneaux has here!"

Jimmy reached into his fish bag and pulled out the biggest bass. The crowd erupted. These were people who really appreciate a bass of that size. Jimmy put the big bass back into the bag and placed the bag on the scale. The crowd buzzed as the numbers on the digital scale climbed.

"Folks, I do believe that this total may stand today. I gotta say, that's one of the finest bags of bass I've seen in the history of Global Bass sponsored tournaments. Nice job Mr. Fresneaux! How'd you do it – and in only half a day of fishing?" He handed the microphone to Jimmy.

"Well, sir, I hit a couple of rocky points way up river that I know will hold fish under these conditions. I took a big risk making such a long run first thing, but I made it for the morning bite and put this limit in the livewell before the sun hit the water. I got most of them on kiwi Jimmy Jams grubs and I stuck the big one on a frog pattern Chompy Chunkbait. Tell you what – the big fish was strong, but with an Accu-Poke hook at one end and a Slidewinder Reel at the other, I knew I needn't worry. My partner, bless him, was one of the best net men I've ever had. I'd like to thank him and my sponsors."

The crowd cheered as Jimmy's name replaced the other fisherman at the top of the leader board.

At the award ceremony Jimmy held up the first place trophy and oversized ceremonial check for photographers. And then he mingled around the buffet table until the bluegrass band had packed up.

"Well, that was quite interesting," said Trukk-9. "I think we have a hit on our hands. Agreed?"

The crew agreed, and Jimmy was marked for future use.

WULU GRIFFER-1 INTRODUCES HIS PLAN

"Oh, there's one more thing I'd like to get your approval on, sir," Wulu Griffer-1, Vice President of the Galactic Pool, said as he was wrapping up his weekly personal briefing in the President's office.

"You got it! Uh, what is it?" replied the President.

"Well, as you know, our majority isn't big enough to pass our most critical initiatives. It sure would be nice to get another friendly representative on the Galactic Assembly," said the Vice President.

"Heh-heh," replied the President, "or we could blow up one of the unfriendly planets…"

Wulu Griffer-1corrected him. "No, Mister President, we don't have the weaponry for that, sir."

"Oh come on, Griffer, that was a joke. Remember what the Discreet Service told you about me? When I go 'heh-heh' before I say something it means it's going to be a joke. Everyone on my staff has been informed. Can't you please pay closer attention?"

"Well, sir, I wish you wouldn't use jokes with me. They're inefficient."

"I can't help it. I don't rehearse the jokes. They come right off the top of my head. You have to adjust to me, Griffer. I'm the President, and you are the Vice President. We can't have it look the other way around. I'm the joker."

***

For his entire life, President Gren Wee-1 had been trained, sometimes brutally, to defer to those who were older or richer. Vice President Wulu Griffer-1 was both.

For example, when he was a petulant teen, Gren Wee-1 said 'heh-heh' to the wrong rich old lady. With precision thrusts of her cane, she dinged him from his ears to his groin. And each time he raised his hands to defend himself she chided him for being a cowardly punk. His friends had to hold him still so he wouldn't embarrass himself with his constant flinching. At one point she broke his nose from one side, and then re-set it with a quick pop of her cane from the other side. She finished by marking him with a small red target – made by grinding the rubber tip of her cane into his forehead.

And as a young man Gren Wee-1 was tossed into the sea from his own yacht by his own elderly skipper for not saluting properly. Poor Gren Wee-1 was forced to purr an apology to his skipper after he was rescued by a press boat. The whole thing ended up on the Galactic News Channel.

***

"Well, my efficient mentor," said the President, "if we want another planet on our side, we'd have to find another whole planet that just happened to be on our side, and then get it approved. Don't tell me you've got a friendly planet under your claw."

"Well, sir, I'm working on it," replied Griffer-1. "The PLUMBOB scanned a planet called Dirt some decades ago. It came up for a preliminary review and was quickly rejected."

"Too primitive?"

"Yes, sir. The Dirtlings tend toward violence and superstition."

"So they've made some big improvements lately?" asked the President.

"No, sir."

"I don't understand."

"Well, sir, last year, on a hunch, I sent some covert Crickets to Dirt's system to have another look at their television broadcasts. Dirtlings are apparently very easy to manipulate through fear – and so far it's only being done to them by their own species. We could ride them to riches. I mean ride them to their own riches, of course – they will benefit tremendously, sir," explained Griffer-1.

"What does Gro Skoo think of the idea?" asked the President.

"He supports it," lied Griffer-1, as he scribbled in his notebook.

"Are the Dirtlings humanoid?"

"Yes."

"Heh-heh, are the women symmetrical?"

"Almost perfectly bi-lateral," said the Vice President.

"But doesn't the PLUMBOB thing make it impossible to sneak in a ringer planet like that?" asked the President.

"Yes sir. The PLUMBOB Act requires an objective evaluation of a candidate planet, etcetera, but there's a lot of flexibility in how one achieves that. I think we'll get the most efficient objective evaluation if we bring in some outside experts. I have enlisted a consultant to help our poor, overworked bureaucrats."

"Oh good, anyone we invest in?"

"Well, I don't know. My investments are held in a blind trust," said the Vice President.

"Oh. Who is it?"

"Well, I have Trukk-9."

"What!? Trukk-9? You're kidding, right? Why would he want to get involved in your political schemes?"

"He wouldn't and he isn't. That's like asking why the hammer wants the nail to go into the wood. He'll simply be a tool doing what a tool does," replied Griffer-1.

"Wood?" asked the President.

"Sir, Trukk-9 is trusted far more than a regular bureaucrat would be, and that's what we need above all else – implicit trust. Few people will question Trukk-9's work. We just have to ask him to answer the wrong question."

"Huh?" replied the President.

"You see, he will answer the question we give him in complete honesty."

"Of course he will – he's Trukk-9."

"Right, but then we take the answer to this… special question, and we use it to answer a slightly different question – the question that the PLUMBOB standard requires. But nobody besides a small group of agency people, and a few radicals, understands that standard."

"I don't understand it either, but that's because I'm a man of the people," said the President.

"Right, so Trukk-9 will assume that the underlying legal standard is consistent with his special skills. Because… Why else would we ask him to do it? He will do excellent work, and will not question whether it is proper. At least not soon enough to matter…"

"Oh, I see," said the President, "the old bait and switch…"

"There you go! And even if someone sues, the

PLUMBOB Act is so convoluted that the courts won't be able to sort it out until after it's too late. Dirt will be in, and there's no way to get it out."

"Wow, that's really smart! You sound like you've done this kind of thing before. And you got away with it, right?" asked the President.

"Relax, Mister President. It doesn't matter whether we 'get away with it'," said Vice President Griffer-1 as he gave vigorous air quotes with his ears.

"We leave no trace. You know sir, 'plausible deniability' and all that. 'Mistakes were made'..." he said, looking like he was trying to keep small insectoids away from his head.

The Vice President changed direction. "And I have a rookie egocite handler from Chuffed-18 for the mission too."

"Chuffed-18!?" asked the President.

"Yes, but the important thing about her is that she has a link to Trukk-9. We have obtained video records showing that he had primary contact with the girl's mother at the egocite mines."

"You mean she's from the Lost Lineage?!" asked the President.

"She's had the wardrobe treatment too. She's a recently retired conversation hostess of the highest grade."

"Heh-heh – she's probably richer than you!"

"No joke, sir. She probably is. Though she says she's looking for more, as she put it, life-enriching experiences."

"More life enriching than being rich? I don't understand," said the President.

"Well, oddly sir, yes, but think of the times you've been on the sea and successfully navigated treacherous waters, for example. Don't you feel enriched for the experience?" asked Griffer-1, as if he hoped to exercise the President's deeper thinking.

"I see what you mean. At those moments I realize that I would be dead if I wasn't rich enough to have a seaworthy yacht and a skipper to sail it," said the President. "This girl and I have a lot in common."

"Uh, right sir. But anyway, here's how I figure the girl can help further richen us. She's going to be so sick of being cooped up with a Dnooblian that she will form a natural bond with Trukk-9 when the ships meet. Then if the Dnooblian starts spewing conspiracy theories about their mission, she and Trukk-9 will naturally be allied against him and, therefore, more likely to ignore him. And since she's a rookie, she, like Trukk-9, won't understand the subtleties of the PLUMBOB Act. Finding her was a nice piece of luck and a nice piece of insurance."

"Heh-heh, and a nice piece of ass!" added the President, looking pleased with himself for such a classically fine joke. "It's brilliant the way you plan these things. Everything falls into place... nothing ever goes wrong..."

"Well, the beauty of a plan like this is that it only gets more effective as more things go wrong. That's another reason for rushing this mission. The need to rush gives us cover for not giving the Dnooblian a self-destruction tablet, and not having his cloaking device maintained, among other things. So if they were to crash, for example, or break down on Dirt for some reason, that opens the door to irreversible contact with Dirt. We could invoke the PLUMBOB Emergency Contact Committee and declare Dirt a de facto member of the Galactic Pool."

"You know, Griffer, watching you work is like watching a galaxy class yachtsman at work. Every move is precisely timed and planned to lead to the next maneuver." The President was getting very excited. "But why did Trukk-9 agree to take a bureaucrat's job?"

"We are allowing him to film anything he wants for

himself with full rights to the footage. Those underground cinema fools are always clamoring for the unused footage from PLUMBOB monitoring. It would be a huge hit for him."

"Wait, I know, by the time the courts rule against him owning the footage, it will be too late anyway! I get it! Right?" said the President.

"You got it, sir. And our objective is…?" asked Griffer-1, sounding like he was leading a student toward another correct answer as a reward for the first correct answer.

"Uh, we want more power!"

"Well, yes, but specifically…"

"More money?"

"Yes, of course, but how do we get the money?"

"Oh, uh, wait, I know… We get Dirt in the Galactic Pool! So then we can win all the votes?" replied the President.

"Correct. And it gets better. You know the trouble we've been having on Scablands-17?"

"Uh, yeah… labor pains," stated the President.

"Sort of, yes… The fact is, Scablands-17 has been the sweatshop of the Galactic Pool for far too long. The people have finally figured out how much they are owed."

"Chuffed-18…" said the President as he absentmindedly gave his ear a working over.

"Mister President, do you see what I mean? We owe it to the citizens of Scablands-17. They vote with us in the Assembly, so it's the right thing to do."

"Right," replied the President. "This thing that you are planning will make the galaxy shine brighter, right?"

"Very astute, sir. As Rim Ram-1 said right here in this office, 'New planets make the galaxy shine brighter'."

"Wow, Rim Ram-1…"

"Yes sir. He said it on the eve of Scablands-17's first

contact. In fact, you looked like Him in this light when you said it."

"New planets make the galaxy shine brighter," repeated the President.

"Sir, you even sound like Him right now," added Griffer-1. "And ever since the passing of Rim Ram-1, I've been concerned that we'd have a president who misunderstood the true meaning of Ram-O-Nomics. That is why I've stuck around this long. Well, Mister President, you should know that I am relieved, and that He would be proud of you."

He brought the President back to reality with a recapping of the main point.

"So, sir, not only will Dirt give us an unbeatable majority in the Galactic Assembly, it will also be an ideal and much needed cheap labor source."

"Aren't there rich and powerful Dirtlings? What do we do about them?"

"Well, Mister President, we would definitely keep the politicians and media barons that we need. All of the otherwise useless rich people will have to invest in our companies to keep their wealth relevant. Or else they'll join the work force when their wealth becomes irrelevant. We don't have to protect the rich if they can't make us richer."

"We don't have to protect the rich if they can't make us richer," repeated the President, turning his head in a Rim Ram-1 pose.

"Yes sir. Now I have some other affairs to attend to. I will be sure to keep you updated on progress. The acceptance of Dirt could become the defining moment of your Presidency."

"Wow, that long in a ship alone with a wardrobe-enhanced conversation hostess of the Lost Lineage... You couldn't buy that for all the money in the galaxy. And she's with a Dnooblian. What a waste." The President's ears quivered.

MEET ULBTX-123

Dark Matter Pixel Person ULBTX-123 of The Great Hologram paid a visit to the Pixel Person who lives diagonally from his lower right corner. His neighbor, ULBTX-404, had been waiting patiently for the esteemed ULBTX-123.

"Hey 404, how've you been?" asked ULBTX-123 when he arrived.

"Pretty good, all things considered, 123," replied 404. "But I've had some problems on one of my best planets."

"Yeah, tell me about it," replied 123. But instead of letting his neighbor tell him about it, he started in with his own problems.

"I'm getting too many requests for help from all over The Great Hologram. No fewer than a thousand Pixels are planning to replicate my experiments. I still have my own very important work to do on Earth, but the demand is so great. So, anyway, 404, you were saying…"

"Oh yeah, well I suspect that some of my genetic tweaks have been evolutionarily implausible. Giving heads the size of pumpkins to my best humanoids was a bad idea. I've had to make the females' hips as wide as shipping containers so they can give birth. I've tried to genetically engineer the men to be sexually attracted to enormous bottoms, but now they are attracted to the beasts of the forest instead. The men are complaining that the gods are punishing them. I think they are on to me. It's gotten out of control and I think I may have to push the reset button there, unfortunately."

"Oh yeah, I hate it when that happens," replied 123. "I almost lost Earth a few years back when I tried to reintroduce some carnivorous dinosaurs. I thought I had spayed and neutered them, but they reproduced anyway. It took me years of hurling individually-sized asteroids before I killed the last one."

"Bummer. Anyway, I managed to get you about a half million tons of carbon dioxide. Here you go," said 404.

"Thanks! But are you sure you don't need it for yourself? My new planetary reset technique is very promising," said 123.

"No, I don't think so. I'm going to have to do a big asteroid reset on this particular planet. But before I do that, do you have a place where I can transplant some flying trees that I've grown fond of?" asked 404.

"I think I can come up with a good spot for you. I have a bunch of planets that I've given up on since my work on Earth has become such a big phenomenon. I don't think those other planets are good for much else anyway. Although I can tell you that giving humanoids eleven eyes and antlers was worth it just for the comedy. I haven't been back there in millennia. But, yeah, let me know when you're ready with the flying trees. It will give me an excuse to go visit the antler people for a few laughs," said 123.

"Yeah, I would appreciate it, thanks so much. Also, I was wondering what I should do to a new humanoid planet that I think might be ready for some work – any advice?" asked 404.

"One word – feet. I really think we've been messing with their heads long enough. Everyone has been totally focused on The Great Hologram's head. We've done everything we can possibly do with a humanoid head and got nothing. A few have moved to hands, and I even did a little of that work too. But though I've answered the first big question, I still think there is significant work to be done with feet. For example, no one has ever tried backwards feet, or perhaps two feet of unequal sizes… I'd really like to see someone work on luminescent feet, and there's an endless variety of toe and claw options. It could be fun to develop some extra springy feet. Or you could replicate my experiment. There's grant money in that."

"I would be honored to help validate your results, but, well, I want to make my own big discoveries. It must feel great!"

"Yes. Yes, it does," said 123.

"So are you still on schedule with Earth?" asked 404. "Congratulations, by the way."

"Thanks. I think so. The Earthlings are getting pretty close to discovering the fundamental nature of matter and energy, but useful quantum technology is still many years away for them, I believe. With Earthlings though, you just never know."

"There's no evidence that they suspect anything about the true cause of their climate change?" asked 404.

"Well, their response has been complicated so far. In fact, I'm thinking of publishing a paper on it. The small footed segment of the population holds a lot of power. And, of course, they laugh at anybody who suggests that half of greenhouse gasses are of extraterrestrial origin. But best of all, the diseases are responding. It's all very exciting."

"That's great, 123. Keep up the good work. Do you think anyone will be able to repeat your results with the foot-size experiments?"

"I don't see why not. I trust the abilities and integrity of our fellow Pixel People," said 123. "But I'm glad the answer came from right here in the Upper Left Buttocks region!"

The two Pixel People cheered. "HURRAH, HURRAH, Upper Left Buttocks! U-L-B-T-X! GO, GO, GO!"

"Oh, it's good to see you Brother ULBTX-404, but I have to get going on this CO2 injection – seems like I'm behind on everything these days. I tell you, between the monitoring of Earth's technology, the climate change work, and the demand for my expertise; I haven't had time to tidy up my pixel. Seriously, there are so many space-time wrinkles pointed at Earth that it would take centuries of cleaning to make a dent. Can you imagine scrubbing space for hundreds of years? Anyway, I'm really pressed, so I have to say goodbye."

"Okay, Brother ULBTX-123, I should have another load ready next month. I'm also trying to salvage some methane from my ungulatoid planet. Anyway, I hope to see you then."

"I'll be here, Brother. Sure saves me a lot of time."

EARTH 6,000 YEARS AGO

ULBTX-123 was all set. He had altered the Earthlings' stem cells – a tedious task. He had established his control group on another planet. He had selected his test population and developed his hypothesis. He was sure that this time he had found the right combination of characteristics.

Life for 123 over the coming centuries would consist of observing the activities of these humanoids, and using his observations to test his hypothesis. During this extended period he would be unable to make his regular visits to his pet dinosaurs. So he sterilized a pair of his favorite ones and brought them back to Earth. For safety's sake, he placed them in the area from which he had removed his Earthling control group. There were enough wild beasts on the land to feed the pair, he thought. He was sure that it would be okay, which was proof to him that it really was okay.

***

So, in a small village at the end of a long valley some six-thousand years ago, Gug brought his daughter, Gugsdaughter, to the Seer.

Gug said, "Seer, my daughter is developing very large feet. She is but ten years old and already her feet are larger than mine. She is a very bright girl, but I worry about her health."

"Yes, I see," said the Seer. "I have seen this in others as well. Brog came to see me recently. He complained that his son had truly gigantic feet. I did not see his son because he had run off into the woods in shame and the family hasn't seen him since. I saw his footprints though. He was but seven years old, and his footprints were the length and breadth of a pair of spawning salmon. And your daughter isn't the only child with impressively large feet, Gug. Dug has a large-footed son. However, Dug's son's feet aren't so big that it causes him shame. In fact, he exhibits much self-confidence and athleticism."

"Seer, have you seen Flog's son?" asked Gug. "He has the smallest feet I have ever seen. Flog's son is also bright, but he is a sneaky little bastard."

"Yes, Gug, I have seen this. I have also seen Fug's son. He's the little boy who runs around with a big pointy stick and many furs piled upon his head and shoulders. He is dim and has tiny feet. He seems to fear something. I will keep an eye on the situation," said the Seer. "But for now I wouldn't worry about your daughter."

***

As the years went by, many children were born with a wide variety of foot sizes. Not including the children who ran off into the forest, the remaining children grew and took over the rule of society from the elders. The elders were happy to relinquish day-to-day control to this dynamic new generation, because they would drive the elders crazy if they didn't have something to keep them busy.

Gugsdaughter summoned Dugsson. "Look what I have invented. I call it a 'wheel and axel' and I think we can use it to transport our harvests and building materials, and perhaps use it to rescue the sick and injured in times of need."

"How does it work?" asked Dugsson.

"If we can attach a platform to the axel, and then yoke an ox to the platform, and if someone brave can learn to drive it, then we can put heavy things on it and roll them wherever we want with minimal effort," explained Gugsdaughter.

"I understand. That's brilliant. Gugsdaughter, I think I can make this contraption work for you. I would love to drive it. May I?"

"I was hoping you would say that," said Gugsdaughter.

One afternoon a week later, Gugsdaughter heard the sound of whooping and hollering. She put her size-twelve moccasins on and ran out to investigate. There, emerging from a cloud of dust, was Dugsson riding on a crude chariot pulled by a stampeding ox. He tried to steer the beast toward Gugsdaughter's hut, but the chariot flipped and threw him into a pile of dung.

He jumped up, and despite his dislocated shoulder, he said, "I'm okay! No problem. Didn't hurt at all…"

Gugsdaughter ran to him.

"YEEE-HAAA! Your contraption is beautiful! I will learn to control it – I just need more time," said Dugsson.

***

Dugsson's performance caught the attention of the

small-footed schemer Flogsson. He called on his dim friend Fugsson, who answered the door wielding a big sharpened stick. The stone spearhead had fallen off his spear, and he couldn't figure out how to reattach it. He was smart enough, however, to sharpen the stick and then claim to his buddies that he was old-school. And they were dumb enough to believe him.

"Oh, it's you Flogsson. Please come in. Would you like a tuber?" asked a deferential Fugsson.

"No," replied Flogsson. "Have you seen the new weapon that Dugsson has been testing?"

"Oh... that's a weapon, is it? It looks very impressive. But he hasn't been able to kill himself with it yet. How does it work?" asked Fugsson.

"It is used to transport soldiers to and from neighboring villages so they can conquer the people and take back what is rightfully ours. If you want to help the cause, tell all of your spear-wielding buddies to start beating the drums. There are many fools in this village who are too cowardly to demand justice for our people. You know how they are..."

"Yes, they want take away our spears and they don't love our village!" replied Fugsson, getting very agitated.

"Exactly. Good people like you must rise and demand that we use our new weapon to restore tradition! Now go Fugsson – beat those drums!"

Bowing to pressure from Fugsson and his band of blathering brutes, the village council ordered their strongest men to build and pilot a convoy of chariots to invade their rich neighbor. But only one man returned from this mission. The man was Dugsson, and he told a tale of horror.

"People, please listen and believe," groaned Dugsson, after he returned on foot. "We found only a bare patch of rocky ground where a village once stood. Even the topsoil and dung piles were gone. A whole village that once sheltered a thousand souls was... missing. As we stood in silence, a herd of great feathered dragons with teeth like spearheads attacked us. With their great mouths and tails they thrashed us to a man, except for me. I fear that these dragons may find us here. I have detected their tracks nearby."

The village council members conferred, and the chief spoke, "We have determined that you are telling crazy stories to cover up for something else – sodomy and cannibalism, probably. We sentence you to death by stoning."

When the great beasts did appear soon after, the council blamed Gugsdaughter. They said it was obvious that the wheel and axel had led the beasts to the village. They threw her in an underground cell with Dugsson and other wrongly-convicted people awaiting execution.

The prisoners were the village's only survivors after the first wave of dinosaur attacks. Luckily for them, a meteorite smashed open the hatch of their cell. But they survived by returning to the underground cell during many years of beast and meteor attacks.

THE MOTHER ROOST VIDEOS

Dluhosh brought up some video clips that he wanted to show Fleence for training purposes.

"My previous egocite handler, Pip-The-Blue-8, had a natural rapport with the people on our last PLUMBOB planet. I think it helped that he was avianoid like them. That fact might be relevant to you since you are a humanoid who will be working with a humanoid planet."

"That makes sense," said Fleence. "Do you think the avianoid planet has a chance for acceptance into the Galactic Pool?"

"Yeah, I'm not sure. I think the initial analysis will qualify it to go to the televised vote. But these types of flightless drab avianoids haven't done well historically. If they were elegant and colorful like Pip-The-Blue, they might have a better chance. Anyway, these avianoids will probably have a hard time politically too. I'm sure they would be opposed by the Ones," said Dluhosh.

He hit play. "Oh yeah, the planet is called Mother Roost."

The screen displays the view through the ship's window

on Mother Roost. Dluhosh and Pip-The-Blue-8 are looking into the open door of a kitchen where a large female Roostling is carrying a tray of hot muffins and honking a melody to herself. Dluhosh uses the grabber beam to bring her into the ship.

Dluhosh paused the video and said to Fleence, "This is the first time we abducted her. She's the one we called Muffin Hen. She was such a sweetheart, and she made us promise to abduct her every time we found her with muffins. She really took a liking to my partner. Watch how he handles it."

Dluhosh places Muffin Hen under the isolation dome with her tray of muffins. Pip administers the calming agent, probaluates Muffin Hen, and then removes the dome.

"What did you do that for, boys?" she asks.

"Please pardon us ma'am. We are from elsewhere in the galaxy, and we are collecting data about you. In exchange for this intrusion, we cure all of your diseases. I think you'll notice that the arthritis in your thighs is gone, and your cloaca is once again its normal size and color," explains Pip-The-Blue-8.

Muffin Hen takes a look, and says, "Well, I'll be... Would you boys like a muffin?"

"Oh, no thank you. I'm a strict piscivore," replies Dluhosh.

Pip-The-Blue asks, "What kind of muffins are they? They smell delicious."

"They are suet and millet swirl with ants on top. Would you like one?"

"I sure would," replies Pip-The-Blue as he grabs a muffin with his foot. He takes a bite and says, "Oh man, Dluhosh, too bad you don't eat muffins. This is fantastic! Ma'am, I come from a Planet called Millet Fields-8, and I can tell you that this is the finest suet-swirl millet muffin in the galaxy! You people grow a superior grade of millet here. And these ants are extra tangy."

"You can have the whole tray then if you like," she says.

"Oh, yes please!"

Dluhosh paused the video. "The point I'd like to make here is that Pip was brave to try the first muffin. But because he did, he discovered a great personal joy while advancing our relationship with the subject. A good egocite handler, in my opinion, can engage the abductees in cross-cultural experiences like this."

"I see," said Fleence. "I think that sounds interesting."

"Of course, you should stay within your comfort zone, but you may encounter such opportunities. We'll try to abduct someone cooking something yummy for you too!"

They resumed watching the video.

Muffin Hen says, "I'm pleased that you like them. You really are a pretty boy. Did you know that I've won many awards for my muffins?"

"I believe it. Seriously, I have never tasted a better muffin."

Pip reaches for his egocite bag and explains, "We want to do one more test before we wipe your memory and send you back. This is a mineral called egocite."

He pulls the ingot out of the bag – shaped like a nare flute from a previous abduction. The flute transforms into a perfect silver muffin, complete with silver ants on top.

"Oh my, that's very pretty. It looks like one of mine," she says.

"It is, in a way. This test shows us what you are proud of. I guess I'm not surprised at this result. Your muffins surely are worthy of pride, ma'am."

"Well, thank you sonny. You boys be sure to come around again, okay?"

Dluhosh stopped the video and said, "My partner spent

all of his free time during our last month abducting her to get a muffin supply for the trip home. He insisted that the duplicator couldn't capture their freshness or the zest of the ants. It's really a shame that we had to wipe her memory at the end."

"I think I would try a muffin – minus the ants of course," said Fleence.

"Okay, now here's an abduction that was messed up. We needed the individual sports checklist item, and we saw this male subject who we thought was exercising alone on a hummocky field."

Dluhosh hit play.

The video shows a male subject running in patterns around grassy hummocks. There seems to be a complex running course that winds around and over the small mounds.

Dluhosh asked Fleence, "How many subjects do you see?"

"Just the one guy running around... Is that some kind of dance he's doing?"

"No, it is a sport – just not an individual sport. We abducted him to find out what he was doing. Here, I'll zoom in. See anything yet?"

"No. What am I looking for?"

"I'll zoom some more. Anything?"

"Just the runner... It's really quite beautiful the way he moves. He's very graceful. I like the little skip he does over the mounds."

"Okay, I'll pause it and zoom in on a mound – watch when he skips. There."

"Oh yeah, there's a pointy yellow thing in the grass... Oh! Is that a beak?"

"Yep. We never saw them either. Look at the runner's ankles."

"He has a bunch of colored bands around them."

"Yeah, the guys hiding in the hummocks are trying to attach bands to the runner. There are actually two teams competing. Watch what happens when we abduct him."

The screen shows the subject being pulled up through the hatch. Then the view out the window shows the twenty-two players leap up from their lairs. They are pointing and shouting in the direction of the ship, having just seen their runner get pulled into the air and disappear.

The players all panic and run across the sports field onto an adjacent agricultural field. They group into a 'V' formation as they go. The herd is kicking up a cloud of dust and honking with vigor. Dluhosh's ship is chasing them. The abducted subject is under the isolation dome watching as the two aliens try to deal with the situation.

Dluhosh said, "What you should notice here Fleence is how Pip-The-Blue takes control of the subject while I pilot the ship and shoot the others with the memory wiper."

Pip-The-Blue administers the calming agent and probaluation, but waits until Dluhosh shoots the others before lifting the isolation dome.

Dluhosh said, "See Fleence, when wiping their memories, you have to start at the back in case they fall over thinking that they are still sitting in a hole. They'll stop once all of them don't know why they're running. Look right now. See how everyone but the front guy is starting to look around as they run? Now watch as the front guy is zapped."

The image shows the herd stopped together honking about a mile from where they started. Then the scene cuts to the abducted runner on the ship.

"What the hell?" he asks when Pip-The-Blue lifts the dome.

The egocite ingot turns into a jewel-encrusted leg band

on a stand – a championship trophy in this sport.

"Then we released him in the hummock field and wiped his memory."

"They just have to deal with it? Aren't they all a bit confused?" asked Fleence.

"Oh yes, they will be bewildered about what happened for the rest of their lives if they don't get into the Galactic Pool. But did you notice what Pip did?"

"Well, he seemed focused on the abductee."

"Yes. Keep them under the dome until we get the outside situation under control. Don't be afraid to administer a heavy dose of calming agent. I will give instructions and help protect you if the situation calls for it. We'll have to be extra careful on Dirt because humanoids tend to scatter."

"So what happens when you lose a subject that has seen you?"

"Well, we try to hunt them down, but usually it isn't a big deal if they see us and get away. There are lots of false UFO sightings on every planet we visit. So the people who actually see us are just considered crazy too."

"Have you had any botched ones that were a big deal?"

"Yes."

Dluhosh punched it up.

"This subject got a great picture of me standing there in a floating doorway. You could even see my colors. We call it a 'tech fart' in PLUMBOB parlance. Here, you'll see."

The screen shows a shaggy large yellowish individual relaxing in a field and fiddling with a camera.

"This subject was on his back surrounded by tall grass, so I had to position myself directly over him."

The video clearly shows the startled subject taking a picture. Dluhosh grabs him and the abduction looks to go routinely. The egocite ingot changes from a muffin-shape to a small replica of one of the little surf-riding boats. When they are done with him, Dluhosh places the subject back on the same grassy spot. The big bird drops his camera on his beak, but appears not to have registered that anything unusual had happened.

"Later that day I realized that I had forgotten to erase the image from the camera – classic tech fart. The picture itself wasn't going to blow the mission or anything, but I was worried that I could be recognized in it. There's a great picture of Maghosh climbing a tree on Free-15. After Free-15 got into the Galactic Pool, some 'crazy' Bearman finally got to prove to everyone that his alien photograph was real."

"Oh, yeah, that could be embarrassing," said Fleence.

"Exactly. So I didn't want to take the risk. The rules allow me some latitude for evidence cover-up, so I decided this one was worth going on the ground for."

The video shows Dluhosh exiting the ship in his night-time outdoor stealth colors. As he sneaks up on the cabin, his skin develops shadowy spots that seem to crawl across his body as he moves. Then his skin becomes bark-like in color and texture when he gets close to a pile of firewood.

Fleence looked away from the screen for a second, and when she looked back she couldn't find him.

"Wow, you are sneakier than a tapeworm omelet, Dluhosh. You look just like a piece of firewood."

"I searched all over for that camera. I looked in all the obvious places, including in that hovercraft of his. I finally found it on the bed next to him."

"Oh no," said Fleence.

"Yep. I was crawling very quietly when the sun peaked over the horizon and shined through the window. He awoke looking right at me. So now we had to abduct him again, but I had to get him outside first. I didn't want to wrestle him if I didn't have to. But he kept jumping behind furniture and into closets and under his bed as I chased him around the cabin. I couldn't get a tentacle safely on him. And he would not run outside. I had to admire his speed and agility for such a big fellow."

Now the video shows the avianoid come crashing head over talons out the front door. But Pip-The-Blue misses him with the grabber beam and the subject jumps into his hovercraft.

"As you saw, I finally tossed him out the door, but we missed him. So I had to sprint after the hovercraft."

The video shows the hovercraft racing down a dirt track across a meadow toward an opening in the dense forest. Dluhosh spins up his tentacles and goes after it. The hovercraft pulls out ahead on the straight-aways, but Dluhosh gains ground in the curves.

"I was able to catch up to him in a forested section of road, and I mounted his vehicle as we came into another meadow."

The video shows the hovercraft exiting the forest as Dluhosh latches onto the luggage rack. Then he crawls up the back end of the hovercraft toward the driver's compartment. As Pip-The-Blue tries to get in close, Dluhosh's skin flashes with intense psychedelic colors.

"Wow, Dluhosh, you look pumped!" said Fleence.

"Yep, I was definitely feeling the drama. But to get control of the craft, I had to learn how to drive a stick-and-clutch transmission on the spot. And to pull it over I had to find the brakes, deploy the landing gear, raise the skirt, and shut down the air cushion – all while dodging my eye from his beak."

The video shows the two drivers struggling as Dluhosh pulls the hovercraft over. The combatants tumble out onto the road, entwined and grappling, with feathers flying and colors pulsing. Pip-The-Blue gets them onto the ship with the grabber beam and reloads the subject's memory from his earlier abduction. The guy stops fighting and both break out in big beaky grins.

"He was a tough old bird, but a really nice guy too. He said his name was Dayv – a big-time wave rider. So anyway, I explained the picture of me that he forgot taking, he let me delete it, and I helped clean up the mess in his cabin."

"And you weren't hurt?"

"No… it felt pretty good to get stretched out, actually. And did you notice how Pip was ready with the memory reload? If there's one thing to stress here, that's it. Once the subjects regain memory of their first abduction, and remember why they feel so good all of a sudden, the situation diffuses, without exception."

"So are we allowed to abduct subjects just to cure their diseases, or save them from an accident or something?" asked Fleence.

"Well, if our manipulations cause an injury, then yes, we can abduct them to repair them. Otherwise, the rules say that we can't do medical abductions unless we're clarifying a checklist item, covering up our presence, or following up on a previous abduction. We aren't even allowed to do it on our free time. Here, I have a good clip."

The screen shows a steep hillside with a long paved track running straight down it. The track terminates in a built-up ramp surrounded by empty observation decks. The lower part of the hill appears to be a landing area lined by empty grandstands.

"These avianoids are technically flightless, but they do have wings, and some athletic individuals can glide effectively over some distance. They call this sport 'skate flying'. We had been watching them practice for about an hour. It was Pip's free time, and he was enjoying watching these clunkers try to fly. You see the guy at the top of the ramp?"

"Yes."

"He's about to be horribly injured in a crash."

The avianoid skater begins his descent. As he reaches maximum speed at the bottom of the ramp he spins out of control, tumbles along the edge of the ramp, scrapes some landscaping, and crashes into the corner of a concrete barrier.

"Oh wow! That didn't kill him?!" asked Fleence.

"Incredibly, no. He remained conscious and was obviously in great agony. Look at that bone sticking out of his leg. There was nobody nearby, so we had a couple of minutes to abduct him before help arrived – IF we could find an excuse."

The scene inside the ship shows Pip and Dluhosh going over the checklist.

"Why not sports and recreation?" asks Pip-The-Blue.

"Well, we already closed that out," replied Dluhosh.

"How about workplace safety?"

"No. I think this is a poor example of that. Can you hear what he's saying?"

Pip listens in. "He's just groaning and swearing."

"Not praying?"

"No – just a string of swear words."

"That's too bad. If he were praying, we could use the religious practices checklist item to heal him," says Dluhosh.

"It's alright if I reposition him a little – just for comfort – right? His beak is hung up awkwardly," says Pip. "It's giving me the willies."

Dluhosh thinks about it. "I guess if you…"

Before Dluhosh can finish, Pip's invisible grabber beam is trying to reposition the skater by the beak. The injured bird squawks once and then goes silent.

"Oops. I hope that didn't kill him," says Pip.

"Well, I guess now we have an excuse to abduct him."

Dluhosh paused the clip.

"We justified abducting him because we had possibly killed him ourselves. Anyway, the probaluation fixed his paralysis and other internal injuries, including a concussion, a bruised liver, torn dark meat, a dislocated wishbone, and a life-threatening gizzard rupture," said Dluhosh.

"You couldn't fix his broken drumstick?" asked Fleence.

"We could have set and fused the fracture as we probaluated him – and we could have duplicated the missing testicle as well. But it would have been unrealistic for him to come out of that crash completely unscathed. We have to be careful not to confuse people into thinking there's been a miracle."

PLANET ONE PREPARES TO INVADE

"Heh, heh... Why do we always prepare for invasions that we don't want to conduct?" said President Gren Wee-1. "Why don't we put our resources into eliminating the need for the invasion?"

"With all due respect, sir, and I know that was a joke," replied Griffer-1, "invasions are much simpler to plan for. Planning for peace is for fools."

The President, Vice President, and chief advisor Gro Skoo-1 stood in an observation tower watching a heavy fighter craft taking aim on a full-sized granite replica of Mount Rushmore.

The President asked the Vice President, "So how is your plan coming along then?"

"Oh, you'll have to ask Gro Skoo – this whole thing is his baby."

"Yes, I assume that Griffer has informed you of my idea," said Gro Skoo. "What you see here is an equipment test and demonstration for an invasion of a planet called Dirt, which I think will be an ally and trading partner if we can get it into the Galactic Pool."

"Oh," replied the President, stroking his ear and looking at Griffer-1 with a more confused expression than usual.

Griffer-1 jumped in, "Yes, Gro Skoo has a great idea for getting control of the Galactic Assembly. Tell us more, Gro Skoo." Griffer-1 intended this segue to lead the President from one confusion to another without a break for questions.

"The plan is similar to The Fermament-4 Compromise, sir. You remember the rhyme from school…?" asked Gro Skoo.

"Yes, of course…" said the President, closing his eyes in concentration.

"This is the mountain of Furniture-4
The melting of which soiled the floor
You did it once and you'll do it some more
Your mother don't care because she's a whore
Your father snuck in through the back door
He stole everything from shore to shore
So I called on your mother until she got sore
And that is the Compromise of Furniture-4!"

The President looked at his advisor with indignation and said, "I haven't forgotten!"

"Um, yes sir, I suppose there are alternate versions of the rhyme, sir. But the rhyme is supposed to help you remember the order of the planets in the Galactic Pool, sir."

"I know my geography well enough Skooks. There's Furniture-4 with the ugly smelly guys. There's Bluey-5 with those crazy wavy glowy dudes. Then there's Squirrelville-6 with the fury loudmouths climbing all over everything. Press-A-Piss-7 with the Billy Goat fellas... And that bird place with the thingy. I know my people, Skooey Skookums!"

"Yes sir, of course, sir. Anyway, our outreach team, will, of course, include diplomats who will attempt to negotiate with the Dirtlings. Once that fails, we'll melt things until the Dirtlings give in. This is a replica of our primary target."

"That's an impressive mountain you got there Skoober," said the President.

"Yes, Mister President, the Dirtlings have an odd penchant for carving these huge replicas of themselves," said Gro Skoo.

"Very odd, indeed, but I wonder why nobody else ever thought of the idea. Maybe I should have one made. The men are very handsome and distinguished looking. I think I would fit in well with them. The man with the mustache in the back sure looks like one tough customer. And the woman is beautiful!"

Griffer-1 and Gro Skoo-1 glanced at each other.

"Oh, right sir! Quite a rendition... She's fabulous. So, sir, the ship is waiting for the order to fire. Where would you like them to start?" asked Gro Skoo.

"St-start with the woman," ordered the President.

Gro Skoo, not knowing which one was 'the woman', gave the order and hoped for the best. "Okay, go ahead and fire at will upon the woman," he commanded.

Aboard the fighter craft, the Dung Beetle navigator shrugged, but the Cricket captain guessed correctly. And Thomas Jefferson changed from solid granite to a flow of rhyolitic lava.

The President jumped up and down laughing and flapping his ears.

"Sir, we should have our excuse to begin the compromise within a couple of months. However, we may need to go through the voting process first. That shouldn't take long because – and here's the real beauty of my idea – I found us a ringer to film the Dirtlings."

"Trukk-9?"

"Excellent guess, Mister President!" said a surprised Gro Skoo. "And I developed a special checklist for him that will surely make the voters love Dirt. It's practically a done deal. We should start getting indications of progress soon. In fact, it's entirely possible that events on Dirt have already sealed their fate."

DLUHOSH MEETS TRUKK-9

Dluhosh and Fleence made good time as the frequency of wormholes increased.

"I've never heard of anything like this," said Dluhosh. "There are so many wormholes, and they seem to be favorably aligned for getting to Dirt. Statistically speaking, this is unlikely to be an accident."

When they emerged from the final wormhole, Dluhosh said, "Whoa! That was dangerous. I can't believe the Dirtlings haven't travelled out into the galaxy through these wormholes. We're already close enough to contact Trukk-9 by radio. You know, I think we must have bad information about Dirt visiting their moon. I mean, by the time you have the technology needed to land on the moon, you will already have the technology to detect and use wormholes. This many wormholes so close-by would practically be screaming in their ears."

"Well, maybe Trukk-9 has some answers. Are we going to call on him?" asked Fleence with obvious excitement.

"I have to admit, I'm intimidated to radio him. I mean, what should I say? Hello, this is your Dnooblian monitor.

I hope you've been behaving yourself without me here to inspect you. And by the way, why did Welter-3 send you here early? Are you part of a conspiracy? And is it true that you were once quartered by a Dnooblian? It wasn't me…"

"You know, honestly, I bet he's excited to meet you too. He said at least five or six times in his film that he likes Dnooblians very much, and how many other Dnooblians do you think he encounters?"

"Okay, well let's see if we can locate his ping. And how about you try to tap into whatever computer network the planet has?"

His scanner image looked like snow.

"Holy halibut!" said Dluhosh. "The scanner shows THOUSANDS of artificial satellites orbiting the planet!"

"Thousands?" asked Fleence.

"Yeah, and they've never sent one through the wormholes? That is very strange. We're going to have to get closer before we can detect The Duke in all that junk."

A moment later the unmistakable voice of Trukk-9 came over the radio.

"Ahoy! Dluhosh-10! Welcome to Dirt! This is Trukk-9 and crew aboard The Cruiser Duke Sukk-9. We hope you've had a pleasant voyage."

Dluhosh responded. "Hello. This is the PLUMBOB monitoring ship, Dluhosh-10 and Fleence-18, our egocite handler. We are happy to hear your voice. I wasn't sure if we'd be able to detect you with all that satellite traffic."

Dluhosh flew to their location, and there it was – THE DUKE, right there, in real life. Dluhosh's skin turned sky blue in an uncontrolled show of wonderment.

"We figured we might be lost in this mess, so I've had my pilot Dee scanning for your cloaking signature all week." He paused then said, "Did you say Fleence-18?"

"Hello, Trukk-9. I'm Fleence. I have a special message

for you."

Dee watched his friend closely. His body language had changed. His blinking had gone out of sync. Dee thought he knew why, and he also thought it was pretty funny. So he activated the video monitor link to Dluhosh's ship.

And there sat Fleence-18.

Trukk-9 was stunned. He imagined Fleence's mother, so he saw Fleence wearing a home-spun tunic covered in red dust. He could almost feel the dust bath and kind words being spoken.

Dluhosh also realized what was happening, of course, and tried to get things back to business. "That's very considerate of you to look for us. But how did you know our cloaking signature? And how do you know my name?"

"Huh? Uh, oh… Welter-3 told me, I think," said Trukk-9. "I was very pleased to find out that I would be working with a Dnooblian. Uh, you said you had a message…"

"Yes, my mother says HI."

"She said HI? To me? She remembers me?"

Dee snorted and covered his mouth. The autotranslator betrayed him, however.

"My mother talks about you quite often. You must know that. I wish I could say I remember you too, but I was too young when you liberated us. People recognize my mother in your film, of course. Perhaps I will have a chance soon to catch you up on how she's doing."

Dee wasn't going to let the fun stop now. "Oh, no hurry," he said. "Please tell us what your mother says Trukk-9 is like when things get dusty."

"My mother always said that nosey bears are only looking for garbage. Is that true, Mr. Bear?" asked Fleence.

"Uh, yes, but this nosey bear is crawling back to his den…" said Dee, which was a pretty good answer considering that he wasn't used to being spoken to like that by anyone but his own mother.

Buzzy examined this humanoid female, and ever so slightly bowed his respect.

Dluhosh tried to get back to business. "Trukk-9, thanks again for contacting us. Uh, this planet seems very unusual already. It's swarming with satellites, but has numerous undetected wormholes sitting right outside of its solar system. How can it be true that they've made it to their moon?"

Trukk-9 came back to the reality of the moment and introduced his crew. Then he said, "Yes, this planet is very much a marvel to behold. They've sent men to the moon several times and they regularly visit space. They blast off on combustion rockets and actually get home safely most of the time. They even have people in orbit on one of those satellites right now."

"You've got to be kidding! So their technology isn't advanced – they are just crazy? Is that what you're saying?" asked Dluhosh.

"Yes, that would seem to be the case," said Trukk-9.

"And why so many satellites?"

"Well, they have the normal sorts of primitive weather, research, and space observation satellites. But they also have military and surveillance-related ones, and a huge number of telecommunication satellites that seem to be mainly used for entertainment purposes. They have thousands of television and radio channels, and vast telephone and computer networks that are, again, mainly for entertainment. It's really quite fantastic."

"Why? Do they bore that easily?" asked Dluhosh.

"Yes, and they have very many imaginative cures for boredom. There are a few countries with only state-run media and underground cinema like we have, but mostly it's a big-money free-for-all. They have many truly fantastic filmmakers and huge multiplex cinemas in practically every town. Honestly, if I lived here I'd probably be just another unknown. I think we can learn many important truths from these people. I like them very much," said Trukk-9.

"How much of this telecommunication is propaganda?" asked Dluhosh.

"I honestly think that a lot of it is, but it's very entertaining propaganda. Their news is also done as entertainment, as is their advertising, and their sports, and they even broadcast themselves having sex. And they are very skilled at combining propaganda, news, sports, advertising, and sex into a single product. And they love it – they absolutely adore it. What a great audience. I wish I had a market like them at home," said Trukk-9.

"Well, then this mission should be interesting," said Dluhosh. "How are the Dirtlings doing on the checklist items so far?"

"We have already located many items to document all around the planet. The diversity of cultures is amazing, and they have quite an array of fascinating social customs. I've been enjoying this mission very much, and I've been desperate for you to get here so we can do some stylizations. So far it's been very difficult to see their souls," said Trukk-9.

"So it's pretty much been all positive then? How about some of the more negative checklist items – war, crime, pollution, etcetera?" asked Dluhosh.

"Oh, yeah, there seems to be plenty of that stuff, but none of it is on our checklist," replied Trukk-9.

"Not on your checklist?" asked Dluhosh. "Mister O'Buzznid-3, do you not have the standard checklist?"

"We are using the official checklist for this mission in its entirety," replied Buzzy.

"What do you mean 'official checklist for this mission'?

Don't you have the standard PLUMBOB checklist?" asked Dluhosh.

"I know the checklist, of course, but they gave us a special list for this mission. Apparently somebody else is getting the bad stuff," said Buzzy.

"And Welter-3 told me that they had intercepted news broadcasts already. So that might cover your other checklist items," said Trukk-9.

"Don't you think they'd want to get the bad stuff from a verifiable source too – not just from some commercial sexy news entertainment shows?" asked Dluhosh.

"Oh, I do not know, the bad stuff is pretty obvious," replied Buzzy.

"Are they at war anywhere?" asked Dluhosh.

"There are dozens, maybe hundreds of wars, big and small, all over the planet, yes," replied Buzzy.

"Well, then doesn't it seem strange that we are here considering this planet?" asked Dluhosh.

Dee said, "Some of that good stuff is really good! Probably good enough to balance things out some… You gotta check it out. The very first thing that my old Cousin Buzzy found was a picture of the cuddliest ursoid this side of the Bare Bear Bar back home where they have these painted and powdered sows that will let you get behind them and fee-"

Dluhosh interrupted. "Balance out dozens of wars?"

"Well, Dee has a point. You should see some of their films and television programs – they're very very good. It might be a good trade-off if too many people aren't getting killed in the wars," said Trukk-9.

"Are these Dirtlings even rational?" asked Dluhosh.

"I think some of them are, but maybe there's a balance between irrationality and entertainment value in their actions," said Trukk-9.

"Entertainment can be considered by the voters, of course, but entertainment value doesn't figure into the planet's qualification for nomination in the first place. They are nominated based only on an objective evaluation of the items on the standard checklist," said Dluhosh. "So have you documented anything bad first hand?"

"Not on purpose, but we have inadvertently captured some negativity being inflicted on a helpless person or two," replied Trukk-9.

"Well, good, that's a start. Now that I'm here, we will be using the full standard checklist," said Dluhosh.

"Hold on, that's not what I signed up for. I have no use for footage of war and violence. If you are going to film that stuff, then I'll be taking my ship home," replied Trukk-9.

"Fine – I don't think we should be here to begin with. The rules are clear, and this mission isn't following them. You know what we say on Dnooblia. Just rules, broken by fools. Let's go home," said Dluhosh, calling what he was sure was Trukk-9's bluff.

"Hold on, hold on. Okay, I'll help with your checklist, but we visit all of the locations that I have lined up first," said Trukk-9.

"Never mind – we're leaving. Okay Fleence, plot our course back to the last wormhole," said Dluhosh.

Fleence began punching buttons on her navigation panel.

"Hold on! Wait, wait… There's a popular saying on my planet too," said Trukk-9. "It translates roughly as 'Never play poker with a purple Dnooblian'."

Dee interrupted. "Skip, what the Dnooblian says actually makes sense if you think about it. This planet would never get a chance at a vote. At least not until the Bear People rise. Think about it. That Griffer-1 is a dick anyway."

"Griffer-1? So he really is involved?" asked Dluhosh.

"He did call me once – just to wish me luck and remind me how important this mission is... Buzzy, what do you think? Is Dluhosh correct? Is this a bogus checklist?" asked Trukk-9.

Buzzy said, "I think it is reasonable to conclude that the person who developed our checklist is confused about the PLUMBOB process."

Trukk-9 continued. "I'm going to be straight with you, Dluhosh. We have accidentally witnessed and filmed a scene that... reminds us of slavery." He glanced up at Fleence.

"Of course, we haven't pursued anything since it's not on our checklist. But I have a clip that I think you should see. Buzzy, please pull up the scene with Numun discussing the young man with his mother," said Trukk-9.

He continued. "We've been following a couple of families in a small village. One is the blacksmith family and the other is a family of cattle herders. They are very very great people. They have truly ancient elements in their culture, but they are poor. Their social customs are elaborate and quite clever, if not occasionally a bit harsh. I like them very much."

Trukk-9 sent the clip to the shared video server.

"This first clip is of a counseling session between the head blacksmith and a mother who has come to him seeking advice. The blacksmiths seem to provide a sort of independent counseling service. They are discussing her son."

The video shows Numun speaking with a worried-looking woman. They conclude some quiet greetings and benedictions as she crouches, looking at the ground as she explains.

"My brother-in-law wants to send my son to work in the goldmines. My brother-in-law is in debt, and I think he wants my son to work to pay the debt off for him. My husband has debts of his own and he says he is powerless to stop them. I want to find a way to prevent this."

Numun recites several benedictions, then says, "I will think on this matter and try to learn more about it. I will call for you when I am ready, and I will have my older brother with me. We will try to help. I know your son. He should not be taken out of school."

The woman parts as they share more benedictions. "May you find a peaceful path home. Greet the people. Sleep well."

Trukk-9 paused the clip. "It seems pretty clear that her son could essentially be sold into slavery. We've been back several times, but we've been unable to determine the outcome."

"Slavery is an automatic disqualifier," said Dluhosh.

Trukk-9 looked at Fleence.

Fleence, who had been searching through Dirt's computer network, added, "I have credible information here that says there are millions of slaves on this planet. In some places slavery is still widely practiced, and though it is illegal in all countries, there is no risk of prosecution in some places."

"Mister O'Buzznid-3, weren't you curious enough about the missing checklist items to do some research? Fleence found this information and she's not even a text translation specialist. You are the research technician," said Dluhosh.

"Trukk-9 does not need research assistance with items that are not on the checklist," said Buzzy. "Dee has research responsibilities too."

"Yeah, but you know I'm no good at translating computer text, Cousin. I've mostly been watching those funny videos. You know that, buddy. How many videos have I forwarded to you?" Then Dee looked up at Fleence and Dluhosh and said, "You guys, they have this animal here called a kitten... Seriously, I'll send you some links."

"Be quiet, you big goof," said Trukk-9, opening all of his back eyes to look at Dee directly. "This is important. I am starting to get the feeling that I've been played like a fiddle."

Dluhosh said to Trukk-9, "I'm going to lay all my cards on the table. The only reason that I haven't already called off this mission and sent everyone home is because you are Trukk-9 and not just another government videographer. From all the evidence available, I think that your integrity is being used by someone at a higher level for their political gain."

Trukk-9 closed all of his eyes in concentration.

"Essentially, they are asking you to answer an invalid question about this planet. That is, they are asking you 'How wonderful is Dirt?' Then they will take your answer and apply it to the actual proper question, which is, 'What is Dirt really like? And the answer...? Well, Trukk-9 himself says it is THIS wonderful!" Dluhosh spread his tentacles from bulkhead to bulkhead and from stem to stern to illustrate his point.

"We've been bluffed!" yelled Dee, happy to be able to continue the poker analogies.

"Calm down, Dee. Let's think about this for a minute," said Trukk-9.

No one else spoke, but a minute later Trukk-9 opened his eyes and said, "I think maybe I HAVE been bluffed. Well, then, I guess we'll do as Dluhosh instructs. Welcome again to Dirt, Dluhosh-10. I think you'll find that a completely objective analysis will show this planet to be completely insane."

"Well, that was easy," said Dluhosh. "Thank you for

being reasonable, Trukk-9. I don't think the Galactic Academy of Sciences could even be that objective."

"One has to think these things through and not let lofty aspirations fool one," said Trukk-9. "I know that I'm politically naïve so I have to be careful – and I wasn't. I thank you for helping, Dluhosh."

Dluhosh let go a short blast of relief from his siphon.

"But please," said Trukk-9, "let's work together here. I have some great stuff lined up. How about this – as a show of good faith we visit the boy in Hippopotamus for more documentation, and maybe help him too? Then will you allow me to visit a very interesting city and then my favorite Dirtling? I chose both of these locations because I knew I'd be working with a Dnooblian. You'll see – it's very interesting stuff with the possibility of bad things too. I'm sure we can both meet our objectives."

"Okay, that works for me. But Mister O'Buzznid-3, I want you to look for objectives from the whole standard checklist. I want you to line up at least a week's worth of whatever mayhem you can find," said Dluhosh.

"Make it be, Buzzy!" said Trukk-9.

Dee let out his hugest happy-roar and said, "Oh, please… AARRR AARRR AARRR… Oh, that's freaking great! 'Make it BEE Buzzy!' AARRR, that is FUNNY! Get it…? Sometimes that piece-of-crap autotranslator NAILS it!"

Fleence shot back. "Hey Bearman, I bet that Bee would let you lick some honey from its stinger."

At that Buzzy thought: I like this humanoid sticking up for me. No humanoid has ever stuck up for me before. But I am not a Bee. I cannot let this pass…

"I AM A FUCKING CRICKET!" he chirped.

Now the only tense person on either ship was the Cricket, and that's the way it was supposed to be.

Trukk-9, trying to keep the positive tone alive, then said, "Oh, by the way, Dluhosh, I know of you. I read that you discovered the last of the flying weasels."

Dluhosh said, "Well, they sort of discovered me. They nested in my siphon during my Drying Out Time rite."

"That's incredible. I'd like to make a film about the weasel one day. I've been thinking about returning to Dnooblia for a long time. The weasels would be a good angle. They are very charismatic."

Dee said, "Yeah, but those weasel guys are way too small to hug though. Hey, maybe if you had a whole bunch of those little suckers that you could roll around with… Like a mountain of 'em all piled up that you could jump in. That would be sweet! They would be all tickly and everything – as long as they didn't crawl up your a-"

"Yeah, okay Dee," said Trukk-9. "Well, I guess I was lucky that weasels didn't find me. I had enough trouble with those wasps, and I'm sure wasp tastes better than weasel. Anyway, we should talk about a weasel film sometime."

Dluhosh liked that Trukk-9 used the accurate Dnooblian names for the animals, since he hadn't done so in the film. He felt like he was getting an exclusive bonus feature of additional accuracy. And the talk of a possible weasel film magnified the importance of keeping the mood light. Mutual flattery seemed like a good strategy. So he said, "Fleence and I were wondering what one question we would like to ask you about your films."

Fleence cooperated and said, "Yeah, we'd like to hear your firsthand account of the duck dance on Swampy-12, right Dluhosh?"

"Oh, good, you've seen that – probably my favorite moment of all my films. Let's see… Well, we knew that Swamp Master sexual reproduction included gregarious physical interactions – the jubilees. And we knew that the events are triggered when a group of Swamp Masters receives or witnesses a wonderful surprise. Even such a thing as a very very excellent film with a surprise happy ending can lead to a jubilee right in the theater."

Dluhosh asked, "So the jubilee you guys triggered was the biggest one ever, right?"

"Well, I was interested in encountering or creating a jubilee in an outdoor situation where I could film from The Duke. We decided to observe a major Swamp Master rodeo in hopes of having the spectacle trigger a jubilee. The bleachers at this rodeo held thousands of people, and we waited and waited. We sat through the frog tying, the newt throw, eel roping, and the leech barrel race, and got nothing. The events were exciting, and the spectators seemed to enjoy them, but I guess there were no surprises or wonderment, or at least not enough to trigger a jubilee."

"So the ducks – they were part of a rodeo event?" asked Dluhosh.

"Yes, apparently at the end of a rodeo it's a tradition to let children bob for ducks. It was very funny to see the kids swim up under the ducks and grab them by the legs. They pull the duck under, stuff it in a sack, and then get to keep as many as they can catch. The parents were enjoying it and laughing and cheering and we really thought a jubilee was going to happen. But it was not stimulating enough for them."

Dee said, "Yeah, those mommy and daddy Swamp Masters were all standing and cheering and I thought maybe some of the smaller ones were getting slick and frisky down in the front. But the giant old ones in the back didn't seem into it enough. Did you know that Swamp Masters keep growing and growing for their entire life? Can you imagine if Bearmen were like that? What if I was thirty feet tall?

HOOEEE! I could film from amazing angles, and I could fight forest fires with my pi-"

Trukk-9 interrupted. "Anyway, I think it was Dee who suggested that Stick help the ducks escape, right?"

"Yeah, those poor ducks needed help, Skip. I said Stick should dodge the ducks around to frustrate the kids. I figured if the parents were anything like Bearmen, they would think it was super funny to see the ducks beat their cubs."

Then Stick.E said, "Yes, the easiest way to do it with that many grabber beams is to simply have all the ducks make the same moves. So I basically made the ducks do a mass line dance in very fast little zigzag patterns. The ducks were dancing and the children were crying with that horrible noise, the parents must have thought it was hilarious, and it worked."

"So that screeching sound was children crying – not the ducks?" asked Fleence.

"Yes, these were quackless ducks," replied Trukk-9. "At first the audience became quiet. Then they started to giggle and point in amazement. And sure enough, they slimed up and started rubbing together. The next thing we knew the bleachers were covered in a mass of slipping and sliding and twisting Swamp Masters."

"Yeah, it was crazy!" said Dee. "Those Swamp Master suckers pile up and slide in and out of the mass and get all frothed up. It was like a wriggling mass of giant yellow salamanders. Which, you know, would normally be my kind of scene – but the slime… Oh, the slime! The gutters under the bleachers flowed with hot goo. You could hear it gushing! Listen real close to the audio for the gloop, gloop, fwooshing sound. Seriously, that jubilee action was like watching a big old living slimy yellow boog-"

Trukk-9 interrupted. "We only included about five

minutes in the film, but the jubilee lasted for almost an hour. It was certainly the biggest one ever filmed. We started to worry that we'd taken them too far, but then they stopped and all went to the swamp to wash off. During the jubilee the children just sat on the rodeo ground eating their ducks."

"So all the Swamp Master women get pregnant?" asked Fleence.

"No. If they wash the slime off in the swamp they don't. If they want to get pregnant, they leave the slime on until it dries out in a few days. While the slime is wet, the sperm cells from all the males they have rubbed against fight it out. The winning sperm army will then fertilize the female's eggs. They say that this is why Swamp Masters are so peaceful toward one another. Their sperm does their fighting for them."

So the crews watched the clip from the movie, which included microscopic views of armies of sperm with fangs, clubbed tails, and spiked body armor doing battle with sperm armies of rival males.

Trukk-9 said, "Well, I agree that I should be helping to answer the question of what Dirt is REALLY like. But if you are willing to help meet both our objectives, I think I would like to work with you, Dluhosh-10."

"Okay, Trukk-9, let's see what Mister O'Buzznid-3 can find us, and then we'll go from there," said Dluhosh.

Buzzy got to work.

VISIT TO THE ELECTRIC CITY

The two ships' crews got ready for the coming day. Dluhosh had a soak. Fleence reduplicated her uniform, ate a churdle burger, and dug into Dirt's computer network. Dee curled up under his flight console and took a nap. Stick.E gave himself a tune-up by oscillating up and down in specific frequencies and amplitudes of sine waves. Trukk-9 watched his personal video archive of Fleence's mother at the egocite mines, including unused footage that Dee secretly shot of them taking a dust bath together. He muted Dee's laughing.

After a couple of hours Buzzy announced, "Okay everybody, I have a pretty good schedule here. Everything should dovetail well with regulation breaks in between. There is going to be a fire hunt at Balontan tomorrow. And then the next morning is Jimmy Fresneaux's regular fishing time. So right now would be a good time to go to that big city where everyone looks like you, Trukk-9. The fish market is about to open."

Trukk-9 said, "Dluhosh, I'm sure you'll find this city to be very interesting. It's very vibrant, has a big fish market that I think you would enjoy, and is full of people that look similar to me. Of course, they only have two eyes and no antlers, but I could pass for one otherwise. Also, there are some interesting ursoids in a zoo there that Dee wants to meet."

"Yeah, baby!" said Dee.

"And they have a highly developed public transportation system. So there are several checklist possibilities within a small area, and some intriguing free-time options. I like these people very much. And, with your approval, I'd like to infiltrate."

"Well, I don't know…" said Dluhosh.

"Stick.E will have a grabber beam umbilical on me. I'd use a tiny lapel camera and microphone. Plus they do this thing… What's it called Buzzy?"

"Cosplay."

"Right, they dress up like cartoon characters. So if I got caught out, they'd just think I was a really good character. What am I supposed to call myself again, Buzzy?"

"You are an original character – 'OC', as it were – and you are called Dab Tabmow. You are from Planet Atacra, and your power comes from your spherical vision. If you need to be retrieved, you yell out 'Multi-vision tornado attack level four' – I have written it down for you," replied Buzzy.

"Yeah, and can I infiltrate the zoo?" asked Dee. "Please? Those poor fellas in there are in bad need of hugs and wrestles."

Dluhosh replied. "Well, the rules don't restrict interactions with non-sapient beings, of course. So I don't see a problem if you want to wrestle bears. As far as doing this dress-up game thing, I agree that it's allowed on your free time, but only with a self-destruction tablet. Are you sure you want to risk that?"

"HA! He's Trukk-9! He's not afraid of some itty-bitty self-destruction tablet! Right, Skip?"

"Well, it certainly wouldn't be the first time I've carried one. So, no, this opportunity is worth the risk. Anyway, we should start very early at the fish market."

"Okay," said Dluhosh, "I'm ready for it. Are you, Fleence?"

"Like a wound-up Rumbly-11 catapult-worm on a sunny night!"

***

They hovered outside the planet's largest fish market before dawn and watched as people unloaded large fish from boats and prepared them for auction.

"And check this out," said Buzzy, "a single one of those fish has sold for the equivalent of almost two million dollars."

"What!? You could buy ten prime fishing concessions in perpetuity on Dnooblia."

"It says we might be able to get a ticket to see the auction if we get in that line. And I gather that the two-million-dollar fish is an advertising gimmick of some kind, so you would not expect to see that high of a price paid on a random visit," explained Buzzy.

"Well, I don't think it's a good idea for Dab Tabmow to cosplay in the fish market anyway," said Trukk-9.

"Wow, this is making me hungry," said Dluhosh.

After the auction finished, they observed a consignment of the large fish being offloaded at one of the stalls. Men with bandsaws and knives as long as Dnooblian fencing weapons butchered the fish. Other carts delivered a wide variety of sea life to vendors.

As they looked around, Dluhosh said, "It's not unusual

for planets to have a variety of edible tentacled animals, but this one seems especially well endowed. I do know one thing though – I wouldn't want to be worth two million bucks to some humanoid. That sounds like a recipe for extinction."

The rest of the crew regarded Dluhosh as if they thought he could be worth millions in there.

"Okay," said Trukk-9, "are we ready to have a look at the public transportation system?"

"Sounds good to me," said Dluhosh.

Buzzy said, "We should be able to observe some very fast trains on the outskirts of town. And they have a vast network of underground and elevated commuter trains in the city proper. The city seems to be developed around the train system rather than the other way around."

The two ships rose up over the city to spot trains.

"According to this source, the city is regularly attacked by monstrous beasts. Here, I will send you each a link."

The others watched the video clip in horror as a crazed reptiloid monster ravaged the city.

"Those poor people!" cried Fleence.

Trukk-9 scrutinized the clip and said, "Uh, well, I think this looks like an animation."

"Oh, Buzzy. What a doofus!" yelled Dee. "AHHAAHHAAAA…"

Stick.E said, "I have a train approaching at a high rate of speed." He put it on the shared screen. "It's going over one-hundred-fifty miles per hour on tracks!"

After observing the train, Fleence and Dluhosh watched in wonder as plane after plane landed and took off at multiple airports. Finally Dluhosh said, "It's all combustion technology…"

They spent the rest of the afternoon documenting the trains, busses, planes, and ferries around the city.

***

"Okay folks, it's quitting time at the zoo. This is my chance," said Dee.

They flew to the zoo. No visitors remained, and the keepers were busy inside the panda house. One panda sat alone eating bamboo.

"Just drop me right behind him. Look how cute he is. Don't you just want to hug him?"

"No. I think you're the only one," replied Trukk-9.

"Okay, I don't know how he'll react, so it's just a quick hug and yank me back. I don't want to fight him, I just want to feel him and smell him. Make sure you get a picture though. My friends are gonna be so jealous."

Stick.E plopped Dee right behind the panda. He gave a big bear hug and buried his smiling face into the animal's fur. Then Dee spread his arms out wide to indicate that he was satisfied. Stick.E pulled him back to the ship.

"That was awesome! He's sooo cuddly! I wish I could take him home."

"Get a genetic sample and some of his food. Mother's lab can probably clone a few up for you," said Fleence.

"Really? Can I Dluhosh?" asked Dee.

"Non-sapient being…" was all Dluhosh said.

"Sweet! Okay, now how does it look over by the white bears?"

Stick.E said, "Same – the keepers are busy and there is one bear having a swim. What do you want to do?"

"Drop me right by him at the side of the pool. I'll let him get out of the water and come to me if he wants to grapple."

Dee appeared in the polar bear pit. The bear turned right for Dee and climbed out of the pool.

"C'mon, big fella, show me what you got."

Dee got into the universal ursoid wrestling stance. The bear, who was about the same size as Dee, landed a mighty swat to the side of Dee's head. The blow spun Dee around, but didn't drop him.

"Oh, so you play dirty on Dirt, huh? Well take this!" Dee punched the polar bear right in the nose, bloodying it. Both bears roared and the polar bear lunged for Dee's throat with its huge mouth. Right before it could land its bite, Stick.E pulled Dee back to the ship.

"What'd you do that for!? I HAD him. He's a damn cheater, but I had him!"

"Well, Dee, that may be the case, but your roaring has attracted a zookeeper," said Trukk-9. "Anyway, I should start getting ready to go out. Exactly what sort of costume do you have in mind, Buzzy?"

"Well, I have been doing some research on this cosplay business, and I have put together this composite as a suggestion. Please view your screens."

The image displayed a 3-D mock-up of Trukk-9 wearing a black leather tunic and tights with a red sash, a pair of knee-high black platform boots with toe claws, and elbow-high studded gloves with wrist claws.

Buzzy clicked on the virtual Trukk-9's back. "We should add a hood to this black satin cape to hide your extra eyes. We can add a red tornado symbol here. And you should spike up the hair tufts between your eyes – like this. Also, I think you should wear your sunglasses as a back-up. However, if your hood and your glasses come off, I would not worry too much about it. You will appear simply as a super-cool comic book geek with excellent make-up skills," said Buzzy.

"What the... Buzzy!" yelled Dee. "That costume looks just like you! Come on Cousin... Why don't you add another pair of legs while you're at it? AHHH HAAAA

HAAA, oh boy, you wanna dress Skip up like a giant Cockroach!"

Fleence said, "I think it looks great. It's certainly a better look than wearing a dirty shag carpet, like some people I know."

"Ouch," said Dee.

"Great! I like it too. Duplicate me that design, Buzzy," said Trukk-9.

Buzzy scanned Trukk-9 for size measurements and activated the duplicator. A fully tailored costume spilled from the duplicator port. Buzzy and Trukk-9 worked together on the make-up and hairstyling. Dee wanted to laugh at Buzzy as he fussed over the eye-liner and hairspray, but Fleence kept her eye on him.

When Buzzy was done, Stick deposited Trukk-9 into a dark construction site on a side street.

***

Trukk-9 was excited to wander the streets of a new city, and this was a good one. He was thrilled at the thought of being the first alien to interact with this species on a face-to-face basis.

Dazzling colored lights and unusual sounds came from everywhere. Bright storefronts displayed everything from plastic models of the Dirtling digestive system to every style and size of electronic cable you could ever need. And there were even small nook shops that appeared to sell egocite mining equipment.

A large robot stood guard outside of one shop and Trukk-9 tried, but failed, to engage it in conversation. Lots of tiny robots, plastic monsters, and figurines with impossibly large chests were locked in glass cases behind shop windows. Thousands of people streamed up and down the streets. Despite feeling conspicuous dressed as a Cricket, Trukk-9 blended into the crowd and seemed hardly to draw a glance.

He peeked into a bright flashing building where loud electronic noises were coming from. Row upon row of young men, many in white dress shirts, ties, and black pants – some wearing surgical masks – ferociously tapped buttons on video game consoles.

He peeked into the next establishment. People sat on stools around a counter with odd-looking food travelling by on a conveyor belt. It looked like stuff Dluhosh would enjoy eating. He got a good video clip of the chefs at work and the customers selecting dishes as they moved past.

Trukk-9 strolled down the street until he was approached by a very pretty young woman wearing a short black and white frilly outfit. She had white stockings half way up her thighs. She had tall fuzzy ears on top of her head, and it took a second before Trukk-9 realized they were fake. She clutched a toy ursoid. She seemed to be trying to look younger and older and of a different species at the same time. She greeted Trukk-9 and handed him a menu.

"Oh, Great Hero, you have a very nice cosplay! My friends would love to see it. Would you care for a snack or some tea while my friends admire you?" asked the maid. "Our excellent café is right over here."

She whisked him to the café where a covey of maids swarmed him. The maids seated him up front where passersby could peek in and see the attention being lavished on this upscale customer.

"Oh, Great Hero, what is your name? And what is your power?" asked the lead maid as she kneeled at his side.

Trukk-9 pulled out his notes. "I am Dab Tabmow, and my power is the multi-vision tornado."

The maids all cooed, and the head maid waived over a couple more maids.

"Oh, Great Hero, you have lovely hair. May we see all of it?"

Trukk-9 removed his hood. The maids were impressed. They rarely saw anything original anymore, but the eleven-lens sunglasses and hair spikes were pretty good. He was now surrounded by all of the café maids, and the head maid had called in all of the street maids who were handing out menus. The mob of maids all squealed and lavished praise on him.

Trukk-9 gazed into the eyes of all the front-row maids at once, which was dizzying but irresistible.

The head maid asked, "Great Hero, do you really have eyes behind all of those dark lenses?"

One of the maids stuck a fingernail under a lens and gently poked it into his blind orange eyeball as if it were just a very clever prop.

That's when Trukk-9 decided he'd better call for help. He stood up, spread his cape and yelled. "MULTI-VISION TORNADO ATTACK LEVEL FOUR!"

Stick.E clamped down with the grabber beam and yanked Trukk-9 through the crowd of onlookers. Because he was protected by the grabber beam, Trukk-9 didn't feel his head slam the café door's frame. And he saw, but did not feel, all the maids and spectators that he bowled over into the street. He disappeared into the air.

"Are you okay, Skip?" asked Dee. "That sure seemed like you were having fun. I hope you got the shots."

The excited crowd searched for Dab Tabmow. Already a rumor was spreading that a famous actor or stuntman was promoting an as-yet unknown TV show or movie at the maid café. Discussion forums were trending with Dab Tabmow rumors, unconfirmed sightings, and blurry cell phone pictures.

"I hope that level of interaction was okay, Dluhosh," said Trukk-9.

Dluhosh said, "I'm listening in, and they aren't saying that you are a space alien. I could start wiping memories, but I really don't think it's necessary. You seem to have enriched their environment considerably."

"Good, because that small bit of footage was worth the entire trip to Dirt! The stags on Bukk-9 will go crazy for these does."

The crews continued to search the city for checklist items until almost sunrise.

Finally Buzzy said, "It is evening in that poor boy's village. We can take a night break and be there for morning."

So both ships zipped on over to Hippopotamus.

THE FIRE HUNT

Trukk-9 called to Dluhosh. "It looks like stoves are being lit, Dluhosh. Good morning!"

It was before sunrise and the women cooked millet flour porridge as the men were stirring in their beds. Roosters crowed and a donkey brayed.

Fleence said, "Oh, look at that bug!" She had just seen her first butterfly – a big yellow and black swallowtail with blue and red eyespots. She picked out another three or four different species flitting around. "They are everywhere!"

"See? Abundant insectoids can be a beautiful sight," said Buzzy.

Down below, women pulled water from wells to heat for the men. The men did not speak until after bathing. Then everyone wished everyone else a good morning and asked how they'd slept. Young girls with younger girls strapped to their backs pounded corn using wooden mortars and pestles.

"Wow," said Fleence. "That pounding makes it sound like the whole village has a pulse."

Trukk-9 pointed to a family compound at the edge of

the village. "That's where the blacksmith family lives. They should be firing up their forge pretty soon. The hunters will stop here before the fire hunt. So we should abduct Numun to have him show us where the boy lives first."

They spotted Numun walking with an apprentice boy toward the forge.

"I can probably grab them both – might as well. Is anyone looking?" asked Dluhosh.

Stick.E said, "I'm pretty sure it's all clear."

Dluhosh piloted his ship over Numun and his apprentice, opened the hatch, and grabbed them with the grabber beam. And Numun and his nephew became the first Dirtlings ever legally abducted onto an alien ship.

Numun and the apprentice sat on the abductee platform with the containment dome around them. They were then exposed to the calming agent. Numun was immobilized as the probaluation apparatus rose from the floor behind him. The ship's computer uploaded a wealth of data about Numun, including a complete sequencing of his DNA. The probaluation had given him a thorough physical exam and cured him of various minor diseases and injuries, including the chronic pain in his shoulder. And during his probaluation, many dead parasitic worms passed from the boy. Dluhosh cleaned up the worms and added them to the duplicator matter conversion supply.

Fleence reached for her egocite and readied it for her first psychological test. She placed the small metallic ball on the platform next to the handsome man, and then Dluhosh lifted the containment field.

The egocite ingot did not change.

Dluhosh said, "Hello, my name is Dluhosh-10 and this is my partner, Fleence-18. We have come from elsewhere in the galaxy as part of a team that is evaluating Dirt for possible inclusion in our Galactic Pool. We apologize for our rudeness in snatching you up like this, and we especially apologize for probaluating you like that. However, the probaluation has provided us with invaluable data, has cured you of several existing medical problems, and has vaccinated you against several others."

Numun said, "Right on!"

Then Trukk-9's voice and image came over the video display. "Hello Numun! How are you? How are your children? How did you sleep? How is your wife? I hope your health is good! You and your work! You and the hammering of hot iron! You are Numun!"

"Right on!" Numun was otherwise lost for words.

Trukk-9 continued. "Numun, I apologize for my colleagues and their abrupt introductions. I would go around and introduce everyone, but we don't have the time. And besides, we are going to wipe your memory of this. You will get to keep your new health though."

"You and your work!" said Numun.

"Um… Right on!" said Trukk-9. "So Numun, we've been following you and your family for a few months now. You have become an example of a typical Dirt family for the education of the people of our galactic family. I personally hope that I get to meet you again someday. Anyway, a few weeks ago you counseled a woman who has a son that was to be hired out to the woman's brother-in-law. We would like to meet this boy."

"Do you mean the tall boy?" asked Numun.

"We don't know. We have only seen his mother."

"It is probably Yacouba that you seek. I can show you where he is."

"Were you able to help the woman keep the boy?" asked Trukk-9.

"Well, my brother performed some sacrifices with a chicken and kola nuts, and he said words. I am not allowed to witness his work, but my brother is very powerful. Now that you have arrived I think that he has been successful."

"Of course. I like your brother very much," replied Trukk-9

Numun pointed the way to the clay quarry where Yacouba worked before school making bricks for repairs to his family's granary.

Numun said, "That is the boy. He is a very bright and respectful boy, but he is also very strong. His family is in debt, and they can hire him out to work in the gold mines for enough to pay off the creditors."

"Can I ask a question?" said Fleence. "Like this boy – are people forced to work off the debts of other people? Are people made to serve others without a choice?"

"Oh yes, that sort of thing happens," replied Numun.

"Thank you."

Trukk-9 continued. "Will Yacouba be at the fire hunt today? And do you think that if he became a very successful hunter that his uncle might not send him away?"

Numun said, "Yes. Especially if he could get enough meat to pay off the debt..."

Stick.E said, "There are some people coming."

"Okay, Numun," said Trukk-9, "we are going to place you back where we found you. You will go unconscious for a second as we erase your memory of this encounter. You will probably be a little disoriented and wonder how you came to be sitting down. I apologize for that. Greet the people!"

"Right on! They will hear it! But wait, can I get you to do your disease cure on my children, and my friend's children?"

"No. I'm sorry, but the rules do not allow gratuitous disease curing," said Dluhosh.

Numun and his apprentice found themselves sitting face

to face on the ground next to the forge. Numun yelled something and shook his finger at the boy. The boy ran into the forge shed.

"Well, what do you think? Can we intervene on behalf of the boy?" asked Trukk-9 of Dluhosh.

Buzzy replied, "Slavery is a Level-1 checklist item…"

"Well, that's a valid point. And you've already uncovered several other checklist items here. There's still much we can learn from this place…" replied Dluhosh. "Why – what do you have in mind?"

"I think we should get a bunch of animals for Yacouba. Stick here can easily grab up whatever we can find before the hunt. Then he can make the animals run out of the grass right to Yacouba's feet, and we can even help kill the animals for him. We can load him up with meat."

"Alright, I think intervention in this case is legitimate," said Dluhosh.

***

As they flew over the river Dee yelled, "Flippo! I see a flippo!"

Buzzy said, "Yes, that does appear to be a hippopotamus. But I do not know whether the people eat them."

"Well, that's a heck of a lot of meat, Cousin. I think we should try."

"Yes, we should," said Trukk-9. "Can you manage that thing, Stick?"

Stick maxed out all of his grabber beams while pulling the hippo up through the cargo hold hatch. Dee hit it with a mega-dose of calming agent.

"Man, I think this sucker is immune to calming agent! He's really tearing things up in there. Wow! Look at those teeth! I don't think we can keep him Skip."

So Stick returned the hippo to the river.

"HAAAHAAA! That was awesome Stick, but I don't think you needed to flip him. Dang, that is one pissed off flippopotamus!"

The ships continued to the other side of the river. They found a troop of baboons on a small hill, and grabbed a half dozen. Then they spotted a small duiker antelope and grabbed it. They found a mother warthog digging up roots with two piglets, and grabbed the three of them. Down in a dry gulch they grabbed an entire flock of wild Guinea fowl, and also a large rock python and Nile monitor lizard that had been attracted by the birds.

And then they spotted a big prize. It was a bull roan antelope with a harem of females with calves.

"Stick, can you grab a herd of beasts that big?" asked Trukk-9.

"If you have room for them…"

"Dee, how's the cargo hold looking?"

"Well Skip, it's pretty crazy in there. But if I give them enough calming agent there should be room to squeeze 'em in! They'll have to cuddle up, but I think it will do them some good. I might have to go in and join them."

"Make it be. Snag them and let's get back to the village."

***

The ships arrived back at the village as a group of hunters entered the blacksmith compound. The hunters greeted Numun's brother, and he replied with 'Right on!' many times.

One of the hunters – the one with the most shotgun shells, fetish pouches, mirrors, and animal parts hanging from his clothes – carried a ten-liter yellow plastic jug of a honey brew that he had already been sampling. He passed it around to the other hunters finally.

Fleence was distracted by the hunters. They were calm and majestic and seemed to own their space, yet none of them seemed to be posturing. Dluhosh noticed a flicker of unusual life sign readings from Fleence on his monitor. Her heart rate and skin temperature were both elevated. He looked at her and she appeared flushed, but otherwise healthy and alert.

The elder blacksmith smoothed out a patch of sand and drew small clusters of short parallel lines in it. Then he bit off a piece of kola nut and tossed the remaining piece of nut onto the patterned sand. Then he spit some of the chewed kola nut onto the pattern. He consulted a notebook with similar patterns drawn in it. He then drew some lines on a small copper plate with a piece of charcoal. He looked up at the eager hunters.

"I can't tell," he said. "It's neutral. The hunt could go either way."

The hunters seemed satisfied with that prophecy, and they all took another swig of the brew.

***

People gathered on the river floodplain where the hunters were going to light the grass fire. The boys and young men arrived with their dogs, machetes, clubs, slingshots, knives, rope, and sacks. Most of the adult hunters carried shotguns of varying quality – the finest being made by famous local blacksmiths. A couple of the hunters had locally-made muzzle-loaders as well.

Three of the lower-ranking hunters walked to the upwind side of the tall grass field and lit a small fire. They took bundles of flaming grass and jogged along the windward edge of the field, lighting new grass as they went. The wind whipped the flames into a fast-moving wall. The remaining hunters, every boy and his dog in the village, and the two village school teachers, waited in a clearing about a kilometer downwind.

The first creatures to emerge from the grass were hares. Most of the dogs and small boys ran off after these. The hares fought the dogs for their lives, the dogs fought each other for the hares, then the boys fought the dogs for the hares, and then boys fought each other for the hares and portions thereof. Then the school teachers, who had let the boys out of class, took what they wanted.

Small rodents scampered out all along the edge of the grass. Older boys killed these with sticks and collected them in their sacks as they waited for larger animals to emerge.

Trukk-9 located the boy. Then he instructed Dee to lower their cloaked ship into the grass ahead of the fire. "Okay, Stick, start sending the animals out through the grass to the boy. Try to get them to emerge from the grass and die at his feet, but make it look like the boy is killing them! Fire at will!"

Stick.E started with the Guinea fowl to warm the boy up. He squeezed each one to death as he shoved them through the grass. Yacouba appeared to swat expertly with his cane as the birds piled up.

Then Stick.E sent the warthogs in, strangling the mother as he shoved her out of the grass. Yacouba took a wild swing with his hand-hoe club, but seemed to deliver a perfect blow.

As soon as the other boys had caught the piglets, Stick.E shoved the rock python out. Everyone scattered, but the snake lay dead where Yacouba had been.

Based on this feedback, Stick.E decided against using the

big lizard. So he sent the small duiker antelope out next. A hunter took a shot at the duiker and instead shot the pinky and ring finger from Yacouba's left hand.

Then Stick.E shoved out the entire family of roan antelopes with the baboons clinging to their backs. The antelope heard 'gave itself' to Yacouba where he lay on the ground being tended to by the teachers and the other boys. The baboons managed to get the hell out of there.

Dee piloted the ship up and over the grass to get a better look at the result. They saw the injured boy.

"Oh no! Now what do we do, Dluhosh?" asked a panicked Trukk-9.

"Well, we don't have enough space on my platform to abduct everybody at once. I can probably take five. How many can you take over there, Trukk-9?" asked Dluhosh.

"We can probably take twenty if we get rid of the big lizard in the cargo hold, but my ship isn't equipped to probaluate them or erase their memories. Oh, what have I done?" cried Trukk-9.

"I'd say you just shot that boy out of slavery for good, Skip! He can't work in a goldmine now."

"That's a good point. It is very very mysterious how these things work out," said Trukk-9. He felt better already.

***

A crowd gathered at the chief's compound to hear the story and witness the arrival of the meat. Volunteers butchered the beasts and carried the pieces to the village by bike and by back.

The careless hunter explained that the duiker had re-directed the shot away from itself. "They have the most powerful life force in the bush – everyone knows that. How else could such a defenseless animal survive amongst lions and hyenas?" he pleaded.

A few of the chief's councilors were of the opinion that the hunter hadn't taken care to prepare his own life force – otherwise he might have missed the duiker but not hit Yacouba. The chief decided that the guilty hunter should pay Yacouba's medical bills and buy his family one-hundred kilos of rice and condiments for the meat.

The chief's intermediary announced the verdict. Everyone agreed that this was adequate, and the matter was settled.

Buzzy said, "We got several items on that: a legal proceeding with a verdict; application of first aid using traditional medicine; food gathering techniques; animistic beliefs with application of magic and divination; and – depending on which checklist you use – we got slavery and drunken use of weaponry."

"Well, that was a good haul, I'd say," said Trukk-9.

Dluhosh said, "My priority is still to focus on the bad stuff, but I agree that we've done well so far."

"Thanks, Dluhosh," said Trukk-9, "I'm feeling better about being able to work with you to our mutual benefit. Anyway, I really want to do some of the wildest sort of stuff that Stick and his grabber beams can do with our favorite guy. It's Friday, so chances are he'll be fishing tomorrow."

＊＊＊

They arrived at Jimmy's house in time for Dee to win five bucks guessing the contents of the box on Jimmy's porch. And later they watched Jimmy dazzle at the gas stations. The two crews called it a day when Jimmy went to bed.

Fleence made herself a churdleherd's pie for dinner, and Dluhosh scarfed duplicator tuna with fish wine.

Fleence asked, "So who came up with the PLUMBOB checklist anyway? It seems like it has some pretty obscure items on it, and some pretty obvious ones are missing. Like here – you have 'drunken use of weaponry' and 'sober use of weaponry' – but here's 'drunken home improvements' but you don't have 'sober home improvements'. Why's that?"

"Yeah, I hear you. It seems arbitrary sometimes. The law is so cobbled together that things have slipped through the cracks and other things have stuck. I think it's as simple as some things being more attention-getting than other things so the list makers think of them preferentially. My guess is that weapon use is always interesting to someone, whether drunk or sober, and home improvements are only interesting when someone falls off a ladder or spills paint on the furniture. But all-in-all I think the list works well enough. Sometimes when looking for one little obscure thing, you document bigger important things that you wouldn't have noticed otherwise – happens all the time."

Fleence was looking down the list. "Have you ever seen communication by choir? Or how about the next one – communing with energy?"

"Oh yes, choir communication is quite common in avianoids. I'll show you a clip from Mother Roost of that. Communing with energy is a checklist item which is more applicable to plasmanoid-like species. But the Roostlings are fond of communing with forces of nature, and one activity they do was close enough, I thought, to satisfy that checklist item. I have some clips of that too – it's very cool."

"Cooler than skate flying?" asked Fleence with a grin.

"Well, I'd have to say 'yes' to that. My bosses may ultimately reject my classification of it as communing with energy. But, in fact, I think if Mother Roost has a chance, it will be because the voters like how the Roostlings play. So a seemingly obscure thing could turn out big. This particular activity requires a lot of grace, which isn't what you'd expect from such big lumbering avianoids. That contrast is appealing to voters. I admit that I'm trying to get it accepted as a checklist item to give them a boost."

Dluhosh cued up the video clips and hit play.

"Okay, here they are on their little flat boats riding on those ocean waves."

"Wow! They stand up too! That IS really cool," said Fleence.

"Yep, they do it repeatedly just for fun. They must like it tremendously because sometimes they get bitten by large aquatic reptiloids. Unfortunately we didn't see that – would have been a rare checklist item. Anyway, it looks so fun that it makes me wonder why Dnooblians never thought to do this. I'm planning to try it when I get home."

"Yeah, we could do that on Chuffed-18 too, I think."

"Those are simply waves of energy propagating across a body of water, right? And I think the way the riders repeat it over and over demonstrates a communion of sorts. Anyway, I guess I'm illustrating how much of this PLUMBOB work is based on best-professional-judgment."

"They have my vote!" said Fleence.

"Good! Anyway, here's a clip of the choir communication," said Dluhosh.

From high above, the video shows a nesting colony spread out over many square miles on flat salt plains. It's not clear what the intricate pattern on the ground is at first, but as the view gets closer there's the sound of a great honking.

Dluhosh paused it.

"I told the film crew to shoot it starting from very high so it would look like a Trukk-9 sequence, actually. An inner landscape thing that says something about something…"

"Cool though," said Fleence.

Dluhosh explained what the birds are doing. "They live at their time-shares in the breeding colony when they are laying and hatching. But they live and work in town otherwise. So during the day the females leave the colony to go to work while the males sit on the eggs or tend nestlings. At night the females sit on the nests while the males go grocery shopping and do the laundry and stuff."

The video now shows the females getting home from work, and the males taking the hovercrafts for their turn in town. After the males are gone, the females begin to honk.

"It sounds like the loudest bunch of noise you can imagine – you can hear it from miles away. And that's the point – they are communicating with the males."

Dluhosh turns the volume up all the way and yells. "That's really about how loud it is when you get close enough to apply the egocite!"

"I can't understand what they're saying! Is the autotranslator working!?" asked Fleence.

"Yeah, we can only reach so many honkers at once with the egocite, and the rest drown them out. But here, I think I can isolate the ones we gassed from the audio mix. The entire flock of females is working as a team to create enough volume to send messages to the males no matter how far away they are."

"Ah-Scar of Brine Pond Drive! You forgot the diaper pail so you need to pick up some disposables!"

This message is repeated another dozen times, and then the sound breaks down into an unintelligible honking and cackling. And another message begins to form as the request moves through the colony. "Caw-Ner of Mocking Court! Our son made a rude honk again today. I told you to stop seeing that friend of yours while I'm at work!"

Fleence continued to watch the video as Dluhosh looked at the DNA sample from Numun.

The next honking turns into, "My mother is coming to visit! My mother is coming to visit! My mother is coming to visit!"

Fleence said, "This time they aren't saying who the message is for."

Dluhosh was distracted by a peculiarity in Numun's DNA and was only half listening. "Um, sometimes they have public service announcements... Or maybe it's emergency services...

JIMMY'S HAWGS, THE ALIEN PERSPECTIVE

Jimmy Fresneaux's alarm sounded at 0430. As predicted, a high pressure center had set in and it was forecast to be a calm, warm, early spring day – one of those days that bass fishermen dream of all winter long. He grabbed his first energy drink of the day and went out to double check his boat trailer hook-ups.

The space aliens hovering over his house had noticed the lights come on.

"Okay, this is looking good," said Trukk-9.

Jimmy hummed a favorite song as he got in his rig for the drive to the lake.

"We should just follow him. It will give us a chance to see this town wake up," said Trukk-9.

"Sure," said Dluhosh. "It's all new to us, so let me know if there's something you want to shoot. I'll try not to bother you unless something unusually bad is happening."

Jimmy's first stop was for donuts and energy drinks at his favorite mini market. He continued humming his tune as he went inside.

Another car pulled in with four young guys who were

playing very loud music. They piled out and gathered to smoke cigarettes.

Trukk-9 asked Dluhosh if was okay to mess with them.

"Those idiots are drunk. Stick, tie their shoelaces together two by two."

In the blink of an eye, Stick.E yanked their feet together, tied the knots, and shoved all four guys over. Having no one else to blame, each guy screamed at his co-victim. Then Stick.E grabbed an open beer from inside the car and poured it on one of the struggling guys before dropping the bottle on his head. The guy, as hoped, thought it was his partner pouring the beer. He rolled over, grabbed the bottle, and struck his friend across the bridge of the nose with it. The friend threw an elbow. The blood from their nose and mouth, respectively, joined the beer and flowed across the asphalt.

One of the other pair of guys pulled out a knife to try and cut the laces. His partner appeared to mistake his friend's intentions and busted him in the mouth a couple of times. In defending himself, the knife-wielding friend slashed wildly and stabbed himself in the bicep.

Jimmy saw the fight from inside the store and pointed it out to the clerk. The clerk called 911 to report four drunken guys fighting in a pool of blood. The clerk asked Jimmy if he wouldn't mind waiting for a few minutes in case he had trouble from these guys before the cops arrived. Jimmy was only too happy to help.

In a few minutes the cops arrived. They apprehended the drunks and asked the clerk and Jimmy to come outside to describe what they had seen.

Jimmy said, "I just looked up and these two guys were having a knife fight, and those two guys were rolling around on the ground yelling and bleeding. I didn't see how it started. But I think they were playing some kind of shoelace game that got out of hand."

"Oh man, that was awesome," said Dee. "Got some checklist stuff for you too, Dluhosh."

"Yes, I believe we got drunken use of weaponry again, plus spontaneous anger with fighting, and arrest of civilians. And I think we can check off samaritanism on the part of our fisherman. What a great start to the day," said Dluhosh.

Jimmy clutched a complementary bag of donuts as he climbed back into his rig and pulled onto the highway. The two cloaked ships followed.

Buzzy said, "Dluhosh, I do not think we can call it samaritanism if he accepted the bag of food."

"Well, as long as there was no *quid pro quo*, then it counts," replied Dluhosh.

"Ah, yes, I believe you are correct," said Buzzy.

"Great. Okay, he's continuing on his way," said Trukk-9.

As they followed Jimmy to the highway, Fleence said, "Dluhosh, this man has blue eyes."

"Yes, I noticed that too," said Dluhosh.

"I've never seen a two-eyed man with blue eyes. The ancient legends from Bounty say that some of my people once had blue eyes, but the trait was lost before we were stolen. The blue-eyed Bountyans were supposedly shamanistic. And when they died out bad things started to happen. Anyway, I guess that's what makes this man look magical to me."

"I don't know about the bad things happening, but the loss of blue eyes could be a simple case of genetic drift," said Dluhosh.

***

The two ships and Jimmy arrived at the boat ramp to find a long line of trucks and trailers already waiting to launch. Trukk-9 surveyed the scene to see what truths he could tease out.

There was a young woman wearing a government uniform who appeared to be inspecting the boats. She looked at the trailer and hull of one boat and then climbed into it to check the livewells. She asked the questions from her inspection form – what other lakes the boat had been at, etcetera. She explained to each boater the danger of exotic mussels being spread, and she talked about how the mussels had recently been found on a boat at a nearby lake.

"Look at those old perverts," Dee said as he noticed the behavior of the two fishermen having their boat inspected. "They aren't even pretending not to leer at her."

One of the fishermen said, "You should try to find my mussels right here, honey."

"Sexual harassment, check!" said Dluhosh.

"Okay, I'm gonna mess with these two old disrespectful perverts. Any ideas?"

Buzzy, who had done some boating back home, asked, "Stick.E, can you tell whether that boat has a drain plug?"

Stick felt around with a grabber beam until he found something. He pulled it out and said, "Yep."

"They probably have pumps too," said Buzzy.

Trukk-9 said, "Stick, just drop the plug in the water and see if you can disable any pumps they might have."

"My pleasure," said Stick.E.

"In fact, let's watch each interaction with the inspector. If anyone is less than respectful, we'll pull their plugs too."

Most of the fishermen found some way to complain or make a stupid remark. Stick.E decided that the rolling of eyes or exaggerated sighs were also infractions.

As each boat launched, Stick.E pulled the plugs and

yanked the wires to their bilge pumps. Some of the fishermen noticed that they were taking in water before their partners came back from parking the truck and trailer. Others noticed after they were already underway, and had to return to the ramp. Guys laughed at guys until they themselves became laughed at. "Where's the goddamn plug!?" was the most repeated phrase of the morning.

As guys scrambled for plugs and fought to get their boats back on trailers, the whole ramp and dock area became a chaotic scene of sinking boats and fishermen shoving and screaming at each other. A few boats were able to break free and beach themselves.

"Wow, these Dirtlings fight as easily as rutting churdles in a cement mixer," said Fleence.

The park rangers had to call in extra police to break up the small riot. And then they had to call tow trucks in to clear the ramp of sunken boats and tangled trailers. A newspaper reporter showed up to cover the scene.

This delayed Jimmy's launch for a couple of hours, but he was content to eat donuts, watch the fun, and describe his latest plastic worm philosophy to the mussel inspector. She excused herself to 'finish some paperwork'. Jimmy tried to get himself into the pictures that the reporter took. He pointed and smiled so it would be obvious that he wasn't one of the idiots.

Buzzy added some checklist items. "We also got obvious lack of cooperation, spontaneous rioting, crowd control, and news coverage. And if I am not mistaken, I think we can call that a mass embarrassment of more than twenty individuals involving loss and/or destruction of property... Right, Dluhosh? I have not seen that checklist item before."

"I agree Mister O'Buzznid-3. I haven't seen that one either. What a good haul. I have to say, Trukk-9, you and your crew are natural PLUMBOB agents!"

***

Once the mess was cleared, Jimmy triple-checked his plug and launched. There was no wind and the water was flat, so he punched the throttle.

"Man, that is one fast boat!" said Dee. "That's insane. Look at him! He's eating a donut and steering with his knee. He doesn't remember how his partner was killed by that fish? That humanoid is crazy."

"And he's doing it with a gas motor and a steel propeller," added Dluhosh. "Remarkable. And he is totally calm. These people are hardcore."

Trukk-9 said, "See? This guy is going to be huge in underground cinema."

"I think that even Dnooblians could bear to watch – especially if he catches some fish," said Dluhosh.

"Well, that's the problem," said Trukk-9. "This guy can't seem to. In my opinion – and I've never been a fisherman – he tries very hard at all the wrong things. He gets distracted, eats the whole time, pretends he's on TV, fondles those wormy things... That's all great fun for us, but there needs to be an exclamation point at the end. So this is what we've been waiting for – for you to be here so Stick can catch him some fish. We HAVE to see his behavior with some success."

"I'd love to see what you can do. Heck, I'd just like to see what kind of fish are in this reservoir. So I'll simply say this – there aren't any rules that would prevent you from doing whatever you want with this guy, short of killing him, of course."

"Great!" replied Trukk-9. "I'd like to wait until later before we really get him going. He usually starts to get depressed about midday, and then he has a couple of those drinks and gets a second wind. I think he becomes more mentally unstable then. That's when I'd like to hit him."

"Okay, I'd like to observe his baseline behavior for a little longer anyway. So let's see what happens," said Dluhosh.

So the ships flew along on either side of Jimmy's boat as he zipped across the glassy water eating donuts without his visor blowing off.

Jimmy slowed to idle as he drove up a side channel and into a narrow cove near some gray siltstone bluffs that had also drawn Dluhosh's attention. He shut his outboard motor down and gracefully moved up front to drop the electric trolling motor as his boat stopped. Jimmy already had a rod in his hand and made a cast out ahead of his boat.

"Hey, that was pretty smooth," said Fleence. "Sleek as an olive eel ballet."

Jimmy took three very elegant casts. Before each cast he said, "I like to get that first cast as far back into a cove as possible."

"So you say he pretends to be on a TV show?" asked Dluhosh. "I guess that explains him repeating himself?"

"Yes. He seems to be in a fantasy world out here. It's like a rehearsal for a part he hasn't been offered," said Trukk-9.

Jimmy sat down to put on some sunscreen. "Folks, even a darker-skinned lad like me needs to be careful out here in the sun. I favor this SPF-fifty lotion by Bassinoma Corp. It's scented with nightcrawler pheromones – odorless to you and me, but like bacon to bass! No more worries about spooking fish with chemicals. No sir, they'll just think you're a big ol' wiggly earthworm! Look, I'm even rubbing some directly on my Mega-Mouth Poppin' Minnow!"

"He's making a production of applying that lotion. I

think he shaves his legs," said Fleence.

Jimmy took a few more fruitless casts and sat down to go through his plastic worms.

"Ah, there it is. Anise! I love that smell. It's funny that I don't like to eat licorice, y'all. I suppose a bass wouldn't like licorice either, but we both sure go for the essence of anise." He put the bag down and gave it a warm smile.

He stood up and took a few more casts and then sat back down. The sun was getting high and the day was warming. He ate another pack of his new favorite cookies and drank another energy drink.

"There he goes," said Dluhosh. "Is he already getting depressed?"

"No, I don't think so. Give it another hour," said Trukk-9.

Jimmy pulled up the trolling motor and shot back out onto the main lake. He drove around at top speed, crisscrossed the narrow upper river channel, and then turned around to jump over his wake.

After a couple of laps, he took a beeline right back to the same spot where he hadn't caught anything.

And he repeated, "I'm at a great little spot up-river on my local lake today, y'all. The recent weather conditions lead me to believe that a lot of nice bass could be back here in this warmer water seeking prey. The wind has dropped, and the big bass are in pre-spawn mode. That means they'll be looking to store away energy for nesting time."

Jimmy continued fishing and posing and talking to nobody.

***

These gray bluffs had gotten someone else's attention too. Unnoticed by Jimmy and the aliens, the curious scruffy fellow from yesterday's gas station tour had hiked to this bluff with his friend to do exactly what Dluhosh wanted to do. And the two fossil hunters were enjoying some success.

"Hey, Dluhosh, I think we are ready to manipulate him. Stick's been scanning the lower lake and has a variety of large fish located. We're going to grab them and bring them over here. And then can I send Dee out on the ground to get this action from a few different low angles?" asked Trukk-9.

"Yes, but if this guy sees Dee we'll need to abduct him."

Trukk-9 piloted the ship as Stick.E gathered up some nice big fish. He selected as many different species as he could find, and all the largest individuals. Within minutes they had returned to begin manipulations. They flew over to the creek channel downstream from the bluff. Dee jumped out with his camera.

They gave Jimmy a chance to use the Tip-of-the-Week cast that he had been rehearsing. Stick.E created a splash and boil by flopping his biggest bass under the water's surface at the edge of Jimmy's peripheral vision. Jimmy executed his cast and Stick.E hooked the fish up with equal perfection.

Jimmy's reaction to catching this very large fish was as good as Trukk-9 could have hoped for.

"How many hooks does he have on that lure, Stick?" asked Trukk-9.

"It has three triple hooks, so nine points all together."

"What about putting three of the big-mouthed green fish on the next cast, and then on the very next cast put a fish on every point of every hook?" asked an excited Trukk-9.

"Sure, that would leave me with one extra fish that I can probably fit in there somewhere," replied Stick.E.

"Make it be," directed Trukk-9.

The three-bass trick worked. Jimmy's whooping and

hollering got the attention of the two fossil collectors, who hurried to see what was going on. They rounded the last bend in the creek, popped out from behind some bushes, and were staring right at the back of Dee.

Dee turned to see what the gasps were.

The two fossil collectors backed away, and Dee radioed to the ships. "Sorry guys, I've just been seen by a couple of Dirtlings."

Dluhosh took command. "Trukk-9, you grab Dee and I'll abduct the two Dirtlings."

"Okay, I'm on it."

The two Dirtlings were weighed down by rocks and tools, but they were familiar with the terrain and able to move through the rocks and fallen trees with relative ease. Dluhosh was unable to get a lock on them with the grabber beam. When the Dirtlings came to an opening created by a small landslide, they turned to look back. They saw Dee rise a short distance into the air and disappear.

"You should have seen the looks on their faces!" said Dee. "Those poor guys need a hug."

"You should see the looks on their faces now that they've seen you fly," added Dluhosh. "Okay Fleence, I have them in my sights, so be ready with the containment dome."

As Dluhosh tried to grab them, the shorter one turned to run back toward the lake to see what was going on. His fear was supplanted by his strong curiosity. Dluhosh got the taller one and pulled him up into the ship. The shorter one saw his buddy fly into the air and disappear, so he took refuge in a slot behind a large boulder at the base of the bluff.

Fleence got the tall one into the containment dome and hit him with a dose of the calming agent. She performed like an expert, but she was startled by the height of this specimen and the look of sheer terror on his face. So she hit him with another dose of the calming agent.

"Nice job Fleence. Go ahead and hit that one with another dose," said Dluhosh, not realizing that she already had.

Fleence administered another dose, and the tall Dirtling shifted into a more comfortable position – slouched cross legged on the floor with his hands in his lap. He looked around with a silly grin on his face.

"I can't get a bead on the other one. He's hiding behind a rock. Hey, Stick, do you think you could roll that boulder out of the way without crushing the subject?" asked Dluhosh.

"Well, Dluhosh, I'm using almost all of my grabber beams to make our cargo hold into an aquarium for these fish, plus I forgot we still had that big lizard in there, so now I'm holding him on the bridge with us. That's a pretty massive boulder and I only have my emergency beams available. A plasmanoid never likes to say this, but my hands are full."

"Okay, no problem. It would probably be safer for me to go down and flush him out anyway. How's our fisherman doing? Do you think I have time to get on the ground?"

Trukk-9 replied, "He's pretty excited, but he hasn't noticed our activity. He's talking to himself and striking poses with the fish. It's still great material and I don't think he's going anywhere. The light is getting better too."

"Okay, Fleence, this will be good practice for you. Use the grabber beam to set me down, put the ship on autopilot, and then snag the subject when I flush him out. Think you can do that?"

"Just like Pip-The-Blue... I think I can handle it, Dluhosh."

"Good, set me down next to that boulder."

Fleence piloted the ship to within a few feet above the subject. Then she opened the main hatch and set Dluhosh next to the rock.

"Hey, Dluhosh, this big lizard is making Buzzy nervous and he's starting to excrete all over his command module. I'm going to dump it – that okay?" said Trukk-9.

Fleence replied, "I already have Dluhosh on the surface, we should wait to ask him before you dump it."

"Buzzy confirms quite vigorously that it's fine to dump it," said Trukk-9.

"If Stick.E still has hold of it and it isn't an actual threat to Buzzy, we should keep it," said Fleence.

Dluhosh and the hiding Dirtling spied each other. Dluhosh preferred to convince the subject to evacuate without having to yank him out. He slid a tentacle into the hiding place to try and find a tender spot. The enraged Dirtling pounded on Dluhosh's tentacle with his rock hammer. He turned his hammer over to the pointed end and still couldn't dent the tentacle. Dluhosh found a tender spot right where he expected to find one, and the Dirtling bolted.

Fleence grabbed the Dirtling like an old pro, and was able to encase him within the same isolation dome as his buddy. Then she picked up Dluhosh too.

"Nice grab, Fleence! Hey, you might want to hit the shorter one with another dose of the calming agent, he's pretty angry."

Fleence hit him with another dose and monitored his vital signs. "His signs are still elevated. Should I dose him again?"

"Yeah, one more should do it," replied Dluhosh. "How many did you give the other guy?"

"Uh, oops, I put them under the same dome together,"

replied Fleence.

Dluhosh let out a loud belly laugh. "Oh boy, that's some very impressive work, Fleence. Pip-The-Blue would be impressed. So, how many doses…?"

"I think he's been exposed to six, maybe seven. Is he going to be okay?"

"Oh, I'm sure he's better than okay. How are his life signs?"

"Low to normal… He seems okay. He's smiling. Oh, and Buzzy is desperate to get rid of the big lizard. He's afraid it's going to eat him. Stick.E can't put it back into the cargo hold because he turned it into an aquarium."

Dluhosh called over to Trukk-9. "You guys need to either kill the lizard or wait until we can take it back where it came from."

"KILL IT!" screamed Buzzy.

"Aw, come on Cousin," said Dee. "That poor animal has been through so much. Just because it's not cuddly doesn't mean we can't show it some respect. Stick has it, buddy, so just relax."

The two ships got back into position to shoot the next fish trick.

***

Michael and Gregory the fossil hunters sat on the containment platform. Gregory removed his glasses to clean them. They both regarded Dluhosh and Fleence.

Michael pointed at Dluhosh and said, "Look at that…"

Dluhosh called over to Trukk-9's ship. "Hey, guess what, we accidentally gave one of these Dirtlings SEVEN doses of calming agent."

Even Buzzy's nervous laughter was audible over Dluhosh's speaker.

Gregory said, "You know, I want to make sure you are with me on this, Michael. Okay, we just saw a flying bigfoot and now we've been abducted by aliens, right? Do you see this too?"

"Yeah…" said Michael. He pointed out the window at Trukk-9's ship.

"And you see the other flying saucer too, right?" asked Gregory.

"Yeah…"

"Okay, now describe the aliens you see."

Michael pointed at Dluhosh again. "That one looks like a combination between an octopus and a little tiny termite mound. It seems to be talking with… Look at that beak! Wow… I feel great. I think they drugged us. Are you having fun too?"

"Yeah, yeah, I guess you could call it that. I'm a lot calmer than I should be," said Gregory.

"Anyway, the other alien looks human. It almost looks like a woman. You think that's a female?" asked Michael.

Gregory said, "Look, I think she's checking us out! She smiled. I definitely recognize that look. I've seen it on TV. Yes, it's a woman. But she seems kind of severe – mean looking and maybe a little unbalanced. Perhaps it's her boot camp outfit."

"Yeah, I guess it's a she," said Michael. "For a space alien though, it could be worse. That other one might be a girl too…"

***

Fleence regarded the two gorgeous men as they turned their attention to her. She wondered what they would imagine her wearing. She hoped it was something skimpy topped by a big red afro. She'd never found herself aroused by imagining her own outfit before. And she caught herself with a sly grin on her face.

The tall man was handsome and graceful looking. She gave a small gasp when Michael smiled and revealed the gap between his front teeth. Even the gap was symmetrical – right smack dab on the centerline of his face. And yet he was the least intriguing of the three Dirtling males she could see at that moment.

Gregory was shorter, but was still above the average height of a galactic humanoid male. His scruffiness contrasted nicely with his luscious lips. Fleence found herself wondering what Gregory's lips would feel like against her own lips. She wanted to touch his mouth and play his symmetrical belly like a drum. Now she caught herself puckering.

***

"I assume that the bigfoot must be with the aliens too, right?" asked Michael.

"You know, I think that's him in the other flying saucer. I guess that solves that ancient mystery once and for all. Where's your camera?"

The probaluation apparatus rose from the floor behind Gregory, and he was probaluated. Neither fossil collector could move to prevent it. Then the apparatus turned to Michael and did the same thing. Gregory laughed.

The crew in the other ship was ready to perform the nine-hook ten-fish trick.

Dluhosh lifted the containment dome and introduced himself in English with a perfect mid-western American accent. "Hello, my name is Dluhosh-10, and this is Fleence-18. I can see by the way you look at Fleence that the calming agent and egocite have taken effect. We'll finish our tests on you in a moment, but first please turn your attention to the fisherman down there in the boat. You'll probably get a kick out of this."

Down below Jimmy was netting his hoard of fish.

Everyone, except Jimmy, laughed. Jimmy knelt in a daze while the fish flopped around him.

"That was pretty funny. Stick.E really is a genius with a grabber beam. Did you guys see that?" Dluhosh asked Gregory and Michael.

Michael said, "Yeah, you guys did that?"

"Yes, please allow me to explain so I can send you on your way. Fleence is going to expose you to an ingot of a mineral called egocite. How the egocite reacts will tell us valuable information about you Dirtlings."

"It's Earthlings, actually," said Gregory.

"Oh, I'm sorry, Soillings," said Dluhosh.

"What? Earthlings…" said Gregory.

"Loamlings," tried Dluhosh.

Gregory just stared at Dluhosh.

"Oh, I'm sorry. Our autotranslator sometimes has trouble with proper nouns that are common words. Here, allow me to try again. Compostlings?" asked Dluhosh.

Gregory gave up and said, "Yeah, sure, it's Compostlings."

"Oh, Earthlings!" replied Dluhosh. "Earth is actually a fairly common thing for people to name their planets. Dirt, Soil, Compost, Humus, Tillage – they're all standard planet names. There is even a ghost planet called Earth that was once… Well, let's just say things didn't work out for them."

Gregory nodded and waved his hand, and Dluhosh continued.

"Anyway, we are here to test you Earthlings for possible inclusion in our Galactic Pool. We won't have results for at least a year, and Earth shouldn't qualify anyway. We will finish this test and then wipe your memory. By the way, the probaluation that you endured will have cured you of any ailments that you have. It's our way of thanking you for your data."

Dluhosh pointed at Gregory. "You will notice that you no longer need glasses that thick, if at all, and you will cease suffering from your entire suite of allergies." Then he gestured at Michael and said, "You won't have to breathe solely through your mouth anymore, and your breath will smell much better."

Outside, Jimmy was hyperventilating into a bag of plastic worms.

Fleence opened her egocite case and placed the ingot in front of Michael. It transformed into the shape of an elongate toothy skull.

"Whoa… Your golf ball just turned into a replica of our fossil plesiosaur skull," said Michael.

This caught Dluhosh's attention. "A fossil?"

"Oh yeah, that's like a mini version of the plesiosaur skull we found last year. We got our pictures in the paper and everything," said Michael.

"Well, that's very interesting. I do a bit of fossil collecting myself. You should indeed be proud of such a find," said Dluhosh. "Is that from a big animal? Are they extinct?"

"Yeah, they went extinct with the dinosaurs and ammonites about sixty-six million years ago. Our plesiosaur was the short-necked variety and was about thirty feet long with a huge mouth and teeth. Believe me – we are glad they went extinct."

Dluhosh asked, "There was a mass extinction here sixty-six million years ago…?"

Fleence moved the ingot closer to Gregory. It morphed

into a perfect chrome replica of an ammonite fossil that Gregory had found in the bluff.

Michael noticed the plesiosaur skull change shape. "Hey, that's like that one heteromorph you found today," he said to Gregory.

Dluhosh looked up and saw the new shape of the egocite ingot. He started to twitch and ripples of purple danced over his skin. He managed to point a tentacle at the ingot. "What's that?" he asked with a shaky voice.

Gregory was still distracted by Fleence, so Michael replied. "Oh, that's like an ammonite fossil he found today. He's awfully proud of it already – hasn't shut up about it all afternoon. Hey, show it to them Gregory."

Gregory pulled a grapefruit-sized rock from his pack. Exposed along the edge of the rock was the surface of a beautiful corkscrew-shaped ammonite with pronounced ridges and an iridescent mother-of-pearl shell. With careful preparation work, this was going to be a stunning specimen.

Dluhosh knew what he was seeing. He knew better than any Earthling fossil collector could. His head spun and he felt like he was melting. He lunged at Gregory's ammonite with his hunting tentacles, and the rest of his tentacles flailed with such violence that all their tips snapped.

One of his flailing tentacles snapped his helm pad twice and then another brushed over the pad from left to right. This caused his ship to shoot toward The Cruiser Duke Sukk-9 at a high rate of speed. Dluhosh's ship attempted to dodge, but it nicked the edge of Trukk-9's ship. Because they were calibrated to different phases, both cloaking emitters burned out as soon as the fields intersected.

The two flying saucers appeared out of thin air right in front of Jimmy.

Dluhosh's ship's sensors recognized that they were about to crash-land in a breathable atmosphere, so the ship's main hatch began to open in case of life support system failure. When the ship rammed the cliff, the inertia bag deployed so the occupants weren't shaken, but the main hatch doors froze only a hand's width apart.

The stricken ship tumbled down the face of the cliff and rolled like a giant bottle cap across the shore and into the lake. The ship now floated upside-down under the spot where it had been hovering.

Jimmy's daze ended. He pulled up his electric trolling motor, fired up the main engine, and sped out of the cove.

In less than a minute it was too late to abduct Jimmy. He was already out on the main lake where dozens of fishers and hikers would have seen a real uncloaked flying saucer chasing Jimmy's bass boat. They would have seen Jimmy fly up into the UFO. It was no use. They had to let Jimmy go and hope that everyone would think he was a kook when he told his story.

Dluhosh still clutched Gregory's ammonite. Fleence took command while Dluhosh mumbled and drooled into his tentacles. "Dluhosh! Snap out of it!"

He looked up and saw the bottom of the lake above him. "Wha… What happened?"

"You freaked out when you saw that rock. Your tentacles started flailing and grabbing at it. And you almost strangled the scruffy one. We narrowly missed Trukk-9's ship. Actually, I think we grazed it and both cloaking devices stopped working. Then we slammed into the cliff and rolled into the lake."

They could hear Trukk-9 yelling through the narrow gap between their main hatch doors.

"Dluhosh! Fleence! Are you okay?!" he yelled from the open hatch of the now de-cloaked Cruiser Duke Sukk-9.

Fleence peeked through the gap and said, "I think we are okay. But we hit the cliff before the door could open far enough."

Dluhosh was coming back to his senses. "Where's the fisherman guy?"

"He got away," said Trukk-9. "We were concerned about you and he got away before we thought to abduct him."

"Mister O'Buzznid-3! Why didn't you implement abduction protocols!?"

"Sorry Dluhosh, I was distracted by the lizard," replied Buzzy.

"Whatever," said Dluhosh. "Now we have another set of protocols to enact. Trukk-9, if your cloaking device is damaged, you have to leave this planet immediately. Come back when you fix it. We'll try to deal with this. But do not return without a cloaking device."

Stick.E dumped the lizard and began working on the The Duke's cloaking device. "All of the capacitors, conduits, crystals, and circuit boards are melted. The resistors, transistors, and transducers have all been vaporized. The diode is still good though. Even if we could duplicate the parts, we can't activate them without a phase coefficient analysis. There's no point in wasting more time on the cloaking devices."

"Okay, check to see if we can open that hatch enough to get everyone out," ordered Trukk-9.

"Don't let anyone see you!" yelled Dluhosh through the gap.

Stick.E oozed through the tiny spaces in the door's roller mechanism and flowed into the machinery.

"It looks like the gimbal's main fillet is gusseted between joists. I'd say that if you could push hard enough you might be able to force the fillet past the joists, but I can't do anything about it from inside," called Stick.E. He flowed back out. "If we combine all of my grabber beams, and you pull with all your tentacles, we might be able to move it. Everyone else grab where you can!"

Dluhosh pulled until his whole body turned fuchsia. Stick.E strained with a thousand appendages and all of his grabber beams until he flipped to cosine. Dee pushed with his mighty shoulder. Buzzy yanked with his hooks and vibrated until he hummed through his spiracles. And all the humanoids' knuckles turned white. But they failed to move anything.

"Look, you guys have to get off this planet now." Dluhosh ejected a memory card from his computer terminal and handed it up though the gap to Trukk-9.

"These are all my files related to this mission. One of the files is called 'DIRT.BS'. It can be used as an ethics complaint that I want to file in case the PLUMBOB process is not carried out according to the rules. My outpost is the closest place to get help, so I want you to give this card to my supervisor Maghosh. Tell him to submit it officially in my name if Earth goes up for an acceptance vote without a full PLUMBOB checklist."

Fleence said, "And Trukk-9, here's a memory card with pictures, videos, and other documents about bad stuff, including slavery, on this planet that I've collected from the Earthling computer network. I think Maghosh will want to see this too."

She handed the card up to Trukk-9.

"And go see my mother. Tell her that I'm alright. Tell her I'm safely in the tentacles of a Magnificent Bull Dnooblian. Give her copies of all of your video and these cards too. She can be a big help if you encounter any trouble."

"Oh, and you should give Fleence and me your self-destruction tablets," said Dluhosh.

"Sorry Dluhosh-10, but my rules say that self-destruction

tablets are non-transferable."

"Dluhosh, you can get out. You should at least save yourself. Leave with Trukk-9," said Fleence.

"Abandon my ship?! And you? Never."

Trukk-9 continued to argue. "Please, I might be able to get a hydraulic jack or something back in town after it gets dark."

"No, just get out of here," replied Dluhosh. "You'll give away both of us, and these Earthlings will probably open fire. And then this place might end up in the Galactic Pool by default. We can't allow that to happen. All I have to do is open this hatch wide enough to get their heads through. If I can get it moving at all, we'll get out. We might have a chance to hide until you get back, but not if you're seen. Go!"

"You can't move those doors!"

"Well, then I can suck in enough water to sink us if I have to. Please move us out to deeper water, and then get out of here before that crazy fisherman brings back the military!"

Fleence said, "I have an idea that I think will open the door! Just go and find my mother!"

Trukk-9 saw that he had no choice. He directed Stick.E to use his grabber beams to pull Dluhosh's ship out to deeper water, and then he shot straight up and out of the atmosphere at full speed.

Fleence pulled Dluhosh aside and said, "I have an idea. The scruffy one would seem to have a dynamic ego. He changed the ingot into an object that he had only discovered today. I simply have to get him to fixate on how wonderful his rock collecting hammer is. Egocite is incompressible. We can use it like a hydraulic jack. Let me take him to my quarters."

"Go ahead…" He didn't need to look to know that he

had turned yellow.

Fleence grabbed Gregory by the arm and pulled him toward her. Then she led him to her upside-down quarters.

"What are you doing to him?!" said Michael.

"Relax. Does he look upset at all, or in any pain?" asked Dluhosh. "You and I need to talk. Here's what you need to know. If we don't get out of here really soon, I will have to sink the ship with us in it. I figure we have about ten minutes before that fisherman can get somebody out here. If we do manage to get out, Fleence and I are going to need your help to hide. If I think I can trust you two, we might all live. But as soon as I feel I can't trust you, you're a dead man."

To emphasize his point, Dluhosh grabbed Michael around the waist and lifted him into the air. "You should know that since I passed my tolerance test on the first try, I have been denied the pleasure of ripping a humanoid to pieces. Don't give me the excuse I need."

"No problem, man. Just put me down. There you go... I'm honored to know you. Really. You can trust us."

Dluhosh crawled back to his chair and said, "Right, well, we've no choice but to trust each other. I believe you, but what about your friend? Can he be trusted?"

"Well, he can be stand-offish when he gets agitated, but he's smart enough to trust. We are the kind of guys that would like nothing more than to be friends with some space aliens, so we aren't going to turn you in. Um, so what is she doing to him in there anyway?"

"She's going to use her psychic sexual powers to flatter him into obsessing over his rock hammer. His ego will cause the egocite ingot, which is now shaped like his fossil, to change to a hammer shape. If it's held in the correct orientation, it may be able to force the doors open when it changes."

"Her?"

"Yes, she is the most beautiful humanoid in the galaxy and she is sexually telepathic."

Michael stared at Dluhosh and shook his head. "We weren't even sure that she was female. She's mean looking. Maybe some guys are into that, but Gregory... Is she a shape shifter or something?"

"Not exactly, but you can change her clothing, hair, and cosmetics with your mind. You hadn't noticed?"

"Eww, well, no... I don't think her powers are going to work. Not her – not on Gregory..."

***

If Gregory were to have known what the idea was, he wouldn't have expected it to work either. But Fleence was very skilled in her trade.

Fleence set Gregory on her mattress, which had fallen to the ceiling. She would never say what she was about to say unless the client paid extra. But she asked Gregory, "What do you imagine me wearing?" And this was the first time that she ever cared about the answer.

"Uh, a boot camp outfit, I guess."

Fleence's personal translation of 'boot camp outfit' caused her to imagine herself wearing hip-high black latex jackboots with a rawhide thong-and-bodice ensemble topped by a 38-liter churdleboy hat. She wished this ritual could be performed under less stressful circumstances.

She stretched out in front of Gregory and sang his praises.

"Oh, handsome rockhound
Please show me what you found
It is curly, long, and round

Only you could pry it from the ground

Oh, handsome Mister Cool
Any other would be a fool
They have the desire, but not your tool
The way you swing it could take them to school .

Oh, handsome rammer
Please excuse my broken grammar
I know that you are not a scammer
Because you have a beautiful hammer."

Gregory twitched on the floor. He desired to feel his hammer in his hand. He wanted to show this army chick how hard he could swing it.

***

Michael and Dluhosh heard their shrieks and moans. "Maybe it could work…" said Michael.

Fleence jumped down from her quarters and held the egocite ammonite in position between the ship's frozen doors. She oriented it such that the ingot's natural axis was perpendicular to the doors' edges. Then she told Gregory to walk toward the door.

He proceeded with some difficulty, but when he got about three feet away, the egocite ingot exploded sideways, changing into a rock-pick like his, except silver and about an inch longer. It sounded like a shotgun going off when the joist snapped the gusseted gimbal fillet, and the doors slid open.

Dluhosh sprung into action. He grabbed the egocite hammer with one tentacle and the three humanoids with three other tentacles, pulled them all through the door, and swam them to shore.

"Wait here, I have to sink the ship." He shot back out through the water, pumping his siphon and tentacles as fast as he could.

From the three humanoids' perspective, he simply disappeared under the surface, and in the amount of time it took Gregory to yell "Get my ammonite!" Dluhosh resurfaced next to his ship out in the middle of the cove.

Dluhosh gathered large rocks from the bottom of the lake and hefted them through the door of the upside-down floating saucer. Once the ship was sufficiently weighted, lake water flowed in through the door little by little.

Once the ship settled to the bottom, he dove down and stretched all of his tentacles and webbing over the door. Dluhosh hadn't stretched out to his maximum in months, and it felt good. He pumped his web while circulating water inside the ship with his siphon. He was trying to get as much air out of the ship as he could so that bubbles wouldn't give away its location. Then he piled as many more rocks around the ship as he could find. He swam back to shore – grabbing a carp along the way.

Dluhosh crawled up on the bank. He looked at Michael and asked, "Did you guys hike down that creek bed from upstream somewhere?"

Michael looked confused. Fleence rubbed the egocite hammer handle under his nose to make it release some vapor. Dluhosh repeated the question.

"Yes. We're parked maybe two miles up the creek at the campground. It's a small red pickup with a black camper topper."

"Okay, I'm not going to be able to hike effectively over this terrain, and crawling will be too slow. So I'm going to have to sprint up the creek ahead of you. Will I be able to see the vehicle and get in it?"

"Yeah. The back is unlocked. You can hide in there. I seriously doubt that anyone else will be there, but you can hide behind some of the big rocks just in case. Oh, watch out for poison oak. Just don't touch anything green."

Dluhosh said, "I can BECOME a rock if I have to." Then he spun up his running tentacles and shot off in a cloud of leaves and stream water.

TO MICHAEL'S HOUSE

ULBTX-123 detected it, but he couldn't pinpoint the origin of the strange electromagnetic emission from the fried cloaking devices. He figured it must have been a faulty reading, but he worried that it was one of the Earthling supercollider projects that may have created a hitherto unexpected physical state of matter and energy. He wasn't expecting false readings from vagrant aliens.

***

The three humanoids hiked up the creek, with the Earthlings asking questions of Fleence the whole way. Fleence rubbed the egocite hammer handle.

When they arrived at Michael's truck, they found Dluhosh inside the camper, and a fresh carp head and bones outside.

Dluhosh filled the back corner like a big wad of putty the same color as Michael's truck. Fleence motioned for Michael and Gregory to get in the back of the truck too. Once they closed the tailgate, she rubbed the egocite ingot hammer handle.

"Hey, I keep doing this to make egocite vapors so we can understand each other. So stop giggling like little boys. Plus, you've had a mega-dose of calming agent, so please try your best to be rational."

Dluhosh said, "Okay, look, we need to find that fisherman soon. What do you think he'll do?"

"I know that guy," said Gregory. "Well, he's from my town anyway, and I see him all the time at the gas station. I talked to him yesterday. He gave me this hat. Here, check it out. It's pretty decent."

Michael tried on the hat.

"Um, you were saying…" said Fleence.

"Oh, he's some kind of big-time bass fishing pro. His name is Jimmy something. We should be able to track him down. But, yeah, I don't know… Probably if he's already crazy he'd say something to the cops or whatever. But otherwise, without proof… He's a goof though, so who knows what he'll do. I do think that you need to get him as soon as possible."

"Do you think he got pictures?" asked Dluhosh.

"You were watching him. Did you see a camera?" asked Gregory.

"No, but he was acting out a television show. Trukk-9 said he does that a lot."

"You know, I bet he has a small dashboard sport cam or something. We should check to see if he has a video channel. It would be pretty tempting to post a good UFO crash," said Michael.

Gregory asked Dluhosh and Fleence, "What are you doing here anyway? What could possibly be the purpose of playing tricks like that? Don't you guys have a Primary Directive?"

"A what?" replied Dluhosh.

"You know – a directive that forbids you from interfering with people on other planets," replied Gregory.

"Are you kidding? It would take way too long to just float around looking at stuff," said Dluhosh. "In fact, we are directed to get in there and mix things up. We have very specific rules about what we can and cannot do regarding getting caught, and for whether we can or cannot abduct somebody. Um, why do you people have this Primary Directive anyway?"

"We don't – it's from a TV show," said Michael. "But if we had one, I don't think it would be like yours."

"Look guys," said Dluhosh, "I'm sure we all have a million questions, and we need to work out a strategy. Do you have a place to hide us?"

"Yeah, I can hide you at my house. You'll fit right in," said Michael.

"People would just think you were some hideous thing that Michael found washed up on the beach," said Gregory.

"Or we could paint you orange and put you in the middle of the street. Cars would just drive around you." Michael laughed and slapped Gregory in the shoulder with the back of his hand. Gregory laughed too.

Dluhosh turned orange out of pure awkwardness.

"There you go! Now a little reflective tape around your tummy…"

"Alright, alright… Look, I need to say something. I'm sorry that I crashed us and have put you in this situation. This could have huge implications not only for Earth, but for the Galactic Pool as well. This isn't just about us being stranded and needing rescue. Your planet is under inspection. My job is to ensure that the inspection is fair. If I compromise that inspection, there could be dire consequences for Earth. I know we are at your mercy, but I have to remind you that you also need our mercy."

Fleence shook her head from side to side, but somehow Michael and Gregory knew that she meant 'yes, it's true'.

"Now, the reason I freaked out and crashed the ship is that I had a psychological fit when I saw that fossil you showed off. I am ashamed that I have failed. But, you see, I think that my ancestors may have come from your planet. This question is of great importance to me, but it isn't part of this mission. I want all three of you to help me stay focused."

"So you're telling us that you are an ammonite?" asked Michael.

"Well, I don't know, but the fossilized shell you had looks like our earliest known ancestor's shell – and mine. They appeared out of nowhere on Dnooblia sixty-six million years ago – ones just like that."

Michael interrupted. "What!? You're an ammonite! That's when the ammonites disappeared from here! You've evolved a lot, I'm sure, but, damn, look at you…"

"Please take us to your home now. We'll continue this discussion later. Fleence and I will ride back here."

"But, you are an ammonite! You're not really a space alien! Welcome home! Are there a lot of you? Are you all coming home? Where…"

"Look! I can't deal with this right now. Get us to your home!" pleaded Dluhosh.

"Okay, the road is a little rough, but we should hit town in about an hour. It will be dark when we get there. You are gonna like my house, Mister Ammonite," said Michael, as he climbed out of the back. "Hold on to something."

***

Michael and Gregory hopped in front.

"Hey, so what did the alien girl do to you?" asked

Michael.

"Oh…"

"What? What did you guys do?"

"Wait, I'm trying to find the words."

"Oh, come on…"

"You know, it's hard to describe. Okay, well, after she dragged me up there the first thing she said was 'If you touch me, I'll kick your teeth out'."

"Whoa, she's hardcore. Then what did she do?"

"She never touched me. She laid out in front of me obviously trying to look all sexy and everything, and she said 'Let me sing your praises' or something like that. Then she sang a song about me and my rock pick. All she did was sing, and her voice wasn't even that good. She sounded nervous. I mean I could see her laying there singing, but we were also doing anything and everything…"

"Whoa, you're probably the first human to do it with an alien!"

Gregory paused and then said, "So, just hypothetically, if the only sex that some poor guy ever had was telepathic and with an alien, would that guy still be a virgin?"

"Yes, definitely," replied Michael.

They sat in silence for a minute.

"Do you think we should tell him that his flying saucer will be exposed when the reservoir drops?" asked Michael.

"Let's not yet."

"I wonder what they eat?"

"I think Mister Ammonite ate that carp."

"Oh right, but what about the girl?"

"Her teeth look like regular teeth. I bet she'll eat whatever. What do you have at home?"

"Uh… cereal, frozen burritos, and a bagel, sort of. Oh, and a can of baked beans, a couple of string cheeses… Croutons…"

"Do you have any alcohol?" asked Gregory.

"I just got a gallon of 90% isopropyl. Why?"

"No, not for specimens – for drinking."

"No. You think we should have a welcoming party?" asked Michael.

"Well, I'm just thinking that if they drink, we might be able to get more information out of them."

"Good point. So, what, like wine coolers or something?"

"No, nothing fancy. Let's stop at the market for some food and whatever booze is cheap. We'll ask them what they want when we stop."

***

Dluhosh and Fleence weren't as talkative. Finally Fleence said, "Don't worry about it Dluhosh. I understand how important that fossil is to you. It could have happened to anyone."

"Thanks, Fleence, but this is really messed up. What are we going to do?"

"Right, well, I think these two Earthlings are trustworthy. They can hide us long enough for Trukk-9 to come back," said Fleence.

"Maybe, but what about the fisherman? What are we going to do about him?"

"Well, if we can find him before he talks, I think I just need to have a special conversation with him."

"You know what else?" asked Dluhosh. "If a rescue party does arrive, I guess they'll go to the crash site first. They should be able to tell that we escaped. After that, Trukk-9 will look at the fisherman's house. We should try to have a presence of some kind there."

Dluhosh and Fleence could feel that they were now

travelling on a paved road. A few minutes later they could see the lights of town.

They pulled into the market and the guys ran around back. "Hey what do you guys eat? This is the market. What do you want?"

Fleence rubbed the hammer, and Michael stuck his head in to repeat himself.

Dluhosh was getting agitated. "I want to go hide at your house. We can worry about food later."

"Just because you ate a great big carp doesn't mean she's not hungry. We're going in. Do you drink?" demanded Gregory.

"Look, there are Earthlings all over the place here. It's too big a risk…"

"Too late – need food. Are you hungry?" Gregory asked Fleence.

"Dluhosh only eats raw fish. I'm an omnivore. Just hurry, and one of you stay here," said Fleence.

Michael pulled out his wallet. "Here's fifty bucks. Get some pizzas and whatever raw fish they have. Spend the rest on whatever booze looks like the best deal."

Gregory ran in while Michael stood guard.

Michael tuned in his radio for news of flying saucers. He went through the whole dial and realized that none of the stations were local, and probably none were even live. He looked at his phone – no space alien news alerts. So far, so good. He still felt elated. This was by far the coolest thing that ever happened to anybody, including the probaluation. He found some Mexican music at the top of the dial, turned up the volume, and did a little dance.

Some Mexican guys gave the thumbs-up and laughed at Michael's dancing as they passed by.

Dluhosh said, "I can't believe how careless this stupid humanoid is acting. The PLUMBOB clearly needs to find a less euphoria-producing or shorter-acting calming agent. It's the Earthlings' intelligence more than their trustworthiness that I'm worried about."

Gregory returned with a full shopping cart and they opened the tailgate. He said to Fleence, "I got you these chocolate peanut candies. They are probably the best food ever created by humans."

Then he looked at Dluhosh and said, "All the fish they had was bags of anchovies in the bait freezer. You might want to thaw them out first. And I hope you like beer."

They continued to drive.

"Why are you getting all harsh with Mister Ammonite?" asked Michael.

"Well, he's a screw-up, and he lost my most awesome ammonite ever. You should keep being nice to him though. We can do a good cop, bad cop thing like on TV. We can learn as much as possible by keeping them off-guard and dividing their trust in us. They are here to manipulate us, so it's fair for us to do it to them if we can. Know what I mean?"

"Well, sure, if you want to try and be a bad cop, go ahead. But remember – he picked me up with one tentacle. So be careful. Oh yeah, I was gonna say, he also told me that you can make her wear whatever clothes, hair, and make-up you want just by imagining it. And that she's the most beautiful woman in the galaxy. Didn't you notice that when she seduced you?"

"You know... well, no."

"Well, I'm going to try it on her. I'm thinking a cowgirl outfit with huge hair."

***

When they arrived at Michael's house, he backed his

pickup into his driveway and opened the garage door. He cleared some recycling and boxes of rocks out of the way so that Fleence and Dluhosh could make a speedy entry. He opened the tailgate for them.

As Fleence ran, Michael tried to imagine her in a sexy cowgirl outfit, and Gregory tried her as a pro football cheerleader. But nothing happened.

Gregory brought in the groceries and started opening beers.

Fleence rubbed the egocite rock hammer and asked Michael if they could heat the ingot. They put it in some hot water and within a few minutes the whole house was fumigated with egocite.

They tried it again, and now Fleence was dressed as a 1970's airline stewardess for Michael, and as an Oktoberfest beer maiden for Gregory. They were startled to see just how well the costumes fit her.

Michael booted up his computer to search for Jimmy. He typed in a search.

"That was easy. He has a website. His name is Jimmy Fresnox. Oh yeah, there's his boat. Now what? Email him?"

Gregory was looking in the phone book. "Yep, here's a number for a J. Fresnox."

"Well, what do you guys want to say?" asked Michael of Dluhosh and Fleence.

Fleence replied, "How about if you say that you saw him while you were being abducted? You just want to know if he reported it, and tell him to wait if he hasn't. Then invite him over here and I'll convince him the rest of the way. Do you think that would work?"

Dluhosh said, "Maybe, but do we want him to know where we're hidden?"

"You know, maybe we should go to his place with, um,

you," said Gregory, gesturing toward Fleence.

"Oh, sorry, my name is Fleence, and this is Dluhosh. Can you remember those names?"

"Yeah – Fleence and Mister Ammonite. Got it," replied Gregory as he started to enter the number into his phone.

"Hey, slow down," demanded Dluhosh. "I'm not going anywhere."

"You aren't invited anywhere anyway. Settle down, squid," said Gregory.

Michael said, "And don't worry – nobody's going to come around here while we're gone. You should take a look at my ammonite collection. That case there, and all those drawers there, plus the ones on shelves – you might meet some relatives. There's beer right here and you have your anchovies. We'll be back as soon as we can."

Gregory made the call. "Is this Jimmy Fresnox?"

Jimmy's tired voice replied. "Yeah, it's pronounced like Fresno, the city. Who is this?"

"You might not remember me, but we talked at the gas station yesterday. My name is Gregory. My friend and I were at those bluffs today… And we saw the flying saucers too."

Jimmy perked right up. "Oh, uh, wow, yeah, wasn't that crazy? I'm so glad you… Have you reported it?"

"You know, I was going to ask you the same thing. No, the last thing I want is for everyone to think I'm crazy. There's no way I'm reporting it… not yet."

Jimmy said, "Yeah, that's what I was thinking. But I have video of the crash. It looks totally real. You can see the UFO hit the cliff and roll back down. It could be worth a lot, I think. So I don't know what to do. Did you get pictures?"

"I got something better," replied Gregory. "How about if my associate and I come over and we talk about what to do?"

Jimmy gave directions.

***

Jimmy was waiting at the door when they arrived.

"You didn't say there were three of you. But come on in. Hello, ma'am. Hey, yeah, you're the guy who told me about the bluffs."

The egocite ingot shifted audibly within the paper sack.

"Would any of you like an energy drink?"

Fleence held up the sack.

"Oh, I forgot. Fleence doesn't speak English. She needs her translator device. Also, don't let her looks fool you. She's actually very nice," said Michael.

Fleence reached into the bag and pulled out an exquisite silver Mega-Mouth Poppin' Minnow.

Jimmy cried out. "Whoa! Where'd you get that? That's… How did you…?"

"Jimmy," said Gregory, "that's the translator. Why it looks like a lure is something we can explain later. Now, can Fleence put it in some hot water? I know it sounds weird, but it needs to warm up to work."

"Uh, fine, sure, in the kitchen," replied Jimmy. "But hey, do you think the aliens are still at the lake? I mean, that was a bad crash. I mean, there could be dead aliens out there, and a flying saucer… I was thinking of going out there again in the morning, but I'm kind of afraid to. You guys wanna go?"

The guys engaged Jimmy in a conversation about the pros and cons of reporting UFO sightings. When Fleence signaled that the egocite was working, Gregory said, "Jimmy, remember when I said on the phone that I had something better than pictures?"

"Yeah…"

Gregory nodded toward Fleence. "Imagine her wearing something different. Anything you want…"

Jimmy looked at her. He saw Fleence's fatigues change into one of the little sundresses worn by the gas station hair stylists. Her hat disappeared and her hair kept changing between blonde and brunette. Her lips seemed to become moist and full.

"How did you do that, ma'am?" asked Jimmy.

"I didn't – you did," replied Fleence.

"Wha…? You're the space aliens!"

"Jimmy, Jimmy! No," said Gregory. "We aren't the space aliens. Calm down. Somebody will hear you." Then he added, "Well, okay, Michael and I aren't space aliens. But Fleence is."

"Jimmy, don't be afraid," said Fleence. "I'm the one who should be afraid. Think about it. I crashed on a very strange planet full of violent humanoids. This is my very first trip away from home. My rescuers are at least six months away. I'm at your mercy. But if you touch me, I'll kick your teeth out."

"Whoa, ma'am – I'm a gentleman. I'm not violent, I swear."

"Okay Jimmy, we are asking for your help and cooperation. We want you to swear secrecy. Please do not tell anyone about today. I can make it worth your while. I just need your trust."

"Worth my while, huh? What do you have? I really like that chrome Mega-Mouth Poppin' Minnow."

"Uh, Jimmy, I was thinking of something more personal…" said Fleence as she took a step closer. She was about to whisper something nice in his ear.

Jimmy recoiled. "Are you hitting on me, ma'am? Hey, I said I'm a gentleman. I'm sorry, you really are very pretty…

How about you give me your lure instead?"

"Well, I can't give you my translator," replied a bewildered and embarrassed Fleence.

"Hey, I just thought of something. Was that you guys hooking me up with all those fish today?"

Fleence replied. "Yes. Sorry for messing with you like that. It looked fun for you though, right?"

"Well, yeah, I guess... But how did you do that? Can you do it for me again? It would make an awesome fishing show."

"No. That was a fellow in the other ship using a special scanner and grabber beam array. That ship is long gone. We don't have that technology."

"I bet Mister Ammonite could do it without a ray beam," said Gregory. "He grabbed that big ol' carp pretty easy."

"Catching big ol' carp isn't exactly the kind of fishing that gets TV deals in this country – not in the USA," said Jimmy.

"No, no," said Michael. "He can probably catch anything. He caught the carp with his tentacles..." Michael's voice trailed off.

"What!? You have another space alien? With tentacles?"

"Oops..." said Michael.

"We were going to tell him anyway," said Fleence.

"Can he catch bass? They have some pretty sharp spines..."

"Oh, I'm sure he can. He's a Dnooblian."

"Okay. How about this for a deal? I want a TV fishing show more than anything. I will swear absolute secrecy if you can get this other alien to repeat what you did for me today. We can start making shows right away."

"I don't know... Dluhosh isn't going to want to risk

going back to that lake with all those people," said Fleence.

"No, no. I know a perfect spot. It's a vacation rental cabin on a lake in the hills. I've always wanted to go there. It's supposed to have lots of big bass and there's nobody else up there this early in the season. I'll also rent professional video gear, and the cabin comes with a second boat so we can use it to shoot like professionals. It will be totally private. I'll supply everything. All you need to do is show up. I have a brochure around somewhere. It'll be perfect."

Michael said, "Jimmy, how about if Fleence fishes with you instead? I've seen those videos of bikini babes fishing..."

"Nope. That doesn't work unless we catch fish. I'll take Miss Fleence too though. I'll keep my mouth shut for forty-eight hours while we plan this. I hate to be difficult about it, but this could be just the thing to put me over the top after my big tournament win, and I ain't gonna let this one get away."

"Well, I guess I can ask Dluhosh. But I'm warning you, he's small but he is quite capable of ripping you into many small pieces if he gets angry. Don't get sassy with him," said Fleence.

"Okay, okay, I get it. Don't mess with the aliens. They'll kick your teeth out and rip you to pieces. Why do you have to be so violent?" asked Jimmy.

"You know, you'll have to promise not to say anything at all about this. Don't post any of the video. Don't send any emails about it. Don't write any notes. Don't mention that you've met me or Michael. Don't even talk in your sleep. You promise to leave no trace of this, and I'll see if Mister Ammonite will look favorably on you."

"I promise. I swear," replied Jimmy.

"Just don't do anything careless. Oh, and I know what

might help you butter up Mister Ammonite. Do you still have any of those fish?" asked Gregory.

"Uh yeah, I almost forgot. I put all of the bass in my freezer, but I don't know what to do with the rest of the fish."

"Well bag 'em up."

ALIENS AS GUESTS

When they got back to Michael's house, they found Dluhosh passed out in a pile of ammonite fossils. Several expensive pieces of museum glass had been knocked from cabinets, and a chair was tipped over.

Fleence ran in. "Oh no! Dluhosh!" she yelled as she tried to revive him. "I can smell anchovies on his breath, so he's not dead..."

Gregory and Michael came in and saw a bunch of empty beer bottles on the counter and floor, and anchovies in the blender.

Michael reached down to pick up his collection and said, "Hey man, he does have that ammonite you found – looks like he prepped it out for you." Michael tried to pick up the fossil and found that it wasn't a fossil – and that it was stuck to Dluhosh.

Having his shell yanked and his mantle twisted like that woke Dluhosh up with a start. "Ow! Careful with that!"

"Whoa, it's part of him!" said Gregory.

"No way, man. You really are Mister Ammonite. Your shell looks a lot like the ammonite that Gregory found today. I have about a million questions for you…"

Gregory said, "Yeah, like what happened in here? Are you drunk? What did you do?"

"Oh, I'm so sorry. I didn't mean to… Look, it's been a really rough day. I tried to make some fish wine – just to calm me down. Then I started going through your fossils. I made some more fish wine, and it was tasting pretty good. Those little frozen fish are wonderful, by the way. Anyway, I came across several fossils that look Dnooblian, and I lost control again. You have to understand…" said Dluhosh as he worked his shell back into its shark-skin sheath.

Gregory interrupted. "No problem, Mister Ammonite. Make yourself another smoothie. There's something YOU have to understand."

Fleence said, "Dluhosh, we got Jimmy the fisherman to agree not to say anything about us. But he wants something in exchange."

Michael handed Dluhosh a smoothie.

"He wants us to help him make a fishing show. Apparently, he has everything you need except the ability to catch fish, and a pretty girl. I volunteered to be the girl. Do you think you can catch fish for him and put them on the hooks like Stick.E did?"

"Are you kidding?!" asked Dluhosh as he drained his smoothie. "I can't go out. I should probably desiccate until help arrives."

Gregory said, "This Jimmy guy is serious. I think he goes to the cops with his video if you don't do this for him. He has video of you crashing your flying saucer, you know. He'll take the military right to it."

"He sent these along," said Michael, indicating the bags of fish.

Dluhosh looked back and forth between Michael and Gregory. "I guess blackmail is another of your endearing

Earthling characteristics. So when would this start?"

"It'll be a couple of days. Jimmy has to rent some gear and stuff. He says he has a totally private lake up in the hills where we can stay in a luxury cabin with no one around."

"Well, if I don't desiccate, I'll need more fish anyway. As long as I get to keep the fish I catch, I should be able to feed myself without you having to buy me fish."

"The limit on bass is five. Is that enough for you?" asked Michael.

"What? Are you going to get him a fishing license too?" asked Gregory. "You know, I think space aliens are exempt from the regs. Besides, those non-resident licenses are expensive…"

"Oh shush. I'm just trying to be careful. We need to protect Mister Ammonite from every threat," said good-cop Michael.

"So you agree to do it?" asked Fleence.

"What else CAN I do? They have me by the shell. Besides, if I'm going to die, it might as well be while I'm fishing. It does fall within the rules…" Dluhosh's voice trailed off as he pondered this.

"Okay, now can I ask some questions? You want a beer, Fleence?" asked Michael.

"Sure, I guess. No fish in mine, please."

"Okay, where do I start…? Um, why do you look like a human, Fleence?"

"Well, because I'm a humanoid, of course."

"No, no… Why do we look so alike even though you are from another planet?"

"Convergent evolution?" suggested Gregory.

"Convergence in every possible trait? If I'm a bat, she isn't a bird – she's also a bat."

They took a long look at her. Both men independently imagined her in a form-fitting superhero outfit.

"What about mimicry?" asked Gregory.

"Yeah, are you a shape shifter Fleence?" asked Michael.

"Nope, what you see is what you get, plus a little extra," replied Fleence.

"Do you have DNA?" asked Michael. "You know, uh, genetic information packets of some kind in your cells?"

"Oh, yes. Spiral ladder kind of thing with instructions coded into it – something like that perhaps?"

"HEY!" yelled Gregory. "You just discovered that aliens have DNA! A discovery like that would win the Nobel Prize! You want another beer to celebrate?"

The egocite ingot in the kitchen changed shape. Fleence heard it and assumed that it was due to a surge of pride from Michael, probably from mentally accepting the Nobel Prize. She was curious to see, so she looked in the pot on the stove. "What does this prize that Gregory awarded you look like, Michael?"

"Ha ha, funny. Well, I think it's a big medal with a guy's head on it."

"And a lot of money," added Gregory.

"So it doesn't look like a topaz-encrusted hoop with a figurine of the galaxy in it?" she asked.

"No, but that sounds pretty cool," said Gregory.

Fleence looked at Dluhosh, who seemed to be lost in concentration over an ammonite fossil. Dnooblians weren't normally ingot alterers.

"Dluhosh? Dluhosh!"

He finally looked up. "Oh, sorry. I did it again. But look here. I've been taking precise measurements of these fossils. They are virtually identical to some of the earliest known ammonites on Dnooblia. The suture patterns are similar…"

"Wow, that's a huge discovery for you too, Dluhosh. Do you think it could be worthy of the Galactic Loop

Prize?"

"Yeah, that's funny. I just thought of that too," said Dluhosh.

Michael jumped back in. "Come on, Fleence, you are too much like us. What gives?"

Fleence leaned over to Michael and whispered, "Maybe we are similar, but you are much more handsome than the other men in the galaxy."

Michael's knees buckled and he fell to the floor, quivering.

And because Fleence was being truthful, her words had a powerful effect. It convinced Michael that Fleence was some sort of sexy shape-shifter. So he shut up about it.

Gregory and Michael spent the next couple of hours learning amazing things about the Galactic Pool, and Dluhosh learned about the extinction of the ammonites and dinosaurs.

Around midnight Michael said, "We have a lot to do tomorrow, so I'm going to bed. I need to sleep on all of this if I can. We should continue this discussion in the morning. So, do you guys sleep, or what?"

"Yes, and I definitely need some," said Dluhosh.

"Fleence, do you need a toothbrush?" asked Gregory. "I have a brand new unopened one that I bought for this visit. I'll use one of my old fossil-cleaning toothbrushes. Mister Ammonite, there's a beak brush in a nifty little cradle on the floor next to the toilet."

"Yes, I'm quite capable of navigating a humanoid bathroom, thank you. However, I will need to soak in the morning. I need a tub, a shower, or a pond – or your kitchen sink might work if nothing else."

"Will the hot tub work?" asked Michael.

"You have a hot tub – like outdoors?" asked a very surprised Dluhosh.

228

"Yeah, it came with the house. I don't put a lot of chemicals in it so it's kind of like a pond. But it works fine. It's not really outside – more sort of in a little covered nook off the back deck. No one can see you in there."

"Are you sure it's private?"

"Sure, I'd be comfortable naked out there – like with a girl – like, you know, when, if, uh…"

"Do you think I could sleep in there?"

"Yeah, sure. You mean in the water?"

"Yes. It's pretty normal for a Dnooblian. It's homey. And it happens to be a good hangover cure – helps filter the system. So I guess I'll see you in the morning?"

"Yeah… let's see… what else does one tell a space alien on his first night on Earth? Oh, if there are little animals hopping around by the hot tub, don't worry about them, they are just toads. Don't eat any of them though. There might be a few insects in there too, but there's a skimmer net if you need it. Uh, some cats might come around, but they are pets. So are the fish in the aquarium. Just so you know…"

TRUKK-9 MEETS ULBTX-123

The Cruiser Duke Sukk-9 was two weeks into the return flight, and Trukk-9 was spending most of his time reviewing his dailies and test-editing footage. The material was golden. He knew that all he had to do was string random images together and add some dramatic music, and it would be considered a work of genius. With this material he would be able to continue his reign over the underground cinema for years to come.

The editing had kept his mind occupied. However, he was distracted by a number of things. These concerns made this feel like a much longer journey than it really was.

First, of course, he was worried about Fleence. He was having a difficult time believing that she and Dluhosh could be alive. But he knew he had to act as if it were possible. He had to come up with a plan, but all of his ideas seemed sluggish and futile.

"Was it really worth abandoning them to slightly lessen the chance of contaminating some faraway planet? Dnooblians and their rules..." said Trukk-9 for the hundredth time to no one in particular.

"Dee, which would you prefer – take the chance of pissing off Griffer-1 for possibly no good reason, or continue letting him use you for some nefarious purpose?"

"Skip, you always have to make things complicated, don't you? If you weren't going to let that jerk use you, you should have done a little more homework before accepting the deal. Just deliver the material and focus on the rescue. One day you might have to admit that you were used, but so what?"

"You make some good points, my friend. This is all very big, isn't it? Galactic politics, the fate of a planet, cinema, love…"

Dee and Trukk-9 were unaware that their ship had come to a halt. Stick.E detected it and came out of his wave state.

"Why did we stop?" Stick.E asked in the middle of Trukk-9's philosophizing.

"Huh?" Dee looked down at his control panel. "Holy nuts and berries! We're at a dead stop…"

A hologram of a headless naked humanoid male now rotated in front of the main video display. It floated there in a standing position with a neck that ended at the Adam's apple, arms that ended above the elbows, and legs that ended in the middle of the knees. The incomplete arms and legs were spread wide.

A very big voice bellowed. "What's this?! I didn't expect to find a ship out here!"

"Who are you?!" yelled Trukk-9.

"I am ULBTX-123."

"I don't mean your name. I mean what are you doing on my ship!?"

"I am not on your ship. I am a quantum thingularity that lives within a volume of space that contains your local group of galaxies. We call ourselves Pixel People. Each of us and our exclusive space is a single pixel in the dark matter Great Hologram that reaches across the Universe, a representational avatar of which you now see rotating before you. My consciousness is contained within a relatively small cluster of precisely vibrating quanta, but I exist wherever I think to exist at any given moment within my pixel space."

"Let us go, asshole!" yelled Dee.

"Hold on, you – I'm not done yet," said ULBTX-123. "And I am not the asshole. I am a single pixel. Look at the avatar now as it rotates before you... There, you see that bright pinpoint of light? That's me. As you can see, it is in the Upper Left Buttocks Region. I have friends in the rectum, and they would prefer that you not refer to them in the pejorative."

"Asshole," repeated Dee.

"Stop it. You'll notice that The Great Hologram has neither head nor complete limbs. As the Universe expands, new Pixel People are born at the ends, gradually forming the rest of The Great Hologram. We should be complete with head and limbs in about another two billion years at this rate. We are terribly excited to see how big our feet are. But the avatar you see is an otherwise anatomically correct humanoid."

"Ha! Compared to Trukk-9, I wouldn't call you anatomically correct, buddy. I've seen Skip many times in all weather conditions. And I can tell you right now, if you ever wanted to use your one complete appendage, you would have to marry a flip-"

The big voice interrupted. "Yes, I imagine that you refer to our penis. More than eight billion light years long, it is. But this is proportionally correct for a male Earthling. You can verify this with a simple search on their computer network. Anyway, I picked up a strange radiation pulse a fortnight ago. And now here you are flying around in sensitive space. I need to keep people like you away from this sector."

"Uh, Big Voice Entity – I hope you don't mind me calling you that – I'll never remember your real name – please let us continue and we'll fix the problem," said Trukk-9.

"Hey, bub, we have an important mission here. Lives are at stake. Let us go!" said Dee.

"Tell me what you are doing here so I can start cleaning up this mess. By the way, humanoid, you are from the planet they call Bukk-9, right?" asked The Big Voice Entity, not paying any attention to Dee.

"Yes, but how do you know that?"

"Because I am your Pixel Person, mister. I see that you have removed your antlers. What is the reason for this?"

"Oh, they're a pain sometimes – always getting in the way… And they're dangerous when you have eight or ten points, and everyone has eleven eyes."

"Hmm, I hadn't thought of that," lied The Big Voice Entity. "But otherwise, do you enjoy having the eyes?"

"It can be disorienting when all of them are open at once, however I see extraordinary things."

"Well good. My hope is that The Great Hologram has many eyes and big antlers too. That way we'll be able to see the whole Universe at once, and it will have to keep expanding for a long time to accommodate the antlers before it starts to contract. I don't want to die. Oh, and I hope you like flying trees."

"Uh, sure… But please, our two friends are stranded on a planet awaiting rescue," said Trukk-9.

"Oh, no. You better not mean you infected Earth!"

"No, I think it's called Dirt. So we can be on our way then?" asked Trukk-9.

"No! Prove to me where you were first!"

Buzzy brought up a random clip of someone jumping out of a hot-air balloon.

"That can only be Earth! What the hell are you doing there anyway? You have to remove this infection, or else I'm going to have to do something drastic. You have to remove them now!"

"That's exactly what we are trying to do, dumb-ass," said Dee. "And you are stopping us."

"But why are you going AWAY from Earth then? Your friends haven't been captured by Earthlings have they?"

"No, but we need a new cloaking device before we can pick them up – the Dnooblian insisted. The closest one is months away. They are going to have to survive until we get back," said Trukk-9.

"Why are you so concerned with being cloaked? Are you conducting surveillance?"

"Well, yes, in a way, yes... We are evaluating whether we should invite the planet into our Galactic Pool."

"Oh, we can't allow that. They didn't see you did they?"

"No. Well, three people did."

"And you didn't terminate them?"

"They got away."

"Damn! Your friend who insists on you being cloaked is right, though. You best not be seen there. If Earthlings gain knowledge of you, it could complicate a very important experiment before the results are officially accepted. And it would not end well for you."

"Well, how about if we go back, find our colleagues, and you can rescue them for us. And then we can work on preventing the bigger infection from arriving," said Trukk-9.

"HA! I'm much too big for that. Me removing two of your kind would be like you trying to remove two viruses from the inside your nose with your finger. I'd have to swab up their whole town. I work well at very small scales and very large ones – this in-between stuff is difficult for me. I might as well hit them with asteroids."

"Well, can you speed up our trip for us, perhaps?" asked Trukk-9.

"Sure," said The Big Voice Entity. "Well, first tell me where you last saw them and I'll have a look. Give me their coordinates."

Dee reluctantly gave him the coordinates.

"I'll be right back," said The Big Voice Entity. "Okay, I'm back. Their ship is at the bottom of a lake. I don't see any sign of them."

"Is the ship's door open?" asked Trukk-9.

"I can't tell. It's stuck down in a pile of rocks."

"Then can you go check out this guy's house? This is one of the Earthlings who saw us. Can you see this picture on my screen?" asked Trukk-9.

"Yes, give me the coordinates."

"Okay, check to see if this boat is there too."

"I'll be right back... Okay, there's nobody home and no boat. Now what?"

"Can you get us to the next wormhole? That would save us a few days," asked Trukk-9.

"Wormhole? Do you mean a space-time wrinkle?"

"It's just a freaking wormhole! We don't know what it is!" Dee lowered his massive head and charged the avatar. He attempted to grapple with it and slammed headlong into the video screen instead.

"I was afraid this might happen. It's very difficult to bend space to yourself without leaving those wrinkles behind. It's getting pretty bad around this sector. I should have known. Someone was bound to start using them, even if it wasn't the Earthlings," said The Big Voice Entity.

"Okay, bend some space then!" yelled Dee. "I'll feed you

coordinates!"

"No. Not yet. What's your plan first? Tell me your plan to get EVERYTHING under control again."

Trukk-9 explained the process of PLUMBOB planet evaluation. He read the opening statement of Dluhosh's ethics complaint. He mentioned Griffer-1 by name, etcetera.

"Once the administration sees all that, it should stop any further consideration of invading Earth."

Dee returned to his station walking backwards with his head cocked and his finger pointed at the rotating avatar.

Trukk-9 continued. "I need to drop off this data at the outpost. It might take a couple of days to get authorization for the cloaking device. We can't speed up the bureaucracy. Then we need to go see the mother of the stranded female. She is wealthy and well connected, so she can probably get us a private cargo ship to grab Dluhosh's ship from the lake without the Galactic Pool authorities knowing anything."

"Your plan is incomplete, complicated, and unreliable. However, if it works, it could save me a major headache," said The Big Voice Entity. "Give me the outpost coordinates. I'll drop you a ways out. You fly the rest of the way and I will observe."

The Big Voice Entity bent their space, dropped them off, and they flew to the outpost.

***

A small voice came over the intercom.

"Identify your port of registry, space vagrant."

Dee replied. "What do you mean, 'port of registry' outpost? Don't be dumb, this is Trukk-9 from Bukk-9 on the Sukk-9, not some fukking space vagrant. And I can tell you right now, there's no way that stupid autotranslator got that one. Give me Maghosh-10!"

"Well, are we not all in a tizzy?" replied the radio voice.

"Are you an insectoid?" asked Trukk-9.

"Yes, of course."

"A Cricket?"

"Yes. Thanks for noticing."

"A female?"

"Well, obviously..."

Buzzy turned to look at Trukk-9. He scratched himself and nodded.

"Perfect – I have a present for you. Tell me where Fleence-18's ship is and meet me there."

Maghosh came through on the radio. "Trukk-9? How...? You must have passed Dluhosh..."

"We don't have time to explain how we got here. Dluhosh and Fleence are stranded on the planet. We don't know if they are alive or whether they've been captured. It's been a couple of weeks since they crashed. I need a new cloaking device so I can go back and get them. We'll also need a way to get their disabled ship off the surface."

"I'm also transmitting all of my video monitoring data to you. I was apparently given a bogus checklist, so Dluhosh and Fleence have tried to fill in the blanks with the bad stuff I wasn't tasked with. Dluhosh wants you to pay special attention to a document he has attached. It's an ethics complaint. Got it?"

"Uh, yeah, I guess. I'll try to get authorization for a cloaking device, but you know how those things are. Do you need fuel too?" asked Maghosh. "Honestly, I'm not surprised that this mission is all screwed up."

"No, but we are taking Fleence's ship to Chuffed-18 to notify her mother. Hopefully she can find us a ship big enough to pick up Dluhosh's. We'll be right back."

"Right back...?"

"Sorry, no time to explain, but please get working on the cloaking device request immediately."

"Okay… Oh, let me forward some messages to you for Dluhosh."

Trukk-9 logged the messages and then dropped Buzzy off in the hangar where Fleence's ship was parked.

***

Chuffed-18 appeared outside the window.

As the ship approached, an automated radio voice contacted them. "To all approaching vessels, if you are here to have your praises sung, please proceed to Holding Terminal Six. There is currently a twenty-seven-day waiting list. You will find complementary amenities and gaming facilities there. Please enjoy your wait. If you are here for other purposes, please say 'other purposes' now."

"Other purposes," said Trukk-9.

"Please hold," said the recording. Music came over the radio – it was a Dnooblian tenor – an homage to Trukk-9, actually.

After a few minutes, a live voice came on the radio. "This is Scrufftag-17, how may I help you?"

"This is Trukk-9. I need to speak to Kyleence-18, mother of Fleence-18. Just point me to her – it's an emergency!"

"I'm sorry," said Scrufftag-17. "I'm at a call center on Scablands-17. I can't point at anything from here. I will try to put you through to our headquarters. Is there anything else I may help you with today?"

"Hurry!" yelled Trukk-9.

The Dnooblian tenor returned.

After a few minutes another voice came over the radio. "May I help you sir?"

Trukk-9 repeated his request to speak with Fleence's mother.

"Sir, I'm afraid… Who is this, may I ask?"

"It's Trukk-9! Put us through now!" said Dee.

"Oh! Certainly, sir. Please hold."

More Dnooblian tenor…

Then a face appeared on Trukk-9's video screen.

And there was a stunned silence.

"Oh come on, boys and girls, let's get on with it," said Dee, embarrassed for his friend.

"Kyleence… Kyleence, I don't have time to say much now. Much more later though… Fleence is in trouble. She is stranded on an alien planet. I'm going to attempt a rescue after my cloaking device is replaced."

Kyleence replied, "Oh no, Trukk-9, is Fleence okay?"

"I don't know. She was fine when I left. She's in the tentacles of a Magnificent Bull Dnooblian. I have a way to return to the planet very quickly once I get the cloaking device I've requested, which could be a few days," said Trukk-9.

Fleence's mother pushed a button on her control panel, and said, "Find out which useless bureaucrat is slowing down Trukk-9's cloaking device request, and have it approved and installed immediately."

"Okay, what else do you need?" she asked, turning back to Trukk-9.

"I need a cloaked cargo ship with a super grabber that we can use to pick up the stranded ship, and I also want to give you copies of all of Fleence's data files for safe keeping. They may turn out to be very important."

A voice came over Kyleence's radio. "Excuse me ma'am, the cloaking device for The Duke has been printed and is being installed at the outpost. Can I do anything else?"

"Yes, I also need a cargo ship with a cloaking device and super grabber. The pilot will be under the command of Trukk-9."

Trukk-9 said, "If the Duke's cloaking device is ready, we'll leave Fleence's ship here and take the cargo ship back to the outpost."

"Trukk-9, you will bring Fleence back to me... I mean, personally?"

"Yes, of course," he replied, gulping.

Dee rolled his eyes and piloted Fleence's ship to a landing pad to meet the cargo ship.

"Good bye Kyleence. I will see you again soon – hopefully later today. We may need some additional help from you to fully fix this mess."

***

The cargo ship pilot said, "Mister Trukk-9, I'm very honored to meet you, sir."

"Thank you. What is your name, pilot?"

"My name is Colleence-18, sir." She looked exactly like Fleence dressed in a flight suit.

"Okay Colleence, please fly your ship into orbit, and try not to be alarmed. We will be automatically transported to an outpost."

Trukk-9 explained. "We are on our way to rescue Kyleence-18's daughter and a Dnooblian friend of mine. You will pick up their ship, if we can locate it. With any luck, we'll have you home by dinner."

"Yes sir," replied a bewildered Colleence.

Trukk-9 radioed the outpost.

The insectoid radio voice spoke. "Trukk-9? Did you forget something?"

"No, I've come back for my ship. Please open the hatch

now."

"You have only been gone for five minutes. I have not processed the order for your cloaking device yet…"

"Open the hatch," said Trukk-9.

The hangar doors opened to reveal a plasmanoid mechanic performing the final phase-calibration on the new cloaking device, and Buzzy's headless carcass lying on the floor.

THE TRIUMVIRATE SEES DIRT VIDEOS

Welter-3 received an urgent quantum communication from Maghosh. It had a very large file attached and was accompanied by a note.

Welter-3, please find attached a partial submission of video data from Trukk-9's and Dluhosh-10's PLUMBOB mission to the planet Dirt. I do not know how, but Trukk-9 himself delivered it to me here at the outpost. Dluhosh and his egocite handler are stranded on the planet. Trukk-9 is preparing a rescue mission. Dluhosh apparently has some legal concerns about the mission and his complaint is also attached. Maghosh-10.

Welter did not review the video or Dluhosh's ethics complaint. He forwarded it all right to Griffer-1's office.

The triumvirate of Ones was pleasantly surprised. They dropped what they were doing and set things up to review the material.

The President asked, "So Skooch, your project is bearing fruit?"

"Yes sir, apparently," replied Gro Skoo. "The

Dnooblian and the girl are stranded on Dirt. Trukk-9 is developing a rescue plan. The Dnooblian is having a hissy fit over what he thinks are irregularities in the process."

"Oh no," said the President.

Griffer-1 said, "Uh, well, we have to worry about the Dnooblian and the Eighteen, of course, and pray for their safety and all that. But if they are alive, they will be rescued. The fact of the matter is, Mister President…"

Griffer-1 paused.

And Gro Skoo bit. "Mister President, the way things are going, we may have no choice but to invite Dirt into the Galactic Pool. These little mess-ups can be helpful if you have the right perspective. The Dnooblian and the girl will return as heroes, sir."

"So… it's okay if I'm happy?" asked the President. "Eh, Skookers, I should be happy, right?"

"Of course, sir – that's what I advise."

They sat in the President's office and pulled up the video documents from Dluhosh. The two main folders were called 'The Good Stuff' and 'The Bad Stuff'.

"Hmm, there shouldn't be any bad stuff, or at least not much of it," said Gro Skoo.

"Heh, heh, maybe it really means naughty stuff," said the President.

"Let's see what it is then," said Griffer-1.

The 'Bad Stuff' folder contained dozens of video files with names like 'security forces', 'boat ramp assholes', 'garbage piles', 'wasted teens', 'suspicious labor', 'diseases', etcetera. Gro Skoo clicked play on the first file in the first folder. It began with a montage of war, famine, murder, industrial pollution, disease, terrorism, torture and various other abuses that the three men couldn't find names for. They watched in silence for a couple of minutes.

"Yikes! This isn't what we ordered! What the hell…?"

said Gro Skoo.

The President said, "These people are nuts! Look at 'em go! Did that guy just blow himself up? My god! I bet we can make these people do ANYTHING."

"Uh, yes Mister President, but this could be problematic for us in the voting process. I bet that damn Dnooblian is responsible," said Griffer-1. "Stop this – I don't think I need to see any more. Go ahead and open the 'good stuff' files."

Gro Skoo opened the other folder. It contained many sub-folders with titles that appeared to match the items on Trukk-9's special checklist.

"Well, this looks more like it. Start at the beginning," said Griffer-1.

They watched Numun's homecoming with the greetings and ritualized insults with Djiana.

"Well, this seems like good stuff, and it's shot in much higher quality than that bad stuff," said Griffer-1. "Go back to the bad stuff for a minute."

Gro Skoo opened the next 'bad stuff' file. The scene was pixilated footage of a laborer being lashed with a cane. There was a TV network logo superimposed on the bottom of the image.

"Try another file."

This one showed a stunt plane crashing into a crowd of spectators with icons at the bottom of the frame that said 'LIKE' and 'SHARE'.

"Try another."

This one was a series of pictures that appeared to show the same uniformed police officer casually spraying a chemical at all sorts of victims including helpless animals, children, and celebrities.

"That guy is brutal! I want him on my Discreet Service detail!" said the President.

"Okay, one more," said Griffer-1.

This clip showed a flaming oil spill with a news headline crawl on the bottom of the screen that said:

...SECRET PRISONS LOSE THEIR COMPETATIVE EDGE...
...DRONE PAINTBALL CAMP FOR FAMILY FUN...
..."I WAS IRRADIATED BY METER READERS"...

"Ah! This isn't official material that Trukk-9 or the PLUMBOB Dnooblian shot. This is all stuff they found on television or some computer network..." Griffer-1 paused.

Gro Skoo bit. "This bad stuff is obviously from unverifiable sources. I don't think we have to use it in the PLUMBOB process."

"Well, I personally don't want to verify how much of this horror we can and cannot use..." said Griffer-1.

Gro Skoo faithfully picked it up. "I think the solution is obvious. Let's start broadcasting the good stuff right now, with maybe a five minute delay for some Crickets to review the footage for unreliable material. We should also go ahead and send the diplomatic mission to Dirt – might as well get them moving in that direction. All you need to do is give the order Mister President."

"Okay, Bro Skoo, order given! Now, what about the Eighteen girl? Would it be appropriate for me to give her an award when she heroically returns?"

"Of course Mister President," replied Griffer-1. "That is exactly what's appropriate. That kind of thankfulness and forward thinking are two big reasons for the people's love of you, sir. You can hang the medal around her neck and everything. If you smile she might say something nice to you."

THE RESCUE MISSION RETURNS

Trukk-9 called out for The Big Voice Entity. "Okay, I think we are ready to go back to the lake."

In an instant, the cloaked Cruiser Duke Sukk-9 and cargo ship were in a geostationary orbit above their intended location. They flew on into the atmosphere toward the lake. It was night time.

"I've checked their computer network and I still don't see any credible news of aliens being captured," said Dee.

"Whew, that's good," said The Big Voice Entity.

"Maybe," replied Trukk-9. "Okay, crew, this is when we find out whether this is a rescue or a salvage mission. Colleence, this is the area where we last saw the ship."

"This is Colleence. I believe I have the ship on my scanner."

Trukk-9 was sweating and his voice shook. "Uh, Colleence, can you make out whether their door is open?"

"I can't tell, sir. The ship seems to be stuck in a big pile of rocks. I'm ready to grab the whole thing as soon as you want," said Colleence.

"Okay, Colleence, bring her up."

The super grabber beam surrounded the ship and rocks. Colleence let the water drain and then maneuvered the ship up into her cargo hold. Trukk-9 couldn't make out the ship's door in the dark.

"Sir, I have the ship. I'm going to take a look."

Trukk-9 held his breath.

The Big Voice Entity spoke. "Are we done yet?"

"Sir, there's no sign of the occupants. The door is wide open. The antimatter is contained and stable."

Trukk-9 and Dee gave each other a big Bearman hug. "Alright, that's a huge relief. But now the tricky part begins. Big Voice Entity, our people have abandoned the ship. They will eventually go to that house we sent you to because it's the closest place that we both know. But they aren't expecting us for at least another five months. Let's go check the house, but please be patient."

"Patient!? Don't tell ME to be patient. I've been monitoring this pixel for over eleven billion years. Just hurry, okay? I have some important things to attend to, and I'd like to be able to ignore this little incident."

"Sorry, we're doing our best, but this might take time," said Trukk-9.

"Get on with it," said The Big Voice Entity.

So the two ships headed to Jimmy Fresneaux's house.

***

"It looks like there's nobody home," said Dee as they hovered over Jimmy's house.

"If you can put me down there, I can ooze in and look for clues," said Stick.E. "I'll try to take the shape of the fisherman in case anyone is looking."

"Make it be," said Trukk-9.

They lowered Stick.E onto the front door step. He

slipped an appendage into the lock, opened it, and went inside.

Chickens clucked next door. Stick.E glanced around and didn't see any obvious signs of Fleence and Dluhosh having been there.

The next door neighbor's porch light came on.

Trukk-9's voice whispered through Stick.E's grabber beam snorkel. "Hey, I think the neighbor suspects something. Get out now, and re-lock the door. We will be ready for you on the porch."

The neighbor was already on the phone to the police. "I'd like to report a burglar at my neighbor's house."

"Do you see the burglar, sir?" asked the police dispatcher.

"Yes, through the window. He's still in the house."

"An officer will be there shortly. Can you describe the suspect, sir?"

"I was hoping you wouldn't ask... Um, it looks like my neighbor who lives there, but it's a ghost of him. He floated down from the sky and he glows blue and I can see through him."

"Sir, have you been drinking?" asked the dispatcher.

"Well, yes, a little, but I'm not drunk, I swear."

"I'm sure the officer would like to hear your explanation. Just sit tight."

The neighbor saw Stick.E in the shape of Jimmy step out onto the porch, fly up into the air a few feet, and disappear from the head down.

"I didn't see anything. I hope the neighbor didn't see anything either," said Stick.E once he was back on board.

The police arrived. Trukk-9 hit them with some egocite vapor and listened in for any clues.

"Sir? I hear a ghost has been terrorizing the neighborhood again," said the cop. "I also hear that you've been drinking, and I can smell it on you. Please step over here and wait while I look around."

The cop checked the door and found no sign of entry. He came back to the neighbor.

"Well, I don't see anything, sir."

"He flew up into the sky and disappeared. I saw it, I swear."

"Sir, I'm tempted to take you in for making a false report. Get yourself sobered up. If I hear from you again tonight I'll arrest you."

"But officer, I'm supposed to be watching Jimmy's house while he's away on vacation. Am I supposed to just let burglars ransack the place?"

"Yes. The flying ghosts have free reign over this town and everything in it," the smart-ass cop said, laughing as he departed.

The neighbor went back inside and sat at his window.

"Okay, Stick, go back in and see if you can find anything that might indicate where Jimmy went on vacation," said Trukk-9.

The neighbor watched as Jimmy's ghost rematerialized on the porch. He tried to snap a picture, but nothing showed up in the image. So he got one of his guns and came back to the window.

Stick.E flowed past the front window and looked around for any clues. He found Jimmy's desk and a color brochure of a cabin by a lake. He grabbed it and called back to the ship. "I have something. You're going to have to grab me as soon as I open the door. The neighbor is still there."

Dee had Stick.E safely encased when the neighbor shot. The bullet would have hit Stick.E right in Jimmy's temple. Instead, the bullet ricocheted off the grabber beam and shot out Jimmy's front window.

"More drunken gunplay. Too bad Dluhosh missed it,"

said Trukk-9 as he examined the brochure. "Anyway, how are we going to find this place?"

"Too bad my old Cousin Buzzy had to complete his life cycle so abruptly. He could probably read that brochure, and I bet he could find that lake on the computer. He... He was the best Cockroach ever," said Dee.

They flew back to where Colleence was waiting.

The Big Voice Entity spoke. "So what you got?"

"Just this brochure with a couple of pictures and some writing we can't read. Do you recognize this place?" asked Trukk-9.

The Big Voice Entity said, "No. But it's probably not too far from here. I can look around and recognize it. I'm going to go find an asteroid just in case though. You wait here."

JIMMY'S FISHING SHOW

It was another beautiful morning on the private vacation lake. Dluhosh was in the water looking for the next fish. Fleence, who was getting a nice tan, was wearing an actual paisley bikini, large white-framed sunglasses with 'Fresneauxlunettes' stenciled on the side, and a big red afro wig like the one she liked to imagine herself in for the guys. Michael and Gregory were in the other boat getting ready for the next scene.

The brochure had been correct – the lake was full of largemouth bass. Dluhosh was eating well, and was saving four more bass for lunch in Jimmy's livewell.

Jimmy was ecstatic. He was fantasizing that this show would make him the most famous bassin' man in the world. His picture would be on every magazine cover, his videos would be available for download, he could self-publish an ebook and maybe actually sell some, and it wasn't out of the question that he could be the subject of a video game one day.

The only glitch so far was when Fleence told Jimmy that he had made a very graceful cast, and he fell out of the boat.

She was more careful after that, but eventually she got up the courage to ask him what he imagined her wearing.

"I told you, I can't afford to lose concentration. I'm making a fishing show." He rubbed a plastic worm under his nose.

"It's okay Jimmy. I was just wondering what you see. Dluhosh used to keep me in a crate due to my hideousness."

"That's not a bad idea," said Jimmy. "Originally I had you wearing an old-timey schoolmarm outfit. But even that kept getting skimpier. So now I have you in a clown suit."

Dluhosh surfaced between the two boats and said, "Jimmy I have a nice one for you. What do you want to do this time?"

"How about we have it strike explosively on Fleence's Mega-Mouth Poppin' Minnow?"

"You got it," said Dluhosh.

Dluhosh disappeared for a second and popped up at about casting distance away. "This good?"

Gregory and Michael pulled up the anchor to reposition their boat for the shot. The noise woke up the kittens that lived in the under-seat storage compartment with their mama. The seven kittens had only just begun venturing out, and were now playing with Gregory's shoelaces.

"Hold on, these stupid cats are grabbing at my ankles. Hey, can we put them on shore now? You know? I'm allergic…"

"I thought Dluhosh made you not allergic," said Michael.

"Shhh! I just want to get rid of the damn things."

Michael said, "Jimmy, these cats could give Gregory an asthma attack if they scratch him. He could die. We need to unload them."

"Well Dluhosh has a nice fish right now!" yelled Jimmy.

He forgot that he was wearing a remote microphone.

"I can hear you, Jimmy! The microphone, the headphones – remember?" said Gregory for the umpteenth time. "I can't deal with these cats. Now some are biting at the battery wires."

"Can we bring them into our boat really quick?" Fleence asked Jimmy.

Gregory was on his way with the kittens before Jimmy could answer. They pulled up along-side Jimmy's boat to offload the kittens.

"But you can't have cats in a bass boat. There's hooks and plastic worms and stuff. They'll get their scent on my lures."

"Oh, Jimmy, I'm putting everything away. They'll be fine. OHH, they are SO cute," cooed Fleence.

"Okay, Dluhosh, we're ready!" yelled Michael.

Fleence cast her lure toward where Dluhosh was waiting with the big largemouth bass.

"Okay, ma'am, good cast. Now let your lure rest until all the ripples are gone. Then give it a twitch."

Fleence twitched the lure, which was the signal for Dluhosh to make the fish attack. He opened the fish's mouth with two tentacles and thrust it forward with another tentacle, while simultaneously shooting a blast of water at the fish with his siphon.

Fleence yelled, "FISH ON!" which sounded like something much different on the primitive recording equipment.

Jimmy yelled, "WOOOOOOOOOOOOOOOO! That's a nice one! Keep your rod up!"

Jimmy removed a kitten from the net and went for Fleence's fish. He imagined the bass to be a chicken, and netted it perfectly. He removed the hooks before lifting the netted fish into the boat. One of the kittens scampered over and took a swipe at the bass's snout. Another kitten jumped on the fish's waving pectoral fin. Michael zoomed in on the action. All of the kittens came over to play with the big fish, and Michael let the camera run until all the kittens had piled on.

"Okay, cut!" shouted Michael. "That was awesome, man! Bass fishing with a bikini model AND kittens – I think you have something special here Jimmy. Nice job!"

Dluhosh popped up next to the boat.

"Hey Dluhosh, do you want to save this fish?" asked Jimmy.

"Uh, no, those filthy animals were touching it. Let it go, please."

***

Trukk-9 gave the order to grab everyone.

The order was meant for Stick.E, but Trukk-9 didn't specify this. Stick.E would have individually plucked each castaway, had them probaluated, dosed them, dried them, and ordered them some snacks.

Colleence assumed the order was for her. She used the super grabber to scoop up the whole mess along with a sizable divot of lake bottom. She got everything and everyone, including the water, mud, boats, and cats, and placed them into her cargo hold.

"Oh, um, nice job Colleence – everyone safe and accounted for?" asked Trukk-9.

It took a few anxious moments to get an answer to that question.

Jimmy Fresneaux was the first to react. Like a true bass pro he placed the kitten-abused bass in the livewell before it was too late. Then he yelled, "NOOOOOOOOOOOOOON! Merde!" And that was all he had to say.

Fleence and Dluhosh remained respectfully quiet.

Michael asked, "Now what's going on?"

Gregory asked, "Who's messing with us now!?"

The Big Voice Entity figured that he should field these questions since he was probably the only one who heard them. His glowing, naked, headless, handless, footless, rotating, inadvertently exaggerated humanoid male avatar did appear unto them.

"Welcome aboard. Some of you are being rescued, and some of you are being thrown back. Someone else will determine who is a keeper. You are in the hold of a cargo ship. And, look over there – it's the ship that you recently crashed… Hold on a second."

Trukk-9 was now asking questions of The Big Voice Entity. The rescuees couldn't hear Trukk-9, but they heard The Big Voice Entity's answers.

"Yes, there are many more organisms than I expected, but I think the important ones are all fine. Hold on a second."

"Your colleague from Bukk-9 wanted to know if you are all okay."

"Yes," said Fleence. "Dluhosh? You okay?"

"Yes, comfortable and relieved."

"Yes everyone is fine," said The Big Voice Entity. "Now wipe the Earthlings' memories and put them back. And let's get out of here before anything else can go wrong."

"Well, we neglected to bring a memory wiper with us and I believe Dluhosh's is out of order. Let's take care of them later," replied Trukk-9.

"Oh, come on. We have to come back here again?" whined The Big Voice Entity. "Let's go get a memory wiper then. What coordinates?"

"Yeah, let me think about this. Bring my colleagues up

to speed while I consult with my crew. I'll let you know what we need to do next in a minute," said Trukk-9.

The Big Voice Entity turned his attention back to the cargo hold. "Okay, he'll be a few minutes. So where were we?"

"Who are you?!" yelled everyone.

The Big Voice Entity answered. "I guess I should introduce myself, sorry. I'm responsible for the research on this planet. I found that you aliens had infested Earth, and I'm trying to clean things up. My real name is ULBTX-123, which is apparently too complicated for you, so you can call me The Big Voice Entity like everyone else."

Dluhosh asked, "Research?"

"Oh yes, most of the life in this sector is being experimentally manipulated. You four Earthlings are part of an experiment to test whether highly variable foot size can drive humanoids to the greatness necessary to create my kind."

"Foot size?" asked Gregory.

"Yes, it's been an extremely interesting experiment too. You have made me perhaps the most famous Pixel Person in the history of the Universe. I gave the population of humanoids on Earth a wide variety of foot sizes. You've been a perfect model of reckless, self-absorbed greatness ever since."

"Foot size? Are you kidding?" said Gregory.

"Sure, haven't you noticed the differences? Until about six thousand years ago, your adult feet were all size eight-and-a-half. I vacuumed up a small pre-treatment sample of Earthlings and put them on a similar planet to serve as a control group. Then I genetically reprogrammed the remaining population on Earth for a much larger variation in foot size. This is considered to be an evolutionarily plausible trait."

"Wait, you took a group of Earthlings where?" asked Fleence.

"The inhabitants call the planet Bounty."

"That's where I'm originally from! So I really am an Earthling!"

"Hey, how did you get here?" asked The Big Voice Entity.

"Good question. My ancestors were stolen from Bounty many generations ago, and the location of the planet is no longer known – some say the planet was destroyed."

"Oh, you're one of THEM! A Stolen One… It really is a small galaxy. No, the planet hasn't been destroyed, and, yes, you were taken by the horrible humanoids from the planet they call One. I punished them by shrinking their feet, and I threatened to give them hooves and to rain asteroids upon them if they disturbed my control group again. Sorry I let that happen."

"But how come we can't go back to Bounty? We don't have any men in our population. We are all female clones. And you know what? It's those same horrible small-footed humanoids from Planet One that are giving you this trouble with Earth."

"Extraordinary! Well, Bounty is still a control group, so it's off limits. By the way, everyone there is still a perfect size eight-and-a-half. Sorry."

"Um, well, I'm a nine-and-a-half," said Fleence. "Shouldn't I be eight-and-a-half too if I'm a clone?"

"You measured wrong. But maybe these three Earthling males will agree to move in with you. They can stay with you on your planet if they want, as long as everyone stays away from Earth forever. I'm sure these post-treatment Earth fellows are much more dynamic than Bounty males anyway."

"Well, okay, um, I see your point. But there would be

thousands of us and only three men," said Fleence.

"Clone a bunch of them," said The Big Voice Entity.

"So how come if you are so mighty you don't have a head or feet yourself?" asked Gregory.

"First of all, the avatar you see rotating before you only represents me – gives you something to address. I myself am but one dark matter pixel in The Great Hologram. The reason that The Great Hologram is incomplete is that the Universe isn't big enough to hold it yet. After about another two billion years or so the Universe will have expanded to accommodate us from head to finger to toe. Pixel People are continuously added to the extremities. I was born eleven billion years ago. The expansion of this particular universe – the Big Belly Button Bang – began 13.75 billion years ago."

Michael said, "I've always wondered what the Universe was expanding into."

The Big Voice Entity replied, "It's expanding into the vacuum left by contracting neighboring universes, duh."

"Duh!? What do you mean 'duh'?!" asked Gregory.

"Oh, cool it… Whatever you heard is probably a glitch in your autotranslator, little Earthling."

Trukk-9 interrupted The Big Voice Entity. "Um, we should probably go back to Chuffed-18 first. I think Fleence's mother can help us with a plan to persuade the administration on Planet One to leave Earth alone for you."

The Big Voice Entity replied, "Since I've had to deal with this Planet One before, I'm thinking about hitting them with a big asteroid this time."

"No, no, don't do that. We have some ideas. Let's go to Chuffed-18 and see Kyleence first," said Trukk-9.

The two ships found themselves in orbit above Chuffed-18. It was as if Earth and Chuffed-18 had switched places. Another space/time wrinkle was added to the mess.

The rescuees slogged through the mud to make their way up to the bridge with Colleence-18. Fleence ordered a new uniform from Colleence's duplicator and went to clean up.

When she returned in her normal canvass fatigues and boots, Gregory and Michael thought she was still in a bikini with the afro wig. Michael thought her legs were still muddy. And for Jimmy, Fleence's clown suit had become more form-fitting and low cut, and her big floppy shoes were now high-heeled.

As before, an automated radio voice contacted the ships when they arrived. "To all approaching vessels, if you are here to have your praises sung, please proceed to Holding Terminal Seven. There is currently a twenty-nine-day waiting list."

"Oh, come on…" said Trukk-9. "Alright people, it's going to be a few minutes. Everyone should get their stuff together. We all need to meet with Fleence's mother."

"How did we get here?" asked Dluhosh.

"Oh, yeah, that's slick, huh? I simply bend the space within my pixel to be where I am. My quantum thingularity consciousness doesn't actually move – the space around it does."

"Say, do you know anything about how MY ancestors left Earth originally – sixty-six million years ago?"

The Big Voice Entity regarded Dluhosh. "Hey, you're a cephalopod! Oh yeah, that's a very interesting story. Let's see… When I first started working on Earth I smashed an asteroid into it to put down the dinosaurs. I didn't think the primitive mammals could give rise to a humanoid form with the dinosaurs around. I took some dinosaurs to one other planet, and I also took many kinds of your ancestors and put them on your planet. Your shells and colors are very pleasing. I always thought your kind might have what it took for sapience. That was my first week working on

Earth. It was exactly 66,037,999 years ago. Ah, the memories..."

"Thanks! You just answered the foremost question of my people. And we appreciate the accuracy of the date – it's something we've worked very hard to pin down. We were pretty close. Um, this might be silly, but is it possible to give the date with even more accuracy?"

"You mean like the number of days and hours?"

"Oh, yes please! That would be wonderful." The accuracy was giving Dluhosh the same feeling that an Earthling gets when hearing its favorite song, and he turned blue.

"Well, that IS silly. Do you remember off the top of your head how many days ago you were born? I do recall that it was first thing on a Monday morning though."

"Are you trying to be funny?" asked Gregory, but he was cut off without an answer when Trukk-9 came back over the intercom.

"Okay, people, I've made contact with the surface. Let's meet at Kyleence's landing pad and disembark. Then, Colleence, Kyleence said to take the boats and all the mud and stuff to her lake, and to take Dluhosh's ship to the mechanic. Thanks for all of your help."

The two ships landed on the pad together. Their main doors opened and all the occupants, including the kittens and some crawdads, piled out to greet Fleence's mother.

"Ohhh! Real kittens!" said Dee. "Oh, look how CUTE they are! Can I keep them, Fleence? Can I please?"

"Of course you can, Dee. I thought of you when I first saw them." Then Fleence ran to her mother.

Kyleence said, "Are you okay, honey? I've been so worried."

"Yes, Mother, I'm fine. I have been, as they say, in the tentacles of this Magnificent Bull Dnooblian. Mother, meet

Dluhosh-10."

"Nice to meet you," said Dluhosh, still bewildered and very curious about what was going on.

"And these are the best Earthlings in the world. They rescued me and Dluhosh and took really good care of us. Mother, meet Michael, Gregory, and Jimmy." Fleence whispered something into her mother's ear.

"Nice to meet you," they all said.

Fleence and her mother were almost identical. Kyleence looked somewhat older, and, as Gregory quickly learned, she hadn't undergone the telepathic wardrobe enhancement.

Everyone gathered around. The kittens took to Dee, and all seven of them were now crawling around on his head and shoulders. The mama cat followed him too.

Then The Big Voice Entity's avatar appeared.

"Oh, sorry, I never introduced our friend The Big Voice Entity," said Trukk-9. "He's the one helping us get around so fast."

"Pleased to meet you all," said The Big Voice Entity. "I'd like to explain why I appear with this anatomy and without a head, etcetera, but we are in a hurry here."

Kyleence said, "Well, you may not have a head, but it's obvious where you keep your brain."

The Big Voice Entity didn't get it.

Dee got it though. He had to go lock himself in The Duke's cargo hold for a couple of minutes. When a Bearman hears the funniest thing he's ever heard in his life, it's best for him not to be in mixed-species company.

"Anything happen since this morning?" asked Trukk-9.

"Yes, you won't believe it," said Kyleence. "Alright, first I'm going to flood this deck with calming agent. We have to move fast, and, honestly, the Earthlings in the bad-stuff videos you gave me seem... Well, they seem very excitable.

Sorry, sweeties, no offense – I just want to make sure you are calm for the moment."

"No offense taken," said Gregory. "I think the calming agent is a good idea. We Earthlings are pretty unpredictable, and we have a very high tolerance to your calming agent."

"Anyway," said Kyleence, "those clowns are already broadcasting the voter video. They interrupted regularly scheduled programming with a big announcement saying something like 'the heroic Trukk-9 presents this profile of your new and exciting potential neighbor.' Dluhosh-10's ethics complaint came out this morning too. But the news channel is calling him a disgruntled bureaucrat with an over active imagination and an exaggerated sense of self importance. I think that's how they put it."

"So they must be showing only the good stuff about Earth in the video program, huh?" asked Dluhosh.

"Yes, and it sure makes the Earthlings look lovable and fun – like churdles on trampolines," Kyleence said.

"Well, ma'am, we are, aren't we?" asked Jimmy.

"You appear to be the star of the show, Jimmy Fresneaux. You are being used to represent the average Earthling. Girls all over Chuffed-18 are putting up posters of you in their bedrooms."

"Jimmy's much better than average, Mother," noted Fleence.

"Yes, I can see that, honey. In fact all three of you appear to be better than average," Kyleence said, as she took an extra-long look at Gregory.

All three men dropped to their knees in ecstasy.

Kyleence watched Gregory writhe. She'd never witnessed such a fine balance of scruff and symmetry.

"Okay, people, we need a plan. The Big Voice Entity is insisting that we prevent this vote and stay away from Earth for good. Ideas?" asked Trukk-9.

Kyleence had an idea. "Well, I can call the President and set up a meeting."

"Really?" asked Trukk-9. "You can call him up?"

"Sure, I'm richer than that sniveling punk. I'm pretty sure I can make him do whatever I want. The trouble isn't him though, of course. Griffer-1 needs to be convinced – and that dough-boy advisor of his too. But I think I can get us a meeting."

"Great. Okay, then what?" asked Trukk-9.

Fleence took her mother aside and told her something.

"Fleence reminded me of a particular vulnerability of the Ones. Hmm… Go ahead, honey. Tell them what you think."

Fleence said, "I'm thinking a three-pronged approach is what we need. So first we have Dluhosh confront them with his ethics complaint."

"Yes," said Kyleence, "this should get the President worrying. I bet the knucklehead doesn't know the complaint exists, let alone understand what it means."

"The second prong," said Fleence, "is my data and the bad-stuff video that Trukk-9 shot. They don't know we have a copy of all that video, so we might be able to threaten them with legal action on that. If a court found that they intentionally omitted that footage, then they could face conspiracy charges. I think that will get their attention."

"I don't think The Big Voice Entity is going to settle for legal action though. He wants a done deal," said Trukk-9.

"Right, then we hit them with the third prong," said Kyleence. "Given their particular anatomical vulnerability, they will be terrified of Earthlings. I think that Michael, Gregory, and Jimmy, with certain attributes emphasized, can intimidate the President into signing a decree on the spot."

"How are we gonna do that?" asked Gregory. "Don't they have Secret Service guys and stuff?"

"Oh, they might have some thugs around, but Fleence and I can disable them, and Dluhosh can keep them at bay if worse comes to worse, can't you honey?" asked Kyleence.

"Yes, but I'd have to be very gentle with them."

"Alright, so what are we supposed to do?" asked Gregory.

"Okay, the President's office has a large window overlooking the parade grounds. Stick.E can easily shove you through the glass with his grabber beams, can't you sweetheart?" asked Kyleence.

"Yes, ma'am," said Stick.E. "No problem. Don't worry guys – you'll be totally encased in the grabber beam field. You'll bust right through the window without feeling it."

"Right," said Kyleence, "then each of you grab one of the three puffy and/or stupid looking guys in the room, and act crazed and dangerous and make lots of threats. Do you know any good insults?"

"HOOOEEEE!" yelled Dee. "Ma'am, these are Earthlings! Oh boy – they are THE MOST insulting fellas ever! You should hear them when they get mad. They have this one insult where a guy will tell another guy to take something – could be anything – could be a whole car, or food, or even an animal! And they will tell the other guy to take that thing and sho-"

It was Stick.E's turn to interrupt Dee. "Ma'am, you should know that Earthlings also growl."

"Really? How interesting..." Kyleence took another look at Gregory. "I bet you can growl good, can't you darling? Let's hear what you can do. I'm nice to good growlers."

"Grrrr..."

"Oh, Grrrregory, give us another."

Gregory started another sheepish growl and Kyleence interrupted with a sultry, "Oh Scruffy, that's so beautiful…"

"Grr-EEEE!" said Gregory, falling to the fetal position.

"Mother! That's not fair!"

"Oh, honey, he doesn't mind."

Kyleence continued. "Anyway guys, you must really do it up good. Be threatening – bare your teeth, foam, growl, stomp, emit any noxious odors that you may possess… I'll leave it to you to invent the insults. The autotranslator might miss some of the subtleties, but it shouldn't matter. Try not to actually hurt them though. Then once we have them cowering, we issue our demands and force them to sign a decree."

"Really? They'll be scared of us? I mean, well, we aren't exactly the toughest looking guys," said Michael.

"I think I have just what you need. You can wear these solid gold flip-flops. The flip-flops will highlight your most intimidating feature. Plus the sheer opulence of golden flip-flops will appeal to the Ones' feelings of wealth inadequacy. That should make you look threatening enough as long as you really grrrr it up good," said Kyleence.

RAID ON PLANET ONE

The President sat at his desk looking out the window wondering what a President should be doing right then. His phone rang. He picked it up, happy for the distraction. His secretary put the caller through.

"President Gren Wee-1?" said a very sexy-sounding voice on the other end. "This is Kyleence-18. I have a question regarding some Presidential praise singing."

"Ah, oh boy... I, uh, hope I can I help you with something," replied the President, making a valiant attempt to deepen his voice.

"Of course you can, sugar. Here's how. I just need a meeting in your office with Griffer-1 and that dewlapped advisor of yours. That's all sugar. If you can do that for me, you'd certainly be worthy of praise."

"When?" asked the President, as he clawed at his ear. "Right now?"

"Well, sure sweetie, now would be good. Are the other two fellows already there?"

"Well, no, I forgot about them. I'll see what I can do, and then can I call you back?"

"Sounds great, Mister President. I'll have a couple of associates with me. I'll be waiting for your invitation. Goodbye." And she hung up.

The President was very excited. He called his Vice President. "Griffer, this is the President. Please come to my office. It's urgent."

"Uh, Mister President, Skoo and I are in the middle of a meeting. Can it wait?"

"No!" he said, sounding uncharacteristically presidential. "Both of you drop whatever you are doing and meet me in my office immediately."

"Sir, may I ask what it's about?"

The President, realizing that he didn't know what it was about, said, "It doesn't matter what it's about. I'm the President and that's all you need to know." Then he strutted around his office like he imagined Rim Ram-1 would do before an historic decision.

***

Kyleence gave the group an update. "The fool agreed to a meeting without asking what it's about. We're just waiting for a call. He wants to do it right away, so let's get everything together."

"Okay," said Trukk-9, "Kyleence, Fleence, Dluhosh, and I will take Kyleence's ship. Stick.E and Dee will pilot my ship behind us with Michael, Gregory, and Jimmy aboard. Let's go ahead and have The Big Voice Entity put us in orbit around Planet One. Dee, you stay cloaked the whole time. Everybody load up and get ready to leave."

Dee and the kitties climbed into the pilot's seat. Stick.E helped the Earthlings into their flight suits.

Michael said to Gregory, "Hey man, I just need to hear you say it – we aren't dreaming this, right? This is actually happening… right?"

"I'm with you. This is the real deal. I have a threatening speech ready too."

"Wow, are you going to use the F-word, or what?"

"Yes, I'm going to try. Do you think I should call them 'dude' too?"

"Yes, definitely. How about calling them bitches?"

"Well, I've never been comfortable with that one. Look, we just need to be menacing. You can be a menace. Visualize it like that guy on TV is always talking about. Be a menace like only a huge-footed Earthling like you can be. Look at you. Seriously, foam at the mouth. We can do this."

"I have an idea," said Michael. "This Big Voice Entity guy claims to be able to hurl meteors. Wouldn't it be cool if he could throw a near-miss down on these assholes? I bet he could make an apocalyptic-looking fireball, and we could act like it's us that did it."

"I heard that," said The Big Voice Entity, his rotating avatar appearing before Michael and Gregory. "And I like it. I've thrown some asteroid warnings here before, I believe. Anyway, yeah, I can hit the atmosphere with a glancing blow – make a nice big fireball for you. Just give me the signal. I'll be right back with an asteroid. Okay, I'm back with an asteroid."

Trukk-9 broke in. "Big Voice Entity, we are ready."

Planet One appeared outside the window.

"We're waiting on the President's call," said Kyleence.

Fleence finally had a chance to speak in private with her mother. "Mom, I just found out that we are originally from Earth!"

"What?!"

"Yes, Ma, The Big Voice Entity said that we were part of an experiment – a control group. We were taken from

Earth and placed on Bounty six-thousand years ago. They did an experiment on the Earthlings' feet and made them different from Bountyans. But genetically we are Earthlings, Ma."

Kyleence gasped. "Get back to me on this, will you please, darling. This is worth thinking about."

"Hey everybody," said The Big Voice Entity. "There's something else. The Earthlings still need to have their memories wiped before I put them back on Earth. Let's not forget that again."

Dluhosh responded. "Sure, I'll have a memory wiper once I get my ship fixed. I can take them back. No problem. You can verify the wipe too."

"Or we can save the trip," replied The Big Voice Entity. "I told the Earthlings that they could stay here as long as they promise to never go back to Earth. Losing them won't hurt anything with my project. I foresee no greatness coming from them."

Kyleence's phone rang. "Hello? Yes Mister President, I understand. Tell them they'll find out when we arrive... There are four of us... Tell us where to land, sir. Thank you."

Kyleence hung up and said, "Alright, let's get down there. Follow us, Dee. I'll point out the President's office window before we land. Hover cloaked outside until I give you an OK sign. Michael, Gregory, and Jimmy – don't worry about over doing it. I foresee greatness."

***

Kyleence landed her ship on the President's landing pad. A detail of four Discrete Service guys escorted them to the President's office. On the way, Fleence and Kyleence whispered nice things into the men's ears. Only three of the four men actually fell over, but they were all compromised.

Kyleence took charge as soon as they entered the President's office. She even overwhelmed Griffer-1 with her command style.

"Gentlemen," she began, "we have a mutual problem that we need to work out together. I'm sure you recognize Trukk-9. And this is my daughter Fleence-18, a certified egocite handler. And this is my Dnooblian friend, Dluhosh-10. I think you know who they are too. Never mind how they got here. Dluhosh-10 would like to say a few words. Dluhosh?"

Dluhosh explained his ethics complaint as clearly as he could. The President only understood enough to start looking back and forth between his vice president and his advisor.

But Gro Skoo responded, predictably, by saying, "We reviewed the video material and determined that much of it was unusable due to it being from unverifiable sources. We used all of the verifiable content in the voting broadcast."

Trukk-9 spoke next. "Are you sure you looked at ALL of the video, gentlemen? Mixed in with the bad stuff were a couple of my clips that confirmed present-day slavery – which would automatically disqualify Earth. Did you not see these?"

Griffer-1 and Gro Skoo-1 both stared at Trukk-9 in silence. The President noticed this and started working his ear over.

Trukk-9 continued. "What do you say, gentlemen – are you ready to give up on this scheme of yours? Could save you from some embarrassment perhaps...? Here, would you like to view the clips?"

Kyleence sensed that she had the three Ones on the ropes. It was time for the knockout punch. She gave the signal to Dee.

The window crashed in and the three Earthlings stood in the office wearing their golden flip-flops.

Vice President Griffer-1, with cat-like reflexes, pushed a button under the President's desk – a button that even the President didn't know about.

Six more Discrete Service guys burst into the room through a hidden panel. They drew their weapons and tried to determine who they should shoot first.

Dluhosh did not think about what he did. His body displayed ocellated electric green spots and his skin sprouted thorn-like papillae. He reared up to his full traffic-cone height.

In an instant, all ten Discrete Service guy were disarmed and pinned to the floor with a tentacle around the neck.

Fleence and Kyleence ran around the room saying "You're handsome. You're handsome. You're handsome." to each of the soldiers and their wild thrashing became harmless quivering.

Michael went for the President, who laid his ears back and hissed. Gregory went for Griffer, who arched his back and sprung his claws. And Jimmy went for Gro Skoo, who put his tail between his legs and screamed.

Michael grabbed the President by the knot of his tie and pinned him against the wall. Jimmy saw Michael's effective move and tried to grab Gro Skoo by the knot too, but was unable to find it under a hanging mass of fat. So he switched tactics and grabbed Gro Skoo by the lower lip – holding him out at arm's length like he was posing for a picture with a big largemouth bass.

Gregory pinned Griffer-1 against the wall with nothing more than his foot presence, and then he struck with his speech.

"Dude!" he yelled, with a menacing finger pointed at

Griffer-1's button nose. "Who the fuck do you think you are?! We are fucking EARTHLINGS, dude! What are you thinking? DO NOT fuck with us, or we will fuck you up bad! Do you know what happened to the last piece-of-shit aliens that fucked with us? Huh!? Does the word 'hooves' mean anything to you, dumb-ass?!"

Vice President Wulu Griffer-1 couldn't quite work out what the crazed maniac was saying. He could have sworn that the guy said, "Do not have sex with us, or we will have worse sex with you." It didn't really matter one way or the other though. The galactic autotranslator got the word 'hooves', and that was plenty.

"I want you to have a look at your fate if you continue to mess with us – look to the window!"

Everyone looked out through the broken window. Gregory snapped his fingers.

A giant fireball with a blood-red tail shot through the sky.

Gregory said, "There goes Comrade Larry, I hope he survives again."

The President's tongue was hanging out, but he managed to say, "You mean there's a guy on that meteor!? Like, you mean he's flying that thing!?"

Gregory answered the question. "Yeah, dude, Comrade Larry is totally into it. His aim is improving too. I'm sure he'll be fine. He always is."

"Okay, okay, what do you want?" gasped the President. "Just leave us alone. Oh please let me go…"

"Okay, tell him what you want before I accidentally give him a rash," said Michael. He released his grip on the President's tie.

Kyleence dictated the decree as Gro Skoo's shaking sausage fingers wrote it out. The writing was made more difficult because Jimmy still had hold of Gro Skoo's lip.

"And, add to that," said Gregory, "You shall open the airwaves. I hear you jerks only have four TV channels of nothing but propaganda! I want five-hundred channels, minimum. And I want more funding for science and art in schools, and fishing shows! Write it down and don't make me come back here again! Bitches!"

The President caught his breath and summoned all his inner strength. "I'll sign anything you want, I'll give any order you want, but I get some time in my antechamber with a conversation hostess first."

Now Michael grabbed the President by the lapels and shouted into his face, "You can take your antechamber and sho-"

Kyleence interrupted. "No, that's alright, Michael. I promised him that he was worthy of praise if he would help us."

Michael dropped the President, who fell to his knees staring right at Michael's big gold-bearing feet.

"He hasn't exactly been helpful yet. This decree still hasn't been signed," said Michael.

"No, no, please," purred the President. "If I sign that decree, then you don't need me anymore and I might not get…" The President could only point at Fleence.

"Give us something useful NOW, you big baby!" said Michael.

"Okay, okay…"

Griffer-1 and Gro Skoo-1 shared a worried glance.

"Okay, here's something you don't know. We've already sent the invasion ship to your planet. It left this morning." The President looked in terror at Griffer-1.

"Call it back now!" demanded Michael.

"But, but…" The President pointed at Fleence.

"Mother, I'll handle this little chore. Come with me, Mister President. This won't take long."

The two of them disappeared into the antechamber. Fleence told the President to sit down. The President imagined her dressed in a naughty sailor suit with a mini captain's hat on top of a tabby bouffant hairdo.

Fleence began her praise singing without looking down at the President.

"Oh, Mister President, so elite
I don't see how you compete
Everything about you is petite
Especially your little feet

Oh, little man with wobbly stance
I can see it at a glance
You do not swing when you dance
You are a goat with a clumsy prance.

Oh, politician with teeth so shiny
With mind so small and toes so tiny
When you speak it sounds so whiny
Don't you wish you could kiss my heiny?"

The President hit his head on the corner of his desk as he flopped around.

They came back into the room after a few seconds and the President signed the decree.

"Now call off that ship!" ordered Michael.

"Okay, calm down, I'm doing it," said the President. He pushed the call button on his desk.

Kyleence said, "Jimmy, honey, I think you can release your lip-grip on that poor man now."

Jimmy dropped Gro Skoo.

"Hello, dispatch? This is the President. I need you to call off a mission that left this morning."

"Yes sir, we have had one-hundred and... doot doot... twenty-three ships leave on missions today. I have a list on my computer right here. Which one would you like me to call back, sir?"

"Gosh, that's a lot of missions," said the President.

"Yes sir, we are the busiest port in the galaxy," said the proud insectoid dispatcher.

"We really have that many places to invade?" asked the President.

Griffer-1 rolled his eyes and Gregory unconsciously made a very rumbly and frightening growl.

"Oh that is a good one sir! Very funny, sir. No, most of them are cargo transfers and a couple of mining crews — things like that, sir," replied the dispatcher.

"I need to stop the one that is heading to a planet called... Is it Dirt?" said the President.

"Earth!" said Gregory.

"Compost," said the President.

"Let us see sir... doot doot... Okay, here we go, a ship left for the planet Soil this morning. Its mission purpose is marked as classified, sir."

"That's it. Call it off, please," ordered the President.

"Hey, wait a second," said Gregory. "It's Earth, not Peat, you idiot. How do we know it's the same place?"

"Oh, yeah, right, uh... dispatcher, do you have any ships going to a planet Humus, or maybe a planet Loam?" asked the President.

"Let us see... doot doot... Here we go — I have a churdle cruiser taking one-hundred-thousand head to pasture on the ghost planet Tillage, sir."

Gregory said, "Dude, just have the dispatcher put you through directly to that classified mission."

"Dispatcher, can you put me directly through to the classified mission to Soil, please?" asked the President.

"Oh, you mean Earth, sir?"

"Yes, yes, that's the one. Please put me through."

The ship's Cricket captain replied, "This is Captain O'Riqnid-3, but if you have trouble with insectoid names, you can call me Captain Riqi, go ahead."

"Yes, Captain Riqi, this is President Gren Wee-1 – please cancel your mission and return home."

"What? Come on... is this a hoax? How do I know you are really the President?"

"Don't I sound like the President?"

"Well, sure, but many people do a good impersonation of the President. I have a Dung Beetle navigator here that does a great one. So, okay, if you really are the President, tell us one of your famous jokes."

The President was stuck for a joke, so he looked around his office and said, "Heh, heh, uh, a Dnooblian, two conversation hostesses, and three big-footed humanoids walk into a bar..."

"HAHAHA! Oh, that is brilliant, sir! Go ahead," said Captain Riqi.

The President had no punch line, of course, so he said, "Enough! I'm the President! Stop your mission and come home!"

"Yes, sir! Mission aborted, sir!"

"Wait," said Dluhosh. "Verify their target, just to be sure."

"Right... Captain Riqi, please verify the target called Mount Rushmore."

Captain Riqi said, "Yes sir, our targets are classified information, sir. So I need to have my first officer concur that I can share it with you. Sorry, just a minute, sir, it is simply our protocol, sir."

The Captain put the line on hold and asked his navigator, "Hey, do we have a Continue-To-Hurry

Mountain on the list?"

"Heh, heh, let me see…" replied the Dung Beetle. "Yep, we are supposed to mine the scrap rare-earth elements from an old building that was once called 'Quicker Service Stadium'. I bet that is it."

The Captain replied to the President, "Sir, yes, I am able to confirm that target."

"Good. Turn around. Thank you for your trouble."

SAY GOODBYE

Once everyone was back safely on their ships, The Big Voice Entity took them right back to Kyleence's landing pad and said, "Well, that seemed to work out pretty well. How did you like the meteor, huh? I added the red tail using a little trick I invented myself. I was thinking of publishing a paper on it."

"Yeah, that was really cool, you know. How about if you don't wipe our memories then?" asked Gregory. "I want to be able to tell my kids one day about how awesome you and your meteor were."

"I'm sorry, but if you are going back to Earth, no. Do you realize what kind of trouble I could get in? Sorry, but no."

Dee hugged Jimmy and said, "Jimmy, old buddy! You won me five bucks when you grabbed that fat guy by the lip!"

The Big Voice Entity said, "Come on – let's get the Earthlings back to Earth now."

"Hold on a minute, buster. You have to let us say our goodbyes first," said Kyleence as she stood on the landing pad holding hands with Trukk-9.

Fleence whispered in Jimmy's ear, "Now if you touch me, I won't kick your teeth out…" And Jimmy dressed her in a low cut bass fishing sponsorship jersey with matching satin hot pants and black rubber hip waders.

The Big Voice Entity Spoke. "You know, like I said, I don't care if you Earthlings want to stay here. It would save me some time if you do. No one will know if you stay behind. It won't mess up any of my experiments as long as you promise to stay away from Earth and Bounty. You can keep your memories too. I can leave right now."

"My mother and father would freak out. Are you kidding? And my dog is in the kennel," said Gregory.

"Yeah, man, my folks too. Plus my natural history collection is there," said Michael.

Jimmy turned to Kyleence. "Um, if it's okay with you ma'am, I think I'm going to stay behind. I know it probably breaks all kinds of cosmic rules, but, I mean, well… My boat and tackle are here already. You can clone plastic worms, right?"

"Yes, of course, dumpling," said Kyleence.

"And if I'm already popular on television, then that Presidential Decree means that I can probably get my own fishing show – maybe a whole fishing channel… I even have some live largemouth bass to get started with – and I think the small one is a male. Plus, all of a sudden, I have a girlfriend who understands my lifestyle and has a mother with a private lake."

Everyone was nodding.

Jimmy continued. "It makes as much sense as anything… And now I can look forward to going back to speakeengs weed my raygyoolar ahxahnt *encore, quoi*. Pleess call me Jacques, *madam*. I ahdmeets dat I am *Québécois* – not *un* Cajun *de* Louisiana."

"Jimmy, Jimmy... Just go ahead and speak full-on French if that's what that is, you know? These aliens have no idea what you're talking about. The autotranslator, remember? It all sounds the same to them," said Gregory.

"Oh yeah... Thanks!"

Kyleence said, "Yes, well, Jacques, you'd be most welcome to stay. Please, please, do. But I need to correct something you said. You actually have about fifty-thousand girlfriends who understand you. You can't be selfish with your seed here. There are many women who would like to have the first blue-eyed baby."

Jimmy glanced around the landing area and noticed that a dozen technicians from several clone lineages had stopped what they were doing and were staring at him. The young woman who was monitoring the landing pad's life support system detected a mass medical emergency and got up to sound the alarm. But then she saw Jimmy too and recognized the symptoms.

"Um, actually," said Gregory, "the first generation won't produce any babies with blue eyes. The blue-eye allele is recessive, so you have to receive a copy of the blue-eye allele from BOTH parents to get blue eyes. For example, I have brown eyes, but my dad has blue eyes, so I have one copy of the blue-eye gene, but my brown-eye copy dominates. If your blue-eye allele is extinct, all of your first generation babies will be heterozygous and have brown eyes until that generation breeds together and produces a homozygous baby with two copies of the blue-eye gene. But then you might have inbreeding problems with other deleterious recessive gen-"

Kyleence interrupted. "Um, very well explained, Gregory. So you'll donate some genetic diversity before you leave...?"

"My mom has blue eyes too," said Michael.

"Yes, you too, Michael. So you'll both donate?" asked Kyleence.

"Um, well…" both guys said while shuffling their golden flip-flopped heroic feet.

"Oh, come on," said The Big Voice Entity, "can't we get going now, please?"

"Why are you always in such a hurry, you big sod?" asked Kyleence. "This will only take a minute. Fleence, get a couple of techs to help the boys, and have them bring some test tubes."

Then once that business was done, Fleence hugged Michael and Gregory, and said her goodbyes.

Stick.E did Gregory and Michael the honor of attempting to form the shape of each of them in turn. He made Michael with his teeth too straight and made Gregory too tall. But otherwise the likenesses were very accurate.

Trukk-9 gave a little speech. "Michael and Gregory, though you will not remember any of this, I want you to know that you will always be remembered here. I truly respect the profound and enormous deeds that you have accomplished. And I like you very much. I will make a movie about your heroic adventures. Goodbye, my friends."

Trukk-9 took Dluhosh aside and said, "We will still need to talk about a weasel film. And thank you, Dluhosh, for being a good man and for not quartering me." Trukk-9 winked at Dluhosh with his green eye.

"Come on, let's get going people," said The Big Voice Entity.

Dluhosh said, "I'm still waiting for my ship to be repaired."

Kyleence made a call. "Is the ship that Colleence brought in fixed yet? Uh huh… Uh, huh… Bring it to my landing pad then. Thank you."

Dluhosh's ship arrived, and he climbed in. He took a look around. There was a card in a pink envelope on his command chair. The card displayed a photograph of the cleaning technician, who looked just like Fleence. And in Dnooblian script it said, "My name is Steence-18 and I have had the pleasure of cleaning your command deck. I hope you find it to your satisfaction."

The card was perfumed, but the rest of the ship smelled musty – as if it were still damp. Everything seemed to be in order though. Dluhosh did a full pre-flight check.

The ship had a new cloaking device. The antimatter engine ran at a previously unattained efficiency, and the fuel tank had been topped off. All of the controls were engaged and the electronics hummed normally. The repaired door opened and closed smoothly over several repetitions. The memory wiper and upgraded grabber beams seemed functional. The viewing dome was now variable tint. His ship had doubled in value.

His personal effects were somewhat misplaced around his quarters, but everything, including his Dnooblian fossils, and Gregory's special fossil, was there. There was another pink envelope on his bed. The Dnooblian Golden Rule poster was hung upside-down. He quietly ordered a Dnooblian trout fillet from the duplicator and popped it down before anyone noticed. It was as good as usual.

Fleence's egocite bag and her mostly undamaged sketchbook and pen were on her bridge chair, and she had a new mattress. Only the feather from Pip-The-Blue was missing.

Dluhosh reached out with a tentacle and tapped Fleence on the shoulder without injuring her.

"Fleence! Check it out!" Dluhosh spread his web out to its full width and height. He looked like a roughened brick-red home movie screen. Then he turned to a deep-sea blue, and coral heads and waving gorgonian fans materialized against this background. Sea jellies and colorful tropical fish sprang up from behind the reef and swam back and forth across Dluhosh's body.

Dee thought it was the coolest thing he'd ever seen, and he laughed like a cub being tickled by its mama.

Then the reef scene faded from Dluhosh's skin. He replaced it with an arrangement of black Dnooblian script set against a pure white background. No one but Dluhosh could read it, of course.

So Dluhosh interpreted. "This writing doesn't really have a direct translation. Each of these symbols represents one of the ten Dnooblian tentacles. The order that the symbols are displayed in corresponds to a particular order of tentacles in a laying-on-of-tentacles ceremony. Because Dnooblians have outlawed this practice outside of Dnooblia for safety reasons, this representation of symbols now serves instead. The actual significance of this display lies in the discipline required to learn the patterns, and presenting them in the correct order. For example, on my wedding day I will make a similar display, in a different order, for my wife. And there's another arrangement for when our first larva returns. The order of the symbols as I now display them acknowledges that I owe my life to you. Thank you, Fleence."

Dee was now crying like a newly weaned cub.

"All set," said Dluhosh.

Gregory and Michael climbed in, still wearing their golden flip-flops. Dluhosh closed his door, lifted off, and within seconds Earth appeared outside.

Fleence went to her mother's ship to put the egocite ingot back into its proper bag. She found that the ingot was shaped like a kitten. Dee, who had quickly ducked in to pull himself together, saw Fleence and said, "Fleence! Thanks for the kittens! I already named that tabby one. Look how dumb he looks – it's SO cute. His name is President Gren Mee-Ow. Isn't that just perfect? I'm going to clone millions of them – maybe billions! And pandas too! I think I might be done working for Trukk-9 for a little while, by the looks of it. This will give me something to do. It's gonna be awesome!"

"Sweet!" said Fleence.

MICHAEL AND GREGORY GO HOME

"Okay Dluhosh, where's my ammonite?" asked Gregory as sweetly as he could.

"It's right here, Gregory. Um, can I convince you to swap it for one of my Dnooblian ammonite fossils?"

"Well, yeah, but I won't remember where it came from, right? Are they properly labeled?" asked Gregory.

"Well, they're labeled in Dnooblian script. How about if you choose one and put your own label on it? Then I'll sneak it into Michael's house for you when I clean up. Just don't say anything about it to big you-know-who, okay?"

"That will still confuse us, but I can't pass up that deal. By the way, I was being mean to you on purpose – just trying to maintain some control and learn as much as I could. No hard feelings?" asked Gregory.

Dluhosh shook Gregory's hand and broke his pinky. Gregory screamed.

"Oh, sorry Gregory, I don't know my own strength sometimes. I'll fix that. I should re-probaluate you both anyway in case you picked up an alien pathogen. I'll give you both another hit of the calming agent too, if you like."

"Oh yeah, definitely. Bring it on," replied Michael.

"We need to get Michael's truck at the lake so we won't be implicated in the disappearance of Jimmy Fresneaux," said Gregory.

"Are you kidding? How long is this going to take?" asked The Big Voice Entity.

"My car is maybe two hours from home. We'll drive it home and then you can wipe our memories," suggested Michael.

"I know it seems unlikely, but for me two hours is too long. I have a very important appointment to pick up a load of CO2. I'll compromise. We'll find your car and wipe your memory once you drive to where you won't be lost. How's that sound? Or should I smash your ship with an asteroid?"

Dluhosh said, "Okay, I just want a chance to say goodbye to these guys. Michael and Gregory, I admire your decision to return to Earth. It's a head-scratcher for me though. It's a nice place to visit in a cloaked flying saucer, but I wouldn't want to live amongst you. Thanks for taking care of me and for helping solve the mystery of my people's origins."

"No problem! It's been mind blowing – really," said Gregory. "But can I ask some questions?"

"That's one already!" said The Big Voice Entity.

"Sure, but, I need to know if you guys are sure that we prevented the invasion."

Dluhosh said, "W-..."

The Big Voice Entity interrupted. "Of course we did! You saw that meteor and the looks on their faces! You heard the radio! Quit stalling..."

Michael said, "Okay, Big Voice Entity, you are about to totally confuse us. So I'm asking more questions first. Come on, it's only fair. So first, what is this foot experiment all about?"

"Oh okay... I just added variability in foot size – quite a lot of variability. I knew this would change your self-image a bit – but, WOW! The effect was obvious right from the beginning. And everything that followed was predicted by my original test group."

"Really?" said Michael.

"Yes. And I'm interested in whether you know who the largest-footed are in your population. Any guesses?" asked The Big Voice Entity.

"Sasquatches?" guessed Michael.

"Rock stars?" guessed Gregory.

"Paleontologists?" guessed Dluhosh.

Gregory and Michael looked at Dluhosh as if they thought it was cute that he was playing this game with them.

"Good guesses, but sasquatches don't count anymore. And, yes, musicians are typically big-footed too, but on average, Dluhosh's answer is most correct."

"What?!" said Michael and Gregory.

"Yes," replied The Big Voice Entity, "Your best scientists are the most well-stood of all. Other typically large-footed occupations include literary agents, editors, publishers, and critics – as well as filmmakers, producers, script writers, and recording engineers. In fact, engineers in general are huge, especially bridge builders and broadcast engineers. And you should see the size of the prints that your astronauts left on the moon."

"You must be kidding," said Gregory.

"As soon as I changed the foot sizes on Earth about six-thousand years ago, all kinds of things that I predicted began to happen. The village I studied did great things! I'm quite proud of you Earthlings. We have done great things together, you and me."

"Wait, you only studied one village? Are you sure the

results are statistically significant?" asked Michael. "How many people were in this village?"

"Oh, about five-hundred, give or take," said The Big Voice Entity.

"You measured five-hundred people's feet in one village, six-thousand years ago, and you made a conclusion about seven-billion people living today?"

"No. Maybe you would enjoy measuring five-hundred feet, but I took a subsample."

Michael asked, "Okay, so how many of them did you actually measure?"

"Seven."

"Seven? Seven people? Is that all?" asked Michael.

"No, seven FEET. Four people."

"Um, what about the eighth foot?" asked Gregory.

"I didn't need to measure it. I could see it well enough right next to the other one, thank you very much. Plus, I measured my pre-treatment control group. The first three in a row were size eight-and-a-half! So that was easy."

"Wait, let me get this straight," said Michael. "Your hypothesis is that foot-size variability will lead to 'great things'?"

"Yes, GREAT THINGS!"

"I'm not sure how you measure 'great things', but I'll give you that. I just don't think you can imply a correlation with such a small sample of feet."

"Give me some credit, Earthling! I've watched your species achieve greatness for thousands of years!"

"Fine, but you've still only measured seven of our feet…"

"There's no need to measure feet anymore. I have been witness to the greatest advancements and discoveries of your entire civilization. For example, I personally knew Einstein, Newton, Rosalind Franklin, Abbas Abu Al-Qasim

Ibn Firnas Ibn Wirdas al-Takurini, AND Gugsdaughter! Many others too – the greatest of your species – and you are nobody! Why do you insist on questioning one such as I?"

"And did you measure their feet?" asked Michael.

"Yes! I measured one of Gugsdaughter's feet!"

"And the others?"

"I did not need to measure those because their discoveries and accomplishments spoke for themselves. They obviously had very big feet – minimum of size twelve easily."

"What? That ain't the scientific method, man. You can't use your hypothesis to confirm your data – it's supposed to be the other way around. You're just like one of those whacked-out conspiracy guys. It's what causes the vortex of bad logic where everything re-enforces what is already believed. You have to actually measure feet and run the statistics. You might have been fooled by a mere coincidence. Plus it sounds like you have been influencing your subjects. Did you tell Newton about calculus, man?"

"I may have sung him to sleep with some integrals, but that does not change his foot size!"

Dluhosh said, "So you are saying that Earthlings' feet explain how they landed on the moon with combustion engine technology?"

"Yes. I knew Wernher von Braun personally too. Fabulous feet on him…"

"Alright, but what's with the CO2?" asked Gregory.

"Take it easy little-footed man, I'm getting to that. I've learned everything that I needed to learn on Earth, but I can't let you continue to advance without jeopardizing the continued existence of the Universe. Your scientists are getting close to understanding the fundamental nature of matter and energy. It takes most species centuries to develop practical uses for this understanding. And then the other species don't present a problem. But you Earthlings have such big feet AND your monuments to yourselves keep growing. This is why we need take you back to the stone-age before it's too late."

"The CO2...?" asked Gregory.

"I'm getting there... Well, usually in these cases, we re-set the planet with a big asteroid. You Earthlings have given me another idea though. Your climate change effort made me realize that ideal extinction conditions can be achieved without the harshness of a meteor impact. Why you are doing it is a mystery, but it's going much too slowly for me so I'm helping you with as much CO2 as I can import. It may not work, but we always have the asteroid option. So there you go."

"So what you're saying is that even if we reduce our greenhouse gas emissions, we still get your contribution anyway? And then we get the meteor if we actually succeed in halting climate change?" asked Michael.

"Yep. It's your choice. Now let's get you back to Earth."

"Hold on, you said sasquatches don't count anymore. What does that mean?" asked Michael.

"Well, the jumbo-footed members of the original mutations all ran off into the forest and became very difficult to see, so they are irrelevant," replied The Big Voice Entity. "Plus, gene flow between humans and sasquatches has become rare enough that you are effectively different species now. Sasquatch-human hybrids have never been able to produce viable offspring."

"So you didn't account for sasquatches in your data? You can't just blow off a segment of the population because it's difficult to measure. You can't pretend that sasquatches don't exist," said Michael.

"Silence, small-foot! Home with you!"

"Uh, I'm wearing flip-flops, man. You can see that I'm a size eleven. That is hardly a small foot," said Michael.

"Your insolence is becoming tedious. Go!"

"Wait a second! One more question. Where did YOU come from?" asked Gregory.

"Okay – then it's home with you. The truth is we Pixel People don't know where we came from. This is why we are doing all of these evolution experiments on humanoids. We think that we could plausibly have been created by a biological life form that resembles The Great Hologram – a humanoid. And my experiment confirms the final key hypothesis. I have created the missing link! It's glorious. You Earthlings have demonstrated that a humanoid with the right feet can become capable of having created us. Now, get directly into your truck and drive. Goodbye!"

Dluhosh interrupted. "Wait, I'm enjoying this. Surely you can hang on a little longer. Don't forget, you up-rooted my entire ancestry so you could carry out your experiment. Don't you think you owe me some answers too?"

"I will not be held hostage here!" said The Big Voice Entity.

Nobody moved. Dluhosh was inspired by these Earthlings – his brothers, as he now thought of them. He felt proud to be staring down such a powerful being. A green starburst or two flashed faintly across his skin.

But Gregory had concluded that The Big Voice Entity was an insecure blowhard with nothing better to do than talk about himself all day. He'd blabber on and on if you let him. And Michael had concluded that The Big Voice Entity was abusing science itself, which was getting him worked up.

"Oh, okay, two more minutes," said The Big Voice Entity.

"Five," countered Dluhosh.

"Alright, what do you want to know now?"

"Can my people make a cloaked visit to Earth so that we can study the fossils of our ancestors?" asked Dluhosh.

"No. Next question…"

Dluhosh continued. "Well, since you claim to be done with your experiment on Earth, you no longer need a control group, right? Can't you tell us where Fleence's former planet is and open it for conjugal visits? And what about Trukk-9 – can't you get rid of his peoples' antlers? They really are quite ridiculous."

"No, no, and no. I might need the planet for replicate experiments. And you probably don't realize how tedious it is to reverse-engineer genetic mutations. You can ask me questions, but stop asking for favors!"

The Big Voice Entity lost his temper and returned with a washing-machine-sized asteroid.

"Hey, take it easy there, big guy," said Gregory. "We are just as curious as you are about our origins, and we have a lot less time to figure everything out, you know?"

"I've already told you too much anyway," said The Big Voice Entity.

"No you haven't," replied Michael. "After all we've done for you – and for everything you're doing to us – I think you can be a little more generous with your time. Now, what exactly is it that you're so worried about from Earthlings?"

"You Earthlings will clearly do something stupid with advanced technology. Our main concern is that an Earthling egomaniac will create another hologram in his own image right in the middle of this one. It would prove my hypothesis, but another Big Belly Button Bang right here in the Upper Left Buttocks would doom the Universe. And it will all be your fault if you continue to delay me with your endless questioning. Okay, next question."

"Come on, why can't you just partner with us? You seem like a pretty cool guy. Talk to our physicists and particle accelerator people – the ones with big feet. They'd love to talk to you. Tell them what they want to know on the condition that they stop accelerating particles and stuff. Or maybe make all our feet small again or something," said Gregory.

The Big Voice Entity said, "I shouldn't even be talking to you three guys, okay? If you didn't have that memory wiper I'd have to kill you or strand you on the planet with my dinosaurs, which would be a death sentence anyway. Come on, guys…"

He paused. Nobody else spoke.

"God, the dinosaurs… I almost sunk myself with my careless use of the dinosaurs. Why did I try to bring back such big predatory ones…? Please don't tell anyone about that, guys. Okay? Plus I have all these damned space-time wrinkles to clean up before that mess comes back to bite me – again. You don't understand the pressures. I know that humanoids all over the galaxy are lopsided and smell bad because of me. But I'm not a jerk guys, really…"

There was another awkward pause. Dluhosh flushed orange. Michael and Gregory looked down at their golden flip-flops.

"And there's nothing I can do about it now anyway!" declared The Big Voice Entity, acting all tough again. He lost control of his asteroid and it dropped into orbit around Earth without any of them noticing. "You Earthlings are a threat to the very fabric of the Universe! And I have important things to do, so let's get on with this!"

"Please reconsider the need for the CO_2 experiment, and keep a better eye out for invaders!" said Gregory.

"Off with you!"

"Okay, guys, sorry we can't party some more. Anyway, you can probably use some calming agent to help you through the confusion." Dluhosh domed them and hit the button four times.

"Now drop them at their car, and you two get in and drive home! Now!" ordered The Big Voice Entity.

Dluhosh thanked Michael and Gregory again and set them down next to Michael's pick-up. They saw Jimmy Fresneaux's truck and trailer.

Michael yelled, "Hey! Our stuff is in the cabin!"

"We aren't stupid," said The Big Voice Entity in the smallest voice he could manage. "We'll take care of it. Now go!"

Dluhosh had his memory wiper beam trained on them. He was waiting until they would be able to find their way home, but be far enough away so as not to be able to figure out where they had been. The guys drove up the dirt road toward the highway.

Michael said, "Okay, so I hope they don't hit us with the memory wiper while I'm driving."

"Dluhosh is smart enough, but I bet he hits us as soon as you stop. Dluhosh! If you can hear me – wait 'til we stop!" yelled Gregory.

"Wipe their memories now!" said The Big Voice Entity.

"Are you kidding? As soon as they stop – otherwise they might crash."

Michael asked, "What do you think will happen if I don't stop?" As they approached the paved highway he asked, "Is it clear?"

"Yeah, but you aren't going to…"

Michael gunned it. They both understood that this wasn't the smartest thing to do, but it felt right, and they were very calm.

"I'd really like to remember. Do you think you can lose

295

them?" asked Gregory.

"They are going very fast! How far do you plan to let them go?" asked The Big Voice Entity.

"There's a major intersection in a couple of miles. That's far enough from the lake, I think," said Dluhosh.

Michael asked, "Okay, man, there's a stop up here soon. Should I blow through it if no one is coming?"

"Well, you probably shouldn't, but... Hey, quick, do you have a pen? I want to write down that guy's name. We have to try and remember. UB- what was it?" asked Gregory.

"What?"

"That big voice asshole... Gimme a pen!"

"Uh... How about if you write in the dust on the dashboard?" suggested Michael.

The Big Voice Entity noticed Gregory writing with his finger as they approached the intersection, and he ordered Dluhosh to wipe their memories.

Michael looked left and right, but had to stop for traffic. Dluhosh fired the beam and downloaded all of Michael's and Gregory's memories from this moment back to the night before they were abducted.

Then Dluhosh said, "Okay, I'll clean up the cabin, then we need to go to Michael's house to remove one more piece of evidence."

***

From Michael's and Gregory's perspective, they had just fallen asleep in Michael's house with plans to go fossil collecting in the morning. But they woke up with golden flip-flops stuck to their feet in Michael's truck sitting at a stop sign with cars streaming by in front of them. Michael flinched and popped the clutch, which caused his truck to lurch and Gregory to jam his finger where he was writing on the dashboard.

"AHHHH!" they both said.

"Okay, what just happened!?" asked Gregory as he squeezed his bent finger.

"I don't know, man – you too? What the…" said Michael.

"Yeah, I was just falling asleep at your house."

"Right, we're supposed to be going to the bluffs. This doesn't look like the bluffs…"

"Where are we going? Or coming back from…?" asked Gregory.

"I think I know where we are. Home is right – I assume we're going there, right?

"Might as well, I guess. Are you okay?"

Michael thought about that. He felt great. He went through the mental checklist of all of his usual aches and pains. "Seriously man, I've never felt better. My mouth even tastes good. You?"

"Same thing – except where I jammed my finger on your dash. I'm not as anxious as I'd expect for waking up from a blackout inches from death, you know? Hey! Where are my glasses? I can't see. Wait. Yes I can. Oh… Everything is so clear. But where are my glasses? Hey, I'm wearing golden flip-flops! Hey, check out how heavy these are. I think they are real gold."

"Oh yeah, me too. That's funny… Huh, it's strange that it sort of seems like no big deal. Weird – I'm super calm. And I can breathe through my nose! It feels weird… But shouldn't we be freaking out? Hey, what were you writing on the dash there?" asked Michael.

"Looks like I wrote 'Big V' – I wonder what that is."

***

Dluhosh finished cleaning the cabin and then went to Jimmy's house. There were police out front and loose chickens all over Jimmy's yard. He would have liked to erase whatever video Jimmy had, but he didn't worry too much about it.

So he landed his ship in Michael's back yard and went in through the cat door. He dropped off the cabin items and the backpacks and boots that the guys had left on his ship. He also left Fleence's make-up and bikinis as a red herring. Then he placed the ammonite that he had traded with Gregory in a conspicuous place on the floor. He grabbed the last bag of frozen anchovies and a beer, and he took a water sample from Michael's hot tub.

Dluhosh was pretty sure that there weren't any give-away clues left behind, but the time was too short for a thorough clean-up. He did, however, wonder how Michael and Gregory would deal with the missing time and all the fragments of evidence. Two weeks was a lot of memory to wipe – two minutes could be very disorienting. Dluhosh regretted having to do it, but he was pleased that Michael and Gregory had made it back with their golden flip-flop rewards.

**

Michael and Gregory pulled into the driveway. The first thing Michael noticed was an additional garbage bag next to an already full garbage can. He took a look inside the can. It smelled very fishy. He found the usual food containers, but a lot more than there should have been. He also found several empty anchovy bags. Then he inspected the large garbage bag and found more of the same. The recycling container overflowed with beer bottles, some with anchovy heads in them.

"Gregory, there must be a hundred pounds worth of anchovy bags in the garbage. Did we go fishing? You hate fishing…"

Then he checked the freezer. "There's a big-ass gar head in here. I guess maybe we did go fishing – nice specimen anyway."

Gregory said, "My phone says it's Sunday the 13th!"

"Mine too. No way… I'll turn on my computer."

The guys confirmed that it was the 13th. "I have to work tomorrow – guess I'll be calling in sick. Shit," said Michael.

Michael checked his email. He found order and shipping confirmations for six bikinis, a bunch of make-up, and two pairs of polarized designer sunglasses. "Hey, it looks like I've had some credit card fraud too. But these bikinis and stuff were supposedly shipped to me here on overnight delivery."

"Yeah, here's a bunch of bikinis and girl stuff on the counter, and look at your ammonites lined up on the floor. I guess we enjoyed playing with those."

"We have beer. Plus there's all the empties… Are those ours? I think somebody else has been here."

"Maybe we can't remember anything because we drank all that beer. You know, like maybe it's a blackout. It happens on TV all the time," said Gregory.

"Well, I feel great. We'd feel like crap if it was just the beer. Maybe we partied with some crazy women and they drugged us."

"Who do you know like that?" asked Gregory.

"Hey! Big V could be Big Vicki from the museum!"

"Big Vicki?"

"Yeah, she has some pretty crazy friends, man."

"Well, I assume Big Vicki was yours…" said Gregory.

"Yeah, sure, I'd do Big Vicki."

"So yeah, I don't think Big Vicki can afford golden flip-flops, or else why would she be working at the museum, you know?"

"Well, if I was rich and HAD to have a job for some reason... The museum would be my first choice."

Michael continued to search the house while grinning about Big Vicki. His bedroom looked fine – no anchovies or bikinis in there. He went into the bathroom and looked in the tub. "Hey, I think I'm right about the women. There's a wad of long brown hair around the drain. Wait, no, I think it's black."

Michael held the wad of hair up to the light and thought he saw a glint of red, and then the whole glob turned bright red. "Whoa, man, I thought the hair was brown and now it's bright red. Wait, now it's brown again. Hold on, it has a little bit of a... AH! The whole wad is purple now!"

Michael dropped the wad in the sink and inspected his fingers for dye. He stared at the wad trying to recall the shade of red he thought he had seen, and it turned red again.

"Hey, man! I swear this hair changes color."

Gregory replied from the other room. "Maybe it's some kind of dye that changes color in different light. How about green?"

"Yep."

"Blue?"

"Yep."

"Is it just iridescent or something?"

"Yeah, that too... and pure white... This should be freaking me out. Come in here."

Gregory came in and said, "It's brown."

"Well, try green."

"What do you mean 'try green'?" Gregory looked back at the hair. "Whoa! It's green!"

"I think it's whatever you think it is," said Michael. "You see green, but I see white. Now I see black. Now I see yellow."

Gregory went through every color he could think of in rapid succession, including chrome and camo. "This isn't right… It's a telepathic hair ball."

"Here, I'll put it in a jar. Maybe the drugs need to wear off. We'll check it later," said Michael.

They continued to search the house. Gregory found their backpacks on a chair. "Hey! We did go to the bluffs. We have some pretty nice ammonites in our packs. Huh, there's a pink envelope in my pack. There's a picture of a woman on it and some kind of foreign script writing. It smells really pretty. She's kind of mean looking though. But, still… Hey, you have one too."

Michael came in to see.

"Mine looks a little like your one. Maybe they are sisters. Do you think…? Did we get some foreign girlfriends? I wonder where they're from."

Then Gregory noticed an unfamiliar ammonite on the table. "Where'd you find this?"

"Whoa, that's a nice one. It's not mine. Is it labeled?"

Gregory turned it over. "Yeah, it looks the same as the writing on the card, and the rest looks like my handwriting. It says 'Dnooblian Highlands, collected by… uh, Dluhosh-10'. I don't know anything about this – or I don't remember…"

"Where are the Dnooblian Highlands?" asked Michael.

"Argentina, I think. I'd sure like to meet these girls again. But not if they come back to take the flip-flops, I guess. These things must weigh five pounds each and they sure seem like real gold."

"We must have made these girls really happy, man. Nice job! I guess if they have enough money to give out pounds of gold, they'd have enough money to get a memory drug to cover their tracks. And they probably paid to fix your eyes, since you look a lot better without those bottle-bottom glasses. And maybe they fixed my nasal passages too. These are the kind of girls that could afford psychoactive hair products. They're probably oil princesses or drug lords' daughters," said Michael.

"Yeah, that would explain it. But why the anchovies?" asked Gregory.

"Well, that could be either a fetish or just what they do where these girls are from. It seems nasty, but, well... Maybe we had a very cultural experience."

"So, uh, hypothetically speaking, if some poor guy had never had sex before, but he found a bunch of girl stuff in his house, and maybe a love note and long hair in the tub, but he had no memory of it. Should that guy assume that he was no longer a virgin?"

"Yes, definitely," said Michael.

DLUHOSH RISES

Dluhosh said, "Okay, I think I cleaned up good enough. Those guys will experience some confusion, but they should be fine. You have to admit, they did a great job for a couple of inexperienced humanoids. Of course, I had to feed them enough calming agent to stop a herd of buffalo."

The Big Voice Entity replied. "Well, I didn't like them. They were disrespectful and full of themselves! How dare they…"

Dluhosh interrupted. "I don't know – I admired their understanding of how one achieves accuracy. I think they find the whole process to be aesthetically pleasing – especially the data gathering part. And I think they are right that you should keep a better eye out for invasions, and that you rethink your foot experiment and the plan to wipe them out. I think they point out some valid holes in your methods. Anyway, you might as well take me to Dnooblia now."

The avatar vanished.

"Dnooblia, please."

Still, there was no response.

"Hey! ULBTX-123! Please take me home!"

No big voice replied.

"Damn! Come on! It's three months to the outpost! I'm sorry. I didn't like those guys either. It was unreal how cocky they were in front of one as powerful as you. I assure you, it was the calming agent talking…"

Nothing.

Dluhosh flew some uncloaked maneuvers while releasing antimatter signatures that he thought might alert The Big Voice Entity to his continued, unwanted presence.

He hung around for two full days while periodically calling out. He wouldn't have said he was homesick, but he did find himself becoming nostalgic for Dnooblia. He finally got around to reading the email archive that Maghosh had sent with Trukk-9. Among the messages were some from his old friend Gnudhosh.

Dear Dluhosh. I hope your latest adventure is going well. I'm still stuck on Dnooblia, of course, but I finally passed my sculpture rite. I painted a very flattering portrait of Prince Plujsdjf with his point slicked back. He is displaying a subtle combination of self-deprecation aquamarine and wonderment blue with a script of accurate leadership commitment across his chest. Then I carved a simple wooden frame for it, and submitted the frame as my sculpture. HA HA. You should have seen their faces. They couldn't reject the handsome Prince, so I had them by the shells on that one! Your friend, Gnudhosh. ; >~

Good ol' Gnudhosh, thought Dluhosh. Then he scrolled to the next one.

Dear Dluhosh. I hope this finds you well. I'm doing okay. Unfortunately, I failed my essay a couple of more times. The first one was titled Why the Essay Rite Should Be Abandoned. I think the judges were just mad about my sculpture. I doubt they even read the essay. The second essay was called simply The Good Rogue. The judges claimed that it was full of threats against them. I guess it sort of was. Anyway, I'm going to focus on the family reliance rite for now, and maybe get back to the essay later. : >~

If the poor guy can't pass these rites, he'll become high risk, thought Dluhosh. And rogue-ism will not go well for him. Then he scrolled to the most recent message. It had arrived at the outpost after Dluhosh and Fleence had departed.

Dear Dluhosh. I was hoping we could get together before your next mission. I'm on my third month of trying to pass the family reliance rite. I keep losing my hunting colors when I get distracted by the beauty of the sea, so then I spend all my time fending off sharks. I'm hoping you can teach me how to fish like you. Plus, I was hoping you could review my latest essay before I submit it. It's called Used Aliens. It's a satirical piece meant to mock everyone I dislike very much, but I think it might be too obvious. And I title-drop it at the end for no apparent reason, so I wanted your opinion on that. Also, my fiancé's father is threatening to annul our engagement if I don't make under-bull soon. Hope to see you. Your friend, no matter what... Gnudhosh. : <~

Now Dluhosh was worried for his friend. He kept looking at the upside-down Dnooblian Golden Rule poster.

ECNEIDEBO, YCARUCCA, HTURT

And he wondered why he hadn't bothered to turn it right-side-up.

Naturally, he pondered the rules: What is the rule right now anyway? What do I obey? Well, the rules probably say to head directly back to the outpost and work on my Mother Roost report as I travel. But those are rules made by Planet One, really, and they don't even follow their own rules. I mean, what shitty rule would prevent me from curing Numun's children of their diseases as simple thanks for his help? And Gnudhosh sounds like he needs help – if it's not too late. Seems like there's a bit of a gray area here…

"What would Jimmy do?" he asked out loud.

Okay, just playing what-if games, he thought. If I never returned to the outpost, Maghosh would just have me declared MIA. Hell, I could probably refuel for free at Chuffed-18 and visit home with very little delay. This ship was basically totaled, and I had it fixed at no expense to PLUMBOB, so it's not like I'd be stealing it. I guess I won my ethics complaint, so Welter won't come looking for me. There must be plenty of ways to earn enough to buy a house and fishing concession much faster than working for PLUMBOB. I could become a consultant...

Dluhosh noticed his distorted reflection in the viewing dome. He was a nice rational brick-red color, so he continued thinking.

I could sit here and rationalize all day, like, what was it…? Like spreading jellyfish on chainmail? Who am I kidding? I'm going to do what I want this time.

Dluhosh thought back to the first time he had heard 'Dluhosh-10' spoken aloud. 'Dnooblia, My Dnooblia' started playing in his head. His nostalgia grew stronger, but there was no reverence.

He checked his colors, and then stared for a few minutes at the pin-point of light that was Earth. He pressed the record button on his panel, took a deep breath, and said, "As a symbol of my rejection of Planet One rules, I hereby change my name to Dluhosh-X! I need to gather some more data on what I suspect will prove to be evidence of the origin of Dnooblians, and then I have to help some friends. These things are more important than any rule. Dluhosh-X out!"

For the first time in his life he felt the creeping exhilaration of willful rule breaking. He took down his Golden Rule poster and was about to rip it to shreds. But instead, he rolled it up and placed it in a drawer in case his new outlaw life-style didn't work out.

He sat back in his bridge chair, blew a blast from his siphon, and declared, "This is for you Jacques Fresneaux!"

Rogue Dnooblian Dluhosh-X yelled, "WOOOOOOOOOOOOOOOOOOOOOOOO!" as he dove his ship back to Earth for a whirlwind fossil collecting and disease curing adventure.

ONE YEAR LATER

"Hooves…"

Gro Skoo looked up. "Huh?"

"Hooves, Gro Skoo. My new grandbaby was born with hooves. The maternity ward is full of them," said Vice President Griffer-1.

Gro Skoo stood up behind his desk. "Oh, I'm so sorry. But I thought the Dirt mission…"

"That mining ship with the classified target…? That's all it was – a mining ship."

"You knew? And you let the real mission continue?" asked Gro Skoo.

"Yes, but come on. You didn't really think those were actual Dirtlings did you? It was Trukk-9 and a couple of show girls. It was theater. Nothing but a show… And golden flip-flops? How much more theatrical can you get? Golden flip-flops, Gro Skoo? Golden Flip Flops…"

"Hooves, Griffer? Hooves. Haven't you ever heard of erring on the side of caution? I thought it might be a hoax too, okay? But hooves, Griffer… Are meteors coming next?"

"Not so far, but…"

"But what?" asked Gro Skoo.

"Well, after it melted the mountain, the ship simply went missing."

"If it crashed or was captured by Dirtlings, we need to invoke the Contact Committee. Perhaps we can even salvage this mission. Or maybe we can appease them – get rid of the hooves at least. Shouldn't we send a reconnaissance mission?"

"Already did. They found nothing but a melted mountain and wild speculation in the media. Those three Dirtlings must have been a classified elite strike force."

"Secret supermen…"

"Exactly. We do need to keep a close eye on Dirt, and, yes, they may still be useful in the future. But we don't want to provoke them directly again," said Griffer-1.

"Agreed."

"However, the recon ship found something very interesting, I think. There is a planet with sapient beings not far from Dirt, and there is a virtual highway of wormholes between them. Neither planet seems aware of the other."

"Hmm… What do we know about the people there?"

"Quite a lot, actually. In fact, I'd like you to take a look at these recent raw videos from PLUMBOB. See if they stimulate any ideas in you, Gro Skoo. Then get back to me. The planet is called Mother Roost…"

GUIDE TO THE GALACTIC POOL

Planet One – Somewhat cat-like ~~assholes~~ humanoids
Bounty-2 – Displaced Earthling control group (location unknown)
ZZZZZZ-3 – The insectoid world with many intelligent species
Fermament-4 – Complexly symmetrical odoriferous nosey humanoids
Blue-5 – Ancient plasmanoids
Cache-6 – Carnivorous Squirrel People who eat a different kind of nut
Precipice-7 – Goat People who enjoy having hooves
Millet Fields-8 – Slender and elegant blue or green avianoids
Bukk-9 – Copiously-eyed and antlered humanoids
Dnooblia-10 – Home of the Dnooblians
Rumbly-11 – Stout three-legged humanoids with very thick hair and massive skulls
Swampy-12 – Home of the Swamp Masters
Flat Rock-13 – Sequentially hermaphroditic Crab People
Peat-14 – Snake Apes, bioluminescent
Free-15 – Ursoid Bear People
Sphere-16 – Ichthyoid Mudskippers with fingers
Scablands-17 – Dwarf humanoids with two hands on one arm and a bony hook on the other
Chuffed-18 – Colony of former slaves and descendants, a humanoid pleasure planet
Mother Roost – Large flightless avianoid former dinosaurs who don't know that they are on a candidate planet
Earth – Still a player…

ILLUSTRATIONS FROM CHAPTER BREAKS, ETC.

Title page – The Ancestral Dnooblian
Chapter 1 – Black bear tracks on beach, California
Chapter 2 – JIMMY JAMS!
Chapter 3 – Fleence's sketchbook, Dluhosh in 2x2 sprint
Chapter 4 – Fanciful heteromorph ammonite, ceramic tile
Chapter 5 – Jurassic ammonite fossil from Dorset, England
Chapter 6 – A Dnooblian ancestor ammonite, ceramic tile
Chapter 7 – Largemouth bass caught by author
Chapter 8 – Fossil ammonite die-off, ceramic tile
Chapter 9 – *Nautilus macromphalus* shell, New Caledonia
Chapter 10– *Desmoceras* ammonite fossil from California
Chapter 11 – *Crioceras*-like ammonite in ceramic tile
Chapter 12 – A Dnooblian ammonite
Chapter 13 – An *Aturia*-like nautiloid in ceramic tile
Chapter 14 – Live squid in Tsukiji fish market, Tokyo
Chapter 15 – Blacksmith in forge, Mali, West Africa
Chapter 16 – The *Bostrychoceras* that crashed Dluhosh's ship
Chapter 17 – *Spirula* tests from Australia
Chapter 18 – Fossil *Pachydiscus* ammonite suture detail
Chapter 19 – Buzzy completes his lifecycle
Chapter 20 – An extinct Dnooblian nautiloid
Chapter 21 – An evolute ammonite in ceramic tile
Chapter 22 – *Hauericeras* ammonite from California
Chapter 23 – Ammonite in ceramic tile
Chapter 24 – Dnooblian body script display to life saver
Chapter 25 – Another Dnooblian ammonite ancestor
Chapter 26 – The Dnooblian Golden Rule, upside-down
Chapter 27 – Hanging six on Mother Roost
End – Larval Dluhosh's kindergarten picture

ABOUT THE AUTHOR:

M. Sid Kelly, Earthling, size eleven.

M. Sid Kelly is from the far north coast of California. He served as a U.S. Peace Corps Volunteer in Mali, West Africa from 1992 to 1994. He grew up as an Air Force brat on bases from Germany to The Philippines to Mississippi, etcetera. He formerly worked in the U.S. federal endangered species program on Pacific salmon "issues". For the past nine years he has worked as a consulting fish biologist specializing in helping agencies and contractors avoid impacts to endangered fish and their neighbors while building bridges over rivers. He enjoys tidepooling, nature photography, collecting things from the ground (fossils mostly), jazz, travelling, and observing how awesome his wife and daughter are. And he has the best dog ever. (M. Sid Kelly suggests that you don't argue this last point, or else the dog may attack.)

ABOUT THE ARTIST:

G. Lasine Doumbia, Earthling, modest.

ETCETERA

Thanks for reading! And if you've made it this far, the author assumes that it's safe to ask you to consider leaving an honest review on Amazon. It helps a great deal. Thanks! Here's the Used Aliens page:
http://www.amazon.com/dp/B00BJ602QQ

And Jimmy is busy (ahem), but Dluhosh will try to answer your email questions here: Dluhosh10@gmail.com

OTHER EBOOKS BY THE AUTHOR:

Fire Hunting in Mali, West Africa – A Photo Journal:
http://www.amazon.com/dp/B00BS4VHN6

Tigerfish to Dodofish – Fishing on West Africa's Niger River, A Photo Journal:
http://www.amazon.com/dp/B00D3CDFO0

CHAPTERS OF BOOK II (MAYBE)

BUZZY'S CHILDREN INFEST OUTPOST
JACQUES FRESNEAUX - RIPPED BASSIN' MAN, FATHER
DAYV! GET SOME DOILIES!
DLUHOSH-X HANGS TEN-TACLES
FREE KITTENS WITH PANDA PURCHASE
GRAB THAT DINOSAUR!
MICHAEL AND GREGORY GET SOME, BUT…
JOKES AND JERKS, HUGS AND HOOVES
YOU WANT SOME PRAISE WITH THAT?
GNUDHOSH-X
ODE TO A SILVER MUFFIN
A GIANT BLUE FEATHER
THAT DAMN MESSY SPACE
HELP! BEARS!
'CONTACT' ISN'T A CHECKLIST ITEM
A USE FOR 'EGOCITE MINERS'
THE PHILOSOPHERS RISE – COINCIDENCE?
HUFFING THE PURPLE WORMS OF *AUBERGINE*
SHE WORE A BIKINI OF BEER
DAB TABMOW'S SECRET LIFE
BLACKSMITHS WANTED, CHARCOAL PROVIDED
THE SWARM YOU NEED
CALMING AGENT DERAILMENT
A GENE FOR BAD-ASSEDNESS
HOVERCRAFT TOW-IN
CRICKET CONTAINMENT, RIGHT-SIDE-UP

***

The disclaimer: Except for arguably Werner Herzog as Trukk-9, the characters are the product of the author's imagination. Any resemblance to other actual persons – Earthling or alien, living or dead – is purely coincidental. However, if you think you resemble Gren Wee-1, Wulu Griffer-1, Gro Skoo-1, or Rim Ram-1, then you should consider suing. Gregory and Michael – you owe us, so if you don't like the use of your names, images, personalities, ailments, insecurities, and direct quotes, you can sho-.